THE TULE ELK
Its History, Behavior, and Ecology

"Notch," an adult tule elk bull.

THE TULE ELK
Its History, Behavior, and Ecology

BY

DALE R. McCULLOUGH

UNIVERSITY OF CALIFORNIA PRESS
BERKELEY, LOS ANGELES, LONDON
1971

University of California Publications in Zoology

Volume 88

University of California Press
Berkeley and Los Angeles
California

⋄

University of California Press, Ltd.
London, England

isbn: 0-520-01921-0
Library of Congress Catalog Card No.: 75-626287

CONTENTS

THE TULE ELK: ITS HISTORY, BEHAVIOR, AND ECOLOGY

BY

DALE R. McCULLOUGH

(A contribution from the Museum of Vertebrate
Zoology of the University of California)

INTRODUCTION

THE TULE ELK, or wapiti (*Cervus elaphus nannodes*), once roamed the grasslands of central California in vast numbers and was the predominant animal of the landscape. Competition from Spanish livestock, heavy hunting by fur trappers, meat demands of the 49'ers, and finally development of the land by settlers came in quick succession, reducing the tule elk almost to the point of extinction.

In the late 1800's and early 1900's measures were taken to insure the survival of the species—first, by protection of the remnant population by an interested cattleman, later by establishment of a refuge at Tupman near Bakersfield, and by transplanting attempts. Of the transplants, two eventually proved successful resulting in free-roaming herds at Cache Creek in Colusa County and in Owens Valley in Inyo County. The recent populations have been approximately 32 in the Tupman enclosure, 80 at Cache Creek, and 300 in Owens Valley.

As the Owens Valley population increased, the ranchers began to complain of elk damage to forage and fences, and the stage was set for a controversy. Some livestockmen demanded complete removal of the elk while protectionists demanded complete removal of livestock. The California Department of Fish and Game, charged with the management of the elk, has attempted to maintain the Owens Valley population at a level that insures survival yet gives the stockmen a measure of relief from damage. The present policy calls for holding it at about 300 head; this is accomplished by periodic controlled hunts. Similar conflicts with agricultural interests have characterized the Cache Creek herd, which ranges mainly on private lands.

Charge and countercharge, the necessity of managing the various herds, and the apparent uncertainty of the elk's survival emphasized the need for knowledge of the life history and ecology of the tule elk. Studies conducted by the California Department of Fish and Game have progressed along two lines: (1) aerial census to determine numbers, and (2) analysis of reproductive tracts and stomach samples collected during the legal hunts. These studies have produced valuable basic information, but of a seasonal nature and restricted in scope.

Apart from the need for management information, the elk presents some interesting biological adaptations deserving study. This race is the most specialized elk in North America, living as it does in open country under semi-desert conditions, whereas the species as a whole typically occupies temperate climates and utilizes heavy cover at least seasonally.

My work on this project began in 1962 with an intensive review of the historical literature. The purpose was to ascertain the original range of elk in California and to follow the fate of the tule elk from the earliest times down to the present. At the

[1]

same time, a phylogenetic study was made to determine the evolutionary pathway which gave rise to this specialized form, and its relationships to other North American races of elk.

The field work was supported by a two-year grant from Resources For the Future, Inc. On July 1, 1963, I established residence at Big Pine in Owens Valley. The field study continued until June 30, 1965. Most of this period was spent working on the wild free-roaming population in Owens Valley. Occasional trips were taken to Cache Creek and the Tupman enclosure to get comparative information.

The basic study method was direct observation of the elk in their undisturbed state. These animals are truly wild, and all close observations had to be made by stalking. Although the elk would tolerate the presence of a human at about 150 yards under ideal conditions, they never really became used to me, and under unfavorable conditions they would not allow any kind of approach. Thus virtually all of the observing had to be done without the elk being aware of my presence. Stalking requires a great amount of effort and diligence, but it is rewarded by the assurance that the animals are behaving in a natural manner. My field equipment consisted of 7 × 50 power binoculars, a 15 to 60× variable power spotting scope, and a pencil and notebook.

Within the Owens Valley population, there are five separate herds. Of these, the Independence herd was selected for intensive observation because of its large size (about 90 head), its ease of location, and the relatively undisturbed area in which it lived. The four other herds in the valley were checked at regular intervals to establish their ranges and to obtain comparative data.

Results are based on over 2,000 hours of actual observation, and the sighting of 1,025 elk groups involving 16,621 individuals. Because the total population of Owens Valley was just slightly over 300 head, there were approximately 50 sightings for every animal. Most of the sightings were concentrated on the Independence herd. There were 10,276 sightings in this herd, or about 115 per animal. These figures indicate the amount of evidence upon which my conclusions are based.

A number of special studies were initiated to obtain information not readily available by direct observation. In this category are forage production and utilization, competition studies, nutritional values of plants, comparative diets of different elk herds, mineral metabolism, disease and parasite studies, etc. Methods will will be given when the topics are presented.

TAXONOMY AND EVOLUTION

The world forms of red deer and elk were referred to a single species, on logical grounds, by Ellerman and Morrison-Scott (1951) and Flerov (1952), but they gave no substantiating evidence. The Museum of Vertebrate Zoology, University of California, Berkeley, recently obtained from New Zealand a series of skulls of hybrid red deer from Great Britain × Rocky Mountain elk from Wyoming. The parent stocks had been introduced into New Zealand in separate localities, and as the populations built up (particularly the red deer) they spread until their ranges overlapped. Hybridization occurred in the area of overlap and much of the population shows intermediate characteristics. It is clear that the elk and red deer are genetically compatible and have not evolved specific isolating mechanisms despite separation. They are genetically a single species with a wide geographic distribution in the north temperate zone of the world. The specific name *elaphus* Linnaeus, 1758 has priority over *canadensis* Erxleben, 1777.

The tule elk was originally named as a full species *nannodes* by Merriam (1905) on the basis of specimens obtained near Buttonwillow in the lower San Joaquin Valley. However, it freely interbreeds with other forms in captivity, resulting in intergrade populations, which shows that it is only a subspecies. Because there seems to be no physiological, behavioral, or genetic isolation, there is every reason to believe that hybridization would occur in the wild. Indeed, it has been suggested that it has occurred on several occasions, as discussed below. However, as yet there is no concrete evidence of hybridization other than in captive situations. The proper designation of the tule elk is *Cervus elaphus nannodes* (Merriam).

Other North American forms considered in this study are the Rocky Mountain elk, *Cervus elaphus nelsoni* (Bailey), and the Roosevelt or Olympic elk, *Cervus elaphus roosevelti* (Merriam).

Materials and Methods

I examined 117 elk skulls: 75 of *nannodes*, 15 of *nelsoni*, and 27 of *roosevelti*. A number of these were from juvenile animals, but because only animals of two years and older were used in the statistical comparisons, skulls suitable for measuring were: 45 *nannodes*, 12 *nelsoni*, and 20 *roosevelti*. On each skull, 21 measurements were taken and five qualitative characters examined as described in Appendix A. Only gross qualitative comparisons were made of skins, and these will be expressed in relative terms without recourse to standardized color descriptions.

Phenotypic Variation

Cervids exhibit a great amount of variation in size depending on nutrition, and elk are typical of the family in this respect. Comparison of populations of *nannodes* from the Buttonwillow area* with those from Owens Valley show some consistent differences which are probably nutritional in origin. In one case, an animal which was derived from a transplant from the Buttonwillow area to near Monterey foraged largely on a watered golf course and grew to very large size; in many respects it was more like *nelsoni* than *nannodes*. Within any elk population there is also considerable individual variation.

Sexual Variation

Sexual dimorphism is well developed in elk. The most obvious difference between the sexes is the large branching antlers borne by the males. Also the males are substantially larger than the females, averaging about 25 percent more in weight. In skull dimensions males exceed females by approximately 8 percent, the difference being greater in breadth than in length. Differences are also apparent in the pelage, with males having a more pronounced mane and heavy dark hair on the

---

* These specimens were taken from a free-roaming band of elk known as the Buttonwillow herd, most of which was eventually enclosed in the Tupman Reserve, which occupies a site on the original range.

breast. With the exception of the period immediately following the spring molt, the pelage over the body of the males is lighter in color.

AGE VARIATION

Females reach adult size at about two years of age, and little change in overall dimensions occurs after that time. However, male elk continue to grow slowly through life. This continuous growth is apparent in body weight, size of antlers, and skull dimensions. Any series of skulls from one locality arranged by tooth wear and other age criteria shows a clear increase in dimensions with age. The base of the skull is the most stable, and it is not surprising that measurements in this region show the least age variation, and therefore are of the greatest value for comparison of skulls of the various forms. The radioactive phosphorus tracer studies of Bubenik et al. (1956) showed similar growth relationships in the skulls of male fallow-deer as evidenced by incorporation of the labeled element in various skull bones.

The only skull dimension which decreases with age in adult elk of both sexes is the length of the toothrow, both upper and lower. As the crowns wear down, the teeth converge. Thus the toothrow is longest when the permanent teeth are first fully erupted and the length decreases thereafter as the teeth become worn.

VARIATION AMONG POPULATIONS OF NANNODES

From the skull measurements (Appendix A) it is apparent that the different populations of *nannodes* were quite variable. The Buttonwillow males showed great individual variation while the Owens Valley specimens were more uniform. As was the case with body weight, the average skull measurements for Owens Valley males exceeded those of Buttonwillow males, and this fact can be attributed to diet. The age distribution of the samples from the two localities was similar.

It has been rumored that the Cache Creek herd is a hybrid population resulting from crosses with *nelsoni* that occurred in the Monterey area prior to transplantation to Cache Creek (transplants are discussed in detail later). Examination of three complete female skulls and a broken skull of a fourth gives no evidence that this supposition is correct. In the most reliable characters, these animals are typical of *nannodes*. All dimensions are easily within the phenotypic variation of the subspecies as demonstrated by the response of Buttonwillow stock transplanted to varying habitats. Fall coloration of these animals is typically light, and tooth and antler pigmentation is light. All bulls observed had antlers of the usual *nannodes* size and form. In short, there is no evidence that this herd is anything other than pure *nannodes* stock.

COMPARISON AMONG THE RACES

While antlers within a race vary greatly, certain general differences among races are apparent, as shown diagrammatically in figure 1. The antlers of *nelsoni* are longer and relatively lighter of beam, compared to *roosevelti;* they tend to sweep backward and have a very wide spread; the tines are relatively thin and usually branch perpendicularly to the main beam. The antlers of *roosevelti* tend to be shorter and heavier of beam, compared to *nelsoni,* and they project upward, resulting in a narrow spread; the tines are shorter, heavier, and branch at an acute angle to the main beam. There is also a tendency toward clustering of the terminal tines, leading to palmation in *roosevelti*, whereas in *nelsoni* tines are usually discrete. These observations agree with those of Graf (1955) and Murie (1951).

In *nannodes*, the antlers are similar to those of *nelsoni* in their proportions and spread, although much smaller in gross size. Both the main beams and the tines tend to arch from the points of divergence. In the fresh state with rugose surfaces (which are weathered away on exposed specimens), *nannodes* antlers have a distinctly contorted appearance as though they were forcefully twisted during growth. There is a tendency toward palmation in *nannodes* antlers of massive size.

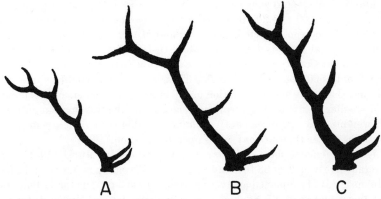

A   B   C

Fig. 1. Schematic diagrams of antler form in three races of *Cervus elaphus;* A, *nannodes;* B, *nelsoni;* and C, *roosevelti.*

While both *nelsoni* and *roosevelti* antlers typically show a deep chocolate brown stain, *nannodes* antlers remain a light brown or taffy color. Staining of the teeth is like that of the antlers. Apparently this difference is traceable to differences in the chemical constituents of the vegetation in the environments of the races. Both *nelsoni* and *roosevelti* occupy habitats with considerable timber and vegetation typical of moderate to heavy rainfall; *nannodes* lives in open country with a xeric vegetation adapted to low rainfall. The most mesic area occupied by *nannodes* was along the coast south of San Francisco Bay. It is significant that subfossil elk antlers from the San Francisco Peninsula (McCullough, 1965a) and the recent specimen which was transplanted to the Monterey area all show deep pigmentation of the teeth and antlers.

Clearly *nannodes* is the smallest of the races considered. On the average, adult bulls weigh about 100 to 200 pounds less than *nelsoni*. Murie (1951) gave 631 pounds as the average live weight of 30 mature *nelsoni* bulls from Jackson Hole and Yellowstone National Park, Wyoming, and Quimbly and Johnson (1951) reported 10 mature bulls to average about 730 pounds. Greer and Howe (1964) recorded somewhat lower weights from north Yellowstone, but observed that they may have been due to range deterioration. Live weight of 7 *nannodes* bulls from Buttonwillow averaged 427 pounds. However, body weight is related to forage conditions, and the above animals were taken when the range was poor; on better range, the Owens Valley males of *nannodes* reach a greater weight. The field-dressed weights of 56 mature bulls taken in legal hunts, corrected to live weight by adding one-third (Quimby and Johnson, 1951), averaged 554 pounds.

Maximum weights express the same relationship. Greatest live weight given for *nelsoni* by Murie (1951) was 1,032 pounds. One bull removed from the *nannodes* herd at the Tupman Elk Reserve weighed 680 pounds. Several very large individuals of *nannodes* in Owens Valley probably exceeded 700 pounds, but this would seem to be near the upper limit for the race.

Weight comparisons between *nelsoni* and *roosevelti* are difficult to make because of scant data on *roosevelti*. It is generally thought that *roosevelti* is larger, and the maximum weights would suggest that this is the case. Graf (1955) gave corrected live weights of 1,000 to 1,200 pounds for three *roosevelti* bulls, and observed that larger bulls have been reported. Schwartz and Mitchell (1945) gave 700 to 1,000 pounds as typical weights for male *roosevelti*. However, 9 adult *roosevelti* males from Humboldt County weighed by the California Department of Fish and Game averaged only 560 pounds live weight. These low weights could be due to range conditions, the young age distribution of the sample, or members of this population may be smaller in size than typical *roosevelti*. From the information on *roosevelti* (both weights and measurements) examined in this study, the assumption that *roosevelti* is larger than *nelsoni* seems open to question.

Weights of females show a similar racial relationship. Murie (1951) reported the average live weight of 38 female *nelsoni* from Wyoming as 520 pounds. Quimby and Johnson (1951) reported an average weight of 562 pounds for 11 females. Corrected live weights of 87 *nannodes* females from Owens Valley averaged 411 pounds. Fifteen adult female *roosevelti* from Humboldt County weighed by the Department of Fish and Game had an average live weight of 459 pounds.

In general, *nannodes* has a shorter coat than the other two forms, and it is clearly lighter in color. The difference in color is particularly apparent in the fall and winter, when *nannodes* bulls become straw-colored over the body. Tule elk cows are considerably darker than bulls, but lighter than female *nelsoni*. Following the spring molt, all three forms are nearly the same in color, but in the winter coat *roosevelti* is darkest, *nelsoni* intermediate, and *nannodes* lightest.

In the skull, *nannodes* is the shortest and broadest besides being substantially smaller than the other two races. The differences between *nelsoni* and *roosevelti* in size are slight, but the form of *roosevelti* tends to be longer and more slender.

Length of toothrow was the only measurement that ran contrary to the usual size relationships of the three forms. As previously mentioned, the toothrows shorten with age. Even taking this factor into account, *nannodes* has relatively the longest toothrow, *nelsoni* the next longest, and *roosevelti* the shortest.

In addition, the cheek teeth show subtle differences in form. The crowns of *nannodes* show a tendency toward selenodonty, with reduction of the cingula, and a more complex folding of the enamel; there is also a tendency toward later eruption of the last molars and slower replacement of the milk premolars. The teeth of *roosevelti* tend toward bunodonty, and are much like those of *Odocoileus* in form. Again, *nelsoni* is intermediate in character.

These modifications of the dentition are no doubt due to selection for differences in diet. The more massive dentition of *nannodes* is a modification to handle fibrous grasses while *roosevelti* dentition is more suitable for a diet heavy with browse.

The measurements showing the least variation with age involve the occipital condyles. The width of the condyles clearly separates *nannodes* from the other forms, and the degree to which the occipital condyles project to the rear distinguishes skulls of *nannodes* from *roosevelti*. In *nannodes*, the condyles project downward so that when viewed from the side, only the rearmost parts can be seen behind the post-glenoid processes. In *roosevelti*, the condyles project decidedly backward, and most of their mass can be seen from the side, extending to the rear of the post-glenoid processes. In *nelsoni*, all intermediate conditions are found. Another character involving the occipital region is the shape of the anteriorly extending indentation of the dorsal portion of the foramen magnum. In *nannodes* this indentation is narrow and V-shaped, with the sides of the V bowing inward, while *roosevelti* usually has a wide U-shaped indentation, with *nelsoni* again being intermediate.

Conformation of auditory bullae differs, *nannodes* having highly inflated bullae with squared anterior profile. In *roosevelti* the anterior edge is less inflated and sloped more gradually into the skull. In most specimens, *nelsoni* is intermediate.

The alisphenoid canal is well developed in *roosevelti* and is usually several millimeters in diameter. Also in *roosevelti* there is a well developed groove running between the alisphenoid canal and the foramen ovale. This groove is lacking in *nannodes* and the alisphenoid canal is reduced to a minute, and all but closed, orifice. Again, *nelsoni* shows intermediate conditions.

A final character of the skull which is useful in distinguishing *roosevelti* is the dished-out appearance of the palate between the upper toothrows, with the toothrows showing a considerable curvature, being closest together at the ends. In *nannodes* the palate tends to be flat, and the toothrows are little curved. In this regard *nelsoni* is again intermediate, but is more like *nannodes,* while in most characters it is more nearly like *roosevelti.*

The wide range of variation and intermediate characters of *nelsoni* suggest a generalized type as opposed to the specializations of *roosevelti* at one extreme and *nannodes* at the other.

From the data presented here, it is obvious that *nannodes* is the most specialized race of elk in North America, and clearly warrants subspecific status. In nearly all characters, it is substantially different from the most similar form, *nelsoni.* The differences between *nelsoni* and *roosevelti* are much less pronounced and are usually not statistically significant. Yet because they are consistently present and compose a more or less uniform trend of differentiation, *roosevelti* is considered to be a valid subspecies.

EVOLUTION OF WESTERN RACES OF ELK

Cervus elaphus originated in Asia and migrated to North America over the Bering Straits land bridge in the Pleistocene period. Wapiti have been a conservative group, evolutionarily, and even today those living in Asia are similar to the New World *nelsoni.* Elk antlers from the Pleistocene dredged up near Anchorage, Alaska, are within the range of the antlers from Recent specimens (Murie, 1951). The same generalized elk spread over most of North America and into the northern edge of Mexico.

The subspecies *nannodes* and *roosevelti* represent the greatest differentiation

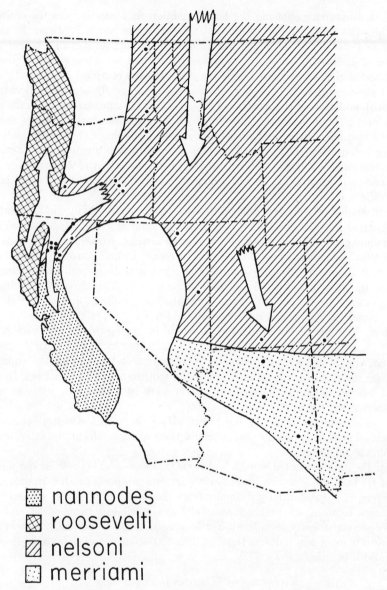

🖾 nannodes
🖾 roosevelti
🖾 nelsoni
🖾 merriami

Fig. 2. Probable spread of elk in western North America based on early records of
nelsoni. Localities are given in Appendix B.

from the generalized type *nelsoni in* North America. It seems highly probable that *nannodes* and *roosevelti* represent separate offshoots from *nelsoni*. Because they diverge in opposite directions, it seems unlikely that *nannodes* was secondarily derived from *roosevelti*.

The Rocky Mountain elk was not previously thought to have occurred in California, but the present study suggests that the records from northeast California should be referred to this race. A sufficient number of historic records have been found to substantiate the existence of a "bridge" of *nelsoni* through southern Oregon and northern California (fig. 2). This was probably the route by which elk originally invaded California.

One specimen of the original elk, a badly worn and broken base of a skull and part antler from the upper Pit River in Shasta County, is deposited in the Museum of Vertebrate Zoology. The only measurement that can be obtained is the width of the brain case (116 mm) which is at the upper extreme for *roosevelti*, but well within the range of *nelsoni*. The alisphenoid canal, which was well developed in all *roosevelti* specimens examined, is absent, and the foramen ovale-alisphenoid canal groove is poorly developed. The antlers, judging from the portion of one present and the placement of pedicels, were wide spreading. These characters suggest that this animal was referable to *nelsoni*. The only other known specimen, a cast antler from Mount Dome in northeastern Siskiyou County, is also in the Museum of Vertebrate Zoology. This antler is of a widely spreading character more typical of *nelsoni* than of *roosevelti*.

It is hypothesized that during more mesic conditions of the Pleistocene, the generalized *nelsoni* extended westward through the Mount Shasta area (the two specimens support this supposition) and invaded the Central Valley and coastal ranges. The populations of the humid coastal areas developed into *roosevelti* while the populations in the more arid Central Valley developed into *nannodes*. Selective factors for specialization, particularly in the case of *nannodes*, probably intensified during the northward recession of mesic conditions.

ORIGINAL DISTRIBUTION OF ELK IN CALIFORNIA

Because of their immense numbers, large size, impressive antlers, and graceful carriage, elk made a strong impression upon early visitors to California. Encounters with groups of elk by early explorers and settlers were frequently recorded in journals, diaries, and other written reports. Thanks to this fortunate circumstance, there exists an unusually complete record of the early distribution of elk in this state. It should be noted that early European visitors associated the elk with the Old World red deer with which they were familiar, and thus, many references to "deer" were actually elk.

Early records are plotted in figure 3. The localities upon which the points are based are given in Appendix B.

CERVUS ELAPHUS NANNODES

Sacramento Valley.—The northern limits of the range of tule elk was given by Grinnell (1933) as Butte County. It now is obvious that tule elk occurred considerably farther north. The John Work trapping party in 1832 and 1833 killed elk

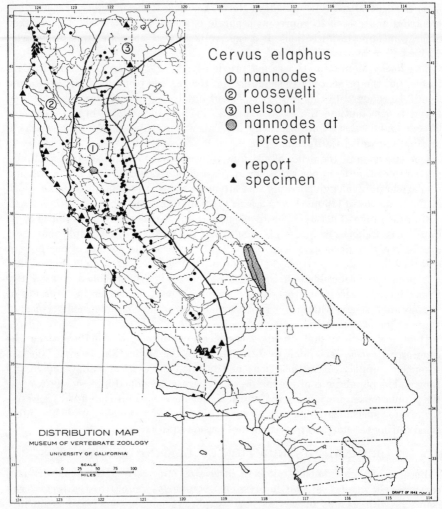

Fig. 3. Original distribution of elk in California. Localities are given in Appendix B.

probably referable to *nannodes* on Cow Creek in Shasta County, some 20 miles north of the present site of Red Bluff (Maloney, 1945). At least 11 elk were killed in this area so there was probably a permanent population present. From this point south there is a nearly continuous string of records, mainly along stream courses which the explorers followed. I know of no preserved specimens from this entire section.

San Joaquin Valley.—Tremendous numbers of elk were found in the Sacramento-San Joaquin Delta, and a good number of records are available from there south through Merced County. Although elk probably occurred through Madera and Fresno counties, the paucity of records suggests that their numbers may have been low. Elk were extremely abundant in the Tulare Lake area of Kings County, and Buena Vista Lake in Kern County. The Tehachapi Mountains apparently served as the southern boundary.

Many specimens are available from the Buttonwillow area near Buena Vista Lake and also from China Grade Bluffs near Bakersfield. The only other known specimen from the San Joaquin Valley is a set of antlers, which is clearly *nannodes,* from the delta area, which is in the possession of Mr. Carlo M. DeFerrari of Sonoma, California. This animal was said to have been shot in the gold rush days. Pictures of this specimen are in my field notes (Sept. 10, 1963) on file in the Museum of Vertebrate Zoology.

Sierra Nevada foothills.—Easternmost records of tule elk are poor, but based on the limited evidence and my observations of tule elk in Owens Valley it seems likely that elk made at least seasonal use of much of the oak-grassland on the lower Sierra foothills. The following quotes from Frémont (ed. Nevins, 1956) give some idea of the relationship of the elk to timber.

April 3, 1844. On a tributary south of the Tuolumne River about five miles east of the San Joaquin River (p. 386):

Skirting along the timber, we frequently started elk; and large bands were seen during the day, ...

April 4, 1844. Latitude 37° 108′ 00″, longitude 120° 45′ 22″ (p. 386):

Elk were running in bands over the prairie and in the skirt of the timber.

December 18, 1845. Merced River, near the Sierra (p. 460):

On the northern side was a low, undulating wood and prairie land, over which a band of about three hundred elk was slowly coming to water, feeding as they approached.

No doubt some small bands occasionally occurred farther east along favorable valleys, but the upper edge of the oak-grassland was probably the effective boundary. For example, there are no records of elk occurring naturally in Yosemite Valley despite a good number of early accounts of the area.

South coast.—The taxonomic status of the elk which originally occurred from the Golden Gate south through the Coast Range to the vicinity of Monterey was formerly in doubt. However a number of specimens unearthed at Pacific (McCullough, 1965a) show that these animals are clearly related to *nannodes*. While they tend to be larger and have more deeply pigmented antlers and teeth, these characteristics are well within the phenotypic variation of *nannodes* as shown by the recent *nannodes* specimen which was transplanted from Buttonwillow to near Monterey. Yet some more basic differences are present. On one of the skulls the condyles project more to the rear than is typical of *nannodes*. All other specimens are typical in this respect. Also a broken specimen from Purisima Creek, San Mateo County, which is in the California Academy of Sciences collection (no. 9845) has wide occipital condyles (±87 mm), at the extreme for *nannodes*. Perhaps these animals show a slight differentiation from typical *nannodes* of the Central Valley due to the more mesic habitat. However, even if these slight divergences are real, they do not warrant subspecific designation. Most characters are typical of *nannodes,* and there is little reason to consider the elk of this area to have been genetically different when the expected phenotypic responses are taken into account.

Scattered records for the larger valleys of the southern Coast Range were found, but many were not specific enough to allow precise plotting. Apparently elk occurred in all valleys where favorable habitat existed. Elk were abundant in the Monterey Bay area, and Indian midden elk remains are available from this locality (Fisher, 1934).

Although there are no definite historic records from the Santa Barbara area, there is evidence that elk occurred there until shortly before the advent of the white man. Fisher (1930) and Gifford (1940) reported finding occasional elk bones and antler artifacts unearthed from Indian middens, and the extensive work of Rodgers (1929) on the mounds of the area yielded quantities of elk remains.

From other archeological and ethnological work it is known that a considerable amount of trade and travel was carried on between the coastal Indians and those of the southern San Joaquin Valley, so the possibility of the coastal mound elk remains being the result of trade must be considered. Yet the studies of Rodgers (1929) would indicate that the elk were being used for food. It does not seem likely that such quantities of unboned, fresh meat would be carried some 50 or more miles from the San Joaquin Valley before the introduction of horses by the Spanish. Dried meat was the preserved product of the age, and bones would have been so much excess baggage.

A number of tools were fashioned from elk antlers and bones, and possibly they were transported for this purpose. Donald R. Dickey (in Rodgers, 1929) reported on the fauna of the Channel Islands, and he thought that the bone and antler remains of deer (*Odocoileus*) found there were the result of trade with the mainland. No mention was made of elk in the island fauna. It seems reasonable to think that if the elk remains along the coast were so important as implements as to be brought from the San Joaquin Valley in trade, then they also should have been an important item in the trade between the coast and the offshore islands. The alternate hypothesis appears more likely. There was probably a natural population of tule elk along the coast in the Santa Barbara region which became extinct sometime before or about the advent of the European explorers.

San Francisco Bay region.—There are several historical records from the San Francisco Peninsula, and the previously mentioned subfossil specimens from this area clearly establish that they were of the *nannodes* type. Elk were found all around the south end of the bay, and throughout the Berkeley Hills. Very large numbers were found near Mount Diablo, Livermore Valley, and eastward into the San Joaquin Valley.

Along the north side of the bay a continuous series of records is available extending to the coast. Previously elk occurring north of the Golden Gate were considered to be of the *roosevelti* form, but detailed accounts point out that these animals occupied the open rolling grasslands rather than the timber. This ecological evidence is supported by the two known specimens from this area. A set of antlers from an elk killed near Sonoma (previously reported by Ellsworth, 1930) is in the possession of Mr. Shirley M. Weise of Sonoma, California. I examined these antlers and they are typical *nannodes*. Photographs are in my field notes (June 25, 1963). A second specimen, a cast antler from near San Geronimo, Marin County, is in the Museum of Vertebrate Zoology. This antler is badly weathered, but its slender and spreading pattern is like *nannodes* rather than *roosevelti*. A questionable third specimen is in the Marin County Historical Society Museum in San Rafael, California, and consists of a set of antlers with the description, "Antlers of an elk killed by John Keys soon after he settled in Tomales in 1850." Tomales is located several miles north of Tomales Bay in Marin County; but from the label, there is no way of knowing if this animal was killed there, or some distance away. The conformation is intermediate between *nannodes* and *roosevelti*, with short heavy beams, but with the tines wide spreading. Without a verified locality, it is impossible to know if the specimen has significance in terms of intergradation between the two forms.

Northern Coast Range.—Because of an insufficient number of specimens, the dividing line between *nannodes* and *roosevelti* in figure 3 is based primarily on ecological grounds; i.e., the transition from oak-grassland and chaparral to redwood forest. The *nannodes* range covers all of the oak-grassland and interspersed chaparral. The present successful occupation of this habitat by the Cache Creek herd clearly demonstrates the suitability of this range for tule elk.

As in the southern Coast Range, elk occurred locally where conditions were most favorable. They were fairly abundant around Clear Lake and in the larger valleys to the west of the Sacramento Valley. A single specimen, a base of an antler with pedicel and a small portion of the cranium, is known from South Yolla Bolla Mountain, and again, its light structure is suggestive of *nannodes* rather than *roosevelti*.

CERVUS ELAPHUS ROOSEVELTI

From the present day distribution of the Roosevelt elk it is apparent that this subspecies reaches its greatest density in rather specific environmental conditions, i.e., thick timber with small clearings in areas of high rainfall.

Historically, the greatest numbers of *roosevelti* were found along the coast in Humboldt and Del Norte counties where they survive to the present time. Roosevelt elk were common along the coast in the Fort Bragg and Point Arena areas, and their range extended south into northern Sonoma County. See Harper et al., (1967) for a more detailed history and present status of the Roosevelt elk in California.

Recent specimens are available from Humboldt County. One specimen is available from the Noyo River. A part of an antler was dredged up about one mile upriver from the coast, and is in the possession of Mr. William Edmands of Reno, Nevada. This antler is of a form like *roosevelti* (photograph in my field notes, June 4, 1965). The southernmost specimens are three cast antlers in the Fort Ross Museum, which were picked up by an early resident at Plantation near Fort Ross. These specimens are clearly of a *roosevelti* type (photographs in my field notes, August 26, 1965).

The cline of differentiation between *roosevelti* and *nannodes* may have been fairly sharp, since each requires a quite specific habitat. On the other hand, the requirements and tolerances of *roosevelti* and *nelsoni* are much more similar, and the zone of integration between these forms was probably very wide, with typical *nelsoni* gradually grading into typical *roosevelti* from east to west.

CERVUS ELAPHUS NELSONI

The subspecies *nelsoni* in California probably occupied the Mount Shasta region and extended eastward into the Great Basin locally where conditions were favorable. The specimens from Mount Dome and the Pit River have already been mentioned.

These elk were extirpated following settlement of the area by white men. The last animal was said to have been killed in 1873 (Doney et al., 1916). In 1913, Rocky Mountain elk were reintroduced to the Mount Shasta area from Yellowstone Park (Tillotson, 1916; Reddington, 1922b; Murie, 1951) and a population exists there today.

HISTORY OF THE TULE ELK
PRISTINE CONDITIONS

The typical habitat of tule elk was found in the large plain which constitutes the Central Valley. Many descriptions of the area before development of the land for agriculture give some impression of early conditions.

About the Butte Creek area in the north central Sacramento Valley, Derby (1932:115) wrote:

There are many clusters of beautiful trees—oaks, sycamores, and ash—upon its banks, but it is not thickly wooded, as is the case with the Sacramento and Feather rivers and their branches. The plain beyond is of rich alluvial soil, covered with fine grass, which was at this time almost dried up, upon which subsisted large herds of wild cattle, horses, elk and antelope.

Derby described the Bear Creek region and western side of the valley as follows (pp. 117–118):

Its banks are thickly wooded towards its mouth, mostly with shrub-oak, buck-eye, and alder. In the summer it has but little water, but is never entirely dry; in the winter it becomes a deep and rapid stream, overflowing its banks to a very considerable extent.

The valley of the Sacramento, on the western bank of that stream, is for the most part a barren plain, with little vegetation or water. It is from thirty to forty-five miles in extent, being bounded on the west by the coast range mountains. There are no streams emptying into the Sacramento from the west .... with the exception of "Puta" and Cache creeks .... the whole country between the creeks is liable to overflow, and is very dangerous to attempt travelling after a heavy rain. The "Tulé" swamp, upon the western bank of the Sacramento, extending to the vicinity of "Butte" creek, and occurring occasionally above, is from three to six miles in width, and is impassable for six months out of the year.

A general picture of the northern part of the San Joaquin Valley was given by Audubon (1906:227) as follows:

The road from Stanislaus over broad prairies of poor sandy soil extends for miles until nearing the edge of the line of beautiful old oaks that fringe French Creek and its swamps; then the earth becomes richer and sends up a growth of clover and beautiful grass knee high, until you reach Stockton.

and (p. 229):

The whole country to the north and east of Stockton through to the Calaveras is most rich and splendid soil, but in many places too low for farming, but the grazing was excellent, quantities of wild oats, rye grass (I think), clover and a species resembling red-top. In many places the grasses were breast high as I waded through them but generally full knee-deep.

That this area was subject to winter flooding similar to the Sacramento Valley is evidenced by Audubon's observation (p. 182) that:

During the dry season this great plain may be travelled on, but now numerous ponds and lakes exist, and the ground is in places, for miles, too boggy to ride over, so we were forced to skirt the hills.

In 1824, the Russian sea captain Otto Von Kotzebue traveled overland from San Rafael to Fort Ross. He described the northern Coast Range in the following manner (Thompson, 1896:25):

The fine, light, and fertile soil we rode upon was thickly covered with rich herbage, and the luxuriant trees stood in groups as picturesque as if they had been disposed by the hand of taste. We met with numerous herds of small deer, so fearless, that they suffered us to ride fairly into the midst of them, but then indeed darted away with the swiftness of an arrow. We sometimes also, but less frequently, saw another species of stag, (elks) as large as a horse, with branching antlers; these generally graze on hills, from whence they can see round them on all sides, and appear much more cautious than the small ones.

From these accounts of the early travelers in California it is apparent that throughout the range of the tule elk, the one common factor was the presence of grassland. The character of the grassland varied from the interspersion of vast marshy areas in the floodplains of the Central Valley to the comparatively xeric rolling hillsides of the coast ranges where trees and brush stands shared the landscape. Then, as today, the tule elk was basically an animal of open country. Allen (Evermann, 1915) verified this situation for elk in Marin County (pp. 91–92):

The elk seemed to inhabit a strip of territory some five or six miles wide. They appeared to have limited their range to the open lands along the coast.

Similarly, descriptions of elk in the south coast leave no doubt that it was in the open grasslands that elk were encountered. This is not to say that elk did not use brush fields; they almost certainly did. Yet the use of brush and chaparral was predicated by the presence of grasslands in the vicinity.

A characteristic of the climate was the periodic occurrence of drought. According to Burcham (1957) droughts occurred in 1820 and 1821; from 1828 to 1830; in 1840 and 1841; from 1845 through 1847; 1853–1854 through 1864–1865; 1876–1877, and 1897–1898. In June, 1864, Brewer (Farquhar, 1949:510) wrote the following account:

we came on to Firebaugh's Ferry, on the San Joaquin, twenty-five miles. Portions of this day's ride, for miles together, not a vestige of herbage of any kind covered the ground; in other places there was a limited growth of wire grass or alkali grass.

He reports that hundreds of cattle died of starvation that year, but does not mention the effect upon elk.

The tremendous numbers of elk that roamed the undisturbed grasslands taxed the descriptive powers of the first explorers. Newberry (1857) stated that the herds of grazing animals in the Central Valley rivaled those of the bison of the great plains or the antelope of South Africa. Bryant (1848) reported numerous herds of elk east of Sutter's Fort in the Sacramento Valley. In the vicinity of the American River Wilkes (1845:113) wrote: "The variety of game in this country almost exceeds belief. The elk may be said to predominate...."

In the Marysville Buttes area, in 1833, the John Work party reported that elk were very numerous, and on one occasion the party killed 52 elk in two days (Maloney, 1945).

In the San Joaquin Valley, the elk were even more numerous. Clarke (1852) observed that nowhere had he seen game as abundant as there. In 1844, Frémont (ed. Nevins, 1956:385) observed that the Tuolumne River at the San Joaquin was:

crowded with bands of elk and wild horses . . . .
In one of the bands of elk seen today there were about two hundred: but the larger bands, both of these and wild horses, are generally found on the other side of the river . . . .

Between Merced and Stockton, Bosqui (1904:62) wrote:

At times we saw bands of elk, deer and antelope in such numbers that they actually darkened the plains for miles, and looked in the distance like great herds of cattle.

In 1844 Frémont (ed. Nevins, 1956) reported multitudinous herds of elk by the Tulare River, and there are numerous accounts of abundant elk in the Tulare Lake area. Similarly elk were abundant about Buena Vista Lake near the southern end of the San Joaquin Valley.

Some of the San Joaquin herds were very large. Audubon (1906) reported a herd of about 1,000 head, and Bryant (1848) estimated some herds at 2,000 animals. James Clyman in 1845 (Camp, 1928:174) on the west side of the San Joaquin near Livermore observed: "one herd of Elk had a grand appearance containing more than 2000 Two thousand head and covering the plain for more than a mile in length. . . ." Even allowing for a wide margin of error, the numbers are astounding.

Apparently the extremely large herds were found mainly in the northern part of the San Joaquin Valley on the west side of the river. In other areas, herds of several hundred elk are the largest reported, and usually 40 to 60 was the typical herd size. Many authors seem to use the term "herd" in a very broad sense to include the animals of a general region. Yet the account of Clyman given above is specific enough that there is little doubt that he was referring to a single aggregation.

Clearly the greatest elk abundance was found on the rich lowlands of both the Sacramento and San Joaquin valleys, in and about the marshes and heavy fertile flood plains. On the higher portions of the valley, such as in Madera and Fresno counties, elk were much less numerous on the poorer sandy soils.

North of San Francisco Bay on Sonoma Creek, Padre Jose Altimira reported seeing a herd of about two or three hundred elk in 1823 (Finley, 1937), and MacKenzie in 1850 found a great herd of elk by Petaluma Creek (Evermann, 1915). The large herds of elk on Point Reyes have already been alluded to.

In San Ramon Valley in Contra Costa County, Brewer (Farquhar, 1949) reported elk once roamed in herds like cattle and although they had been exterminated by 1861 when he visited there, the antlers were abundant over the ground. In 1835 Dana (1840) saw a herd of several hundred on the San Francisco Peninsula at the mouth of the bay. Sailing from Angel Island north to San Rafael, Duhaut-Cilly (1834:239) observed:

The coast we were passing is formed of mountains of moderate height, covered with grass, at that time somewhat parched; in the ravines we saw clumps of oaks. From time to time we descried large deer (elk) herds. They were wandering in bands over these sloping pasture grounds. . . .

In 1786, De Galoup, captain of the "Laperouse," reported elk as very common in the Monterey area (Chinard, 1937). This observation is generally corroborated by the early Spanish accounts, although they are typically vague in natural history matters.

While elk were probably the most important single species in the pristine state, most of its range was shared by numerous antelope (*Antilocapra americana americana*) and deer (*Odocoileus hemionus* ssp.). Even in the Central Valley, deer were commonly encountered.

The predominant predators throughout the tule elk range were grizzly bear (*Ursus horribilis*) and the coyote (*Canis latrans*). The black bear (*Ursus americanus*) was common in the northern Coast Range, and overlapped the tule elk range in that area. The mountain lion (*Felis concolor*) was found in the coastal mountains both north and south of San Francisco Bay.

Conspicuous by its absence is the wolf (*Canis lupus*) which was such an important predator of open country in other areas. Grinnell (1933) stated that no verified record of a wolf was known from west-central California (including all the range of the tule elk) and the more exhaustive study by Young and Goldman (1944) gave the same result.

It seems that in the primitive state, tule elk were not preyed on by an efficient large carnivore. Most of the predators would have been effective against only the young calves and the weak or crippled. The mountain lion, the only predator which would have been effective against healthy adults, was limited to a relatively small portion of the original range, and would have been further handicapped by the preference of tule elk for open areas.

USE OF TULE ELK BY INDIANS

The native tribes of California devised a number of ways to obtain elk and other large animals for food and material for clothing and tools. Kroeber (1953) stated that elk were obtained in long-distance surrounds and drives and that snares and bows were not effective against so large an animal.

Mayfield (1929), who lived with the San Joaquin Valley Indians as a boy, (about 1860) mentioned the use of drives for antelope but not for elk. He reported that Indians used to shoot elk and antelope from blinds erected where they came to water (pp. 34–35).

Antelope were easily killed with arrows, but elk were almost too much for them. It was almost impossible for them to kill an elk outright with their weapons. They would shoot arrows into an elk and then follow it until it was weak enough to be overpowered.

Mayfield also stated that deer and elk, in addition to small game, were occasionally snared, but that ground squirrels obtained by smoking from burrows were the best and most dependable animal food source. Leigh (1928) agreed that rabbits and rodents and also birds furnished more food through the year than the large ruminants, and also that insects were taken where they could be obtained in large enough quantities.

Jedediah Smith (Sullivan, 1934) observed that the Indians in the Central Valley about 1828 were mainly vegetarians. Leigh (1928) concurred with the opinion that the diet of Indians throughout California was predominantly vegetable, with the acorn being the staple. He further observed that the amount of animal food in the diet of the Central Valley tribes was much lower than in the diet of coastal tribes. This difference is partially explainable on the basis of availability of bivalves and mammals such as the sea otter (*Enhydra lutris*). Schenck (1926) found sea otter to be the most often represented mammal among the bones found in the Emeryville shell mounds. Yet, elk were third (deer being second) in these deposits. Humboldt (1811) described an unusual technique for taking elk in which the Indians placed the head of an elk over their heads, and by imitating the movements of the elk were able to get close enough to make a kill. He notes that the method was used in the Monterey region, and curiously, in the Santa Barbara region. The account is not definite, but may further support the presence of elk in the latter locality as previously discussed, and suggests that a few may still have been present there when the first Europeans arrived.

The Indians of San Jose demonstrated this technique to Rezanov in 1806 (Langsdorff, 1927), and Kotzebue gave a similar description from north of San Francisco Bay (Thompson, 1896).

DISCOVERY OF TULE ELK BY EUROPEANS

Humboldt (1811) and Evermann (1915) credited Sebastian Vizcaino, who landed at Monterey in December, 1602, as being the first white man to see tule elk. That he actually may have seen elk is indicated by a letter written to the King of Spain in 1603 (Vizcaino, 1891:71) in which he noted that the Indian's food "consists of seeds which they have in abundance and variety and of the flesh of game, such as deer which are larger than cows. . . ."

However, since the present study establishes that elk in the area from San Francisco Bay north to Point Reyes belonged to the race *nannodes,* Sir Francis Drake was probably the first European to see tule elk. Drake landed on the California coast in the summer of 1579. While the exact place of landing is in some question, Drake's Bay on the south side of Point Reyes, or within San Francisco Bay, are the most probable places.

The account of Bourne (1653) which was collected from the notes of Drake, Philip Nichols, Francis Fletcher and other persons on the voyage, leaves little doubt that it was elk which were seen in July, 1579. This quote was taken from an original edition of the book in the Bancroft Library, University of California, Berkeley (pp. 79-80):

The inland we found to be far different from the shoare, a goodly country and fruitful soil, stored with many blessings fit for the use of man: infinite was the company of very large and fat Deer, which there we saw by thousands as we supposed in a herd. . . .

EARLY SPANISH SETTLEMENT

The first overland expedition to the area of present-day California was made by the Spanish in 1769 with the establishment of a mission at San Diego in the southwest corner of the state. In the following years a chain of missions reached as far north as Sonoma. Besides their religious function of conversion of the natives to Christianity, the missionaries, with native labor, grew grains and fruits, on large and prosperous ranchos, and developed great herds of cattle and horses on the natural pasturelands.

Spanish influence was never extended eastward into the Central Valley. Cook (1960) lists a number of military expeditions into the interior, but these were intended to return escaped neophytes (converts), regain stolen livestock, and punish the Indians to discourage further trespass.

Some hunting of elk for food occurred with first establishment of settlements from Monterey to San Francisco. Fages (Priestly, 1937) in his early description of elk observed that the meat was of good flavor. However the immediate success of the missions in raising cattle resulted in a superabundance of high quality and easily obtainable meat. In the absence of necessity, psychological factors entered into the use of elk meat for food. Duflot de Mofrás (1937) observed that the early Spaniards discarded elk meat, and in 1827–1828, Duhaut-Cilly (1834:312) referring to elk, noted:

They do not like game: they might easily provide themselves with hare and deer. They claim the flesh of the deer is not healthful; it is, they say, a cold meat (*carne fria*); they never eat it.

It seems that the direct impact of the early Spanish settlement upon the original elk populations was probably slight, and localized. Nevertheless, indirect factors resulting from Spanish settlement had a greater and more widespread influence on tule elk.

INTRODUCTION OF ALIEN PLANTS

From his extensive study, Burcham (1957) concluded that the dominant pristine plants of California grasslands were perennial bunch grasses. He records the invasion of aggressive annuals which resulted in displacement of the native flora over most of the grasslands of the state at a very early date. Although there are species of high grazing value among the introduced plants, in general they are not nearly as good as the pristine species they replaced. Also, the shift from a principally perennial vegetation to an annual one resulted in a much greater fluctuation in species composition and forage production from year to year (Talbot, Biswell, and Hormay, 1939). These changes in the character of the food supply no doubt had adverse effects upon the elk population.

WILD CATTLE AND HORSES

As the herds of domestic stock belonging to the missions increased, they were allowed to roam in a semi-wild state over the surrounding grasslands where they were easily stolen by the natives. The San Joaquin Valley was the usual destination of the thieves, and a substantial buildup of cattle and horses occurred despite the punitive expeditions of the Spanish.

By 1819 the natives had begun to breed their own stock and regular fairs were held in the Tulare Lake region for the sale of livestock (W. P. U. Smith, 1932). In 1824 Spanish military leaders reported that the Indians of the San Joaquin had large herds, and the cattle were building up faster than the Indians could eat them (W. P. U. Smith, 1932). Similarly horses were allowed to go wild and they built up vast droves (Bancroft, 1888). When Zenas Leonard (Quaife, 1934) came through the San Joaquin in 1833, he wrote: "The prairies are in many places swarming with wild Horses. . . ." John Marsh (Lyman, 1931), Frémont (ed. Nevins, 1956), Clarke (1852), and others referred to vast herds of horses in the following years. As late as the 1860's Mayfield (1929) reported thousands of wild horses on the west side of the valley.

Feral livestock spread to the Sacramento Valley somewhat after their buildup in the San Joaquin. John Sutter reported few wild horses in the Sacramento when he settled there in 1839 (Bancroft, 1888). However by 1849, Derby (1932) found immense numbers of wild cattle and a herd of over 200 horses near Butte Creek. Derby reported wild cattle and horses in much of this region.

The region north of San Francisco Bay was also inhabited by escaped livestock. Probably this stock was derived from the last missions to be established at San Rafael and near Sonoma. In 1824, Kotzebue (Thompson, 1896) rode through the grasslands northwest of San Rafael toward Fort Ross and made no mention of wild stock at that time. But by 1838 the area around Petaluma abounded in wild cattle and horses (Thompson, 1877). Gibbs (1860) reported immense herds of wild cattle and horses in Sonoma County in 1851.

The influence of these vast herds of wild cattle and horses upon tule elk populations is not evident from the published accounts. But the tremendous amounts of forage diverted to the use of wild stock cannot help but have reduced that available for the elk.

The Hide and Tallow Trade

By the early 1800's the gradual buildup of the human population in Spanish California had created a ready market for manufactured goods of all kinds. And the buildup of the cattle herds furnished a durable export product in the form of hides and tallow, which soon became the currency of the country. Dana (1840) described this trade in detail from his visits along the coast from San Francisco to San Diego in 1835.

In 1833, Leonard (Quaife, 1934) reported that cow hides sold for $1.50 each and tallow for four cents a pound. These prices rose to about $2.00 per hide and six cents per pound by 1841 (Wilkes, 1845); the meat was without monetary value. Bancroft (1888) noted that anyone might kill cattle for food so long as they made sure the hide got to the owner.

It was inevitable that the tule elk, which was free and readily available, would also be exploited for hides and tallow. Duflot de Mofrás (1937:257–258) described the capture of elk as follows:

The rancheros hunt them in groups of eight or ten, using their best horses and armed with the lasso. They attempt first to break up the herd and then scatter them, in order to follow an isolated deer which, after being caught by the noose, is surrounded by a circle of men and pulled down. One of the hunters then dismounts, cautiously approaches the animal, and with his knife cuts his hamstring, or strikes his throat. After a certain number have been caught, they are loaded on horses, and oxcarts and brought in to the ranchos. The does, unincumbered by horns, run more swiftly than the males and are more difficult to catch.

After being melted, the fat is turned, like that of beef, into large hide sacks and securely sewed to avoid leakage in warm weather.

The magnitude of these hunting enterprises can be estimated from Wilkes' (1845) statement that about three thousand elk and deer hides were annually exported from California at a value of fifty cents to a dollar each.

These activities were localized to the areas immediately adjacent to the missions and settlements along the south coast from Monterey north, and around the San Francisco Bay.

THE FUR BRIGADES

The great interior valley of California was first explored by mountain men seeking the valuable pelts of beaver (*Castor canadensis*). In early 1827, the Jedediah Smith party entered the San Joaquin Valley and found an untapped source of beaver. The party left California in 1828 with a large take of skins, and traveled north, planning to reach the Hudson Bay Company outpost on the Columbia River. In southern Oregon the party was attacked by Indians, and only Smith and two others managed to escape and make their way to the Columbia. The Hudson Bay Company helped Smith to regain most of his possessions and were soon convinced that Smith had found an important fur resource. In that same year, Alexander McLeod led a Hudson Bay Company expedition into the Central Valley to as far south as French Camp, below the present-day Stockton. Thereafter, Hudson Bay expeditions came to California every year until at least 1843 (Bolton, in a foreword to Maloney, 1945). In 1832, French Camp was established as a permanent camp, and as many as 400 trappers gathered there at the annual rendezvous (W. P. U. Smith, 1932). In addition, American parties under Pattie, Young, and Walker trapped in California during this time.

The tremendous amount of game taken to sustain the brigades is indicated by the accounts of John Work (Maloney, 1945) who led a Hudson Bay Company expedition in 1833. His journal lists the killing of 166 elk in the four days from January 21 through 24, 1833, and his entry for February 22 (p. 31) referring to the Marysville Buttes area reads:

We have been a month here and we could not have fallen on a better place to pass a part of the dead winter season when nothing could be done in the way of trapping on account of the height of the waters. There was excellent feeding for the horses, and abundance of Animals for the people to subsist on, 395 elk, 148 deer, 17 bears, & 8 antelopes have been killed in a month which is certainly a great many more than was required, but when the most of the people have ammunition and see animals they must needs fire upon them let them be wanted or not. The Animals for a considerable time back have been in general very lean, indeed they could not be expected to be otherwise being hunted without intermission.

Yet notes on animals killed scattered through the journal for the month of January 22 to February 22 total only 213 elk, 63 deer, 8 bear, and 1 antelope, or about one-half the total Work mentions. Thus the total recorded kill of 568 elk, 165 deer, 25 bear and 98 antelope taken by the party between November 16, 1832, and August 25, 1833, underestimates the actual kill. Under the continuous hunting pressure, the elk lost condition and took refuge in the marshes where the hunters could not follow.

Apparently the elk largely disappeared from the south-central part of the

Sacramento Valley around Sacramento and Woodland between about 1835 and 1840. By 1842 Wilkes (1845:183) noted:

Game is represented to have decreased in this vicinity, from the numbers destroyed by the parties of the Hudson Bay Company, who annually frequent these grounds.

The end of the fur-trapping era came in the early 1840's with the exhaustion of the fur resource in California and the consequent diversion of activities to other areas. The 1841–1842 expedition to California led by Francis Ermatinger did poorly (Bolton in a foreword to Maloney, 1945) and the fur brigades in California ended within the next few years.

SETTLEMENT OF THE INTERIOR

When John Marsh settled near the present day Pittsburg in 1838, not a fence or house occupied the countryside (Lyman, 1931).

The first farm in the Sacramento Valley was established in 1839 when John Sutter was granted land 30 leagues square bounded on the west by the Sacramento and on the north by the American River. Here he built Sutter's Fort (New Helvetia) on the present site of Sacramento. By 1841 he had 1,000 horses, 2,500 cattle and 1,000 sheep (Wilkes, 1845). A ranch was established on Antelope Creek in 1842 (Farquhar, 1949) and Frémont (ed. Nevins, 1956) reported ranches on Yuba Creek, Deer Creek, an unnamed creek north of there, and two on Butte Creek in 1846.

Settlement of the San Joaquin Valley did not begin until after the gold rush in 1849. Benjamin Wilson (Cleland, 1929:414) reported:

In that same fall of 1847, I moved up all my stock, about two thousand head of cattle, passed through the Tulare Valley, by way of Cajon de las Uvas; there was not a white man living on that route, from San Fernando Mission to Sutter's Fort.

Similarly in the north bay region, most of the country was not settled until after the gold rush, although Thompson (1877) reported that a ranch was started near Petaluma as early as 1838.

With settlement, fences were constructed and domestic livestock brought under control. Bancroft (1888) reported that wild horses were shot to eliminate competition for forage. No doubt elk received the same treatment. Frequently elk were rounded up and slaughtered along with cattle. Finley (1937) reported that F. G. Blume drove cattle and elk together into a corral on the Petaluma ranch of General Vallejo.

THE GOLD RUSH: MARKET HUNTING

The discovery of gold in California in 1848 and the subsequent immigration of people changed the entire character of the region. The value of livestock soared with the boom in human population. Cattle which had previously been worth $2.00 for their hides now became worth $35.00 for their beef (W. P. U. Smith, 1932), and increased in value rapidly as the wave of immigration continued.

Wild game was free for the taking, and the miners soon exhausted the supply locally. Many men became disillusioned with the hard work and moderate success of the gold mines, and turned to market hunting. Not only the miners, but the burgeoning population centers of San Francisco, Sacramento, and Stockton created a ready market. As early as 1850, Bosqui (1904:53) noted that in San Francisco:

On the bills of fare of most of the restaurants were to be found venison, antelope, elk and bear steaks, wild ducks, geese, and many varieties of fish.

The price paid for wild game during late 1850 is given by Thompson (1877:54):

A good sized deer or antelope brought twenty dollars, the hindquarter of a fat elk forty dollars, quail nine dollars a dozen, and ducks from ten to twelve dollars a dozen.

The market hunting era brought the tule elk to the end of its time as an important element of the fauna of the region. In the 1850's the elk population collapsed under the constant pressure of the market hunters. First to disappear were the remaining herds in the Sacramento Valley. The elk in the Butte Creek area reported in 1849 by Derby (1932) are never heard of again. Nelson Kingsley (Teggart, 1914) spent from June, 1850, to February, 1851, in the Marysville region without mention of elk, although he referred to deer. The elk in the Sacramento Valley were decimated so quickly that H. C. Banta (Evermann, 1915) who hunted the San Joaquin Valley in 1854, stated that the elk originally ranged only as far north as Grand Island, just above the junction of the Sacramento and San Joaquin Rivers. He also stated, "I never heard of any except south of the Sacramento River. . . ."

At the beginning of the gold rush, elk were still abundant north of San Francisco Bay. MacKenzie (Evermann, 1915) found elk in the marshes around Petaluma Creek, and Kingsley (Teggart, 1914) in Suisun Bay. James Clyman (Camp, 1928) found elk in Napa Valley in Napa County in 1845, and this population probably persisted until the gold rush. Revere (1922) hunted elk on the Point Reyes Peninsula in 1846 and reported one herd of about 400. The accounts given by Shafter to Evermann (1915) show that elk were present until 1852 in the Point Reyes-Tomales Bay area in Marin County.

Thompson (1877:54) recorded the beginning of market hunting in the north bay as follows:

In October, 1850, John Lockwood came up the creek with one or two others in a whale-boat, attracted by the reports of the abundance of game. They camped under the oaks on the bank of the creek just above the town, on what is now known as the Bell place. Lockwood and party hunted for the San Francisco market, making regular trips to the city in the Spark, as they called their whale-boat.

Referring to Lockwood's partner, Finley (1937:411) expands upon the above account:

James Hudspeth and his partner . . . were hunters for years before they became farmers. Two regular trading posts were established at Petaluma, their operators buying game from hunters direct and shipping it to San Francisco at advanced prices. Probably fifty men were engaged in Sonoma county either as hunters or game traders . . . .

Most of the elk were probably gone from this region by 1855. According to Finley (1937) the last elk killed in Sonoma County was in November of 1857.

Elk persisted somewhat longer in the tule marshes of Suisun Bay and the delta near the mouth of the San Joaquin. Ellsworth (1931) gives an elk record from the Suisun Bay in April, 1857, and Jim Paine (Evermann, 1915) claimed to have killed the last elk ever seen there, probably in the fall of 1868. California Fish and Game (1918:144) quoted from the Stockton Argus, October 25, 1859, as follows:

An elk weighing some 425 pounds was brought to Stockton on 25th October from Middle River, where it was killed on Saturday last by Robert Dykman, the hunter, to whose superior skill with the rifle we are indebted for the larger portion of game of this description that finds its way into our market. Mr. Dykman was three days upon the trail, in which time he followed his game from near the mouth of the Mokelumne, across the San Joaquin and Middle River, a distance of about thirty-five miles.

The following quotation is from H. C. Banta in Evermann (1915:88–89). The "Bob Dikeman" is no doubt the person referred to above.

In 1854 I found elk plentiful in the foothills west of the San Joaquin as well as in the tule swamp. Bob Dikeman and Lee Phillips were my hunting companions, and we practically finished up all the tule elk in the section between Martinez and San Joaquin City.... They were originally driven from the hills and valley land into the tules by the vaqueros rounding up wild horses and cattle, as well as by hunters. In 1854 they were nearly all driven to the tules, but the finding of horns of six to eight prongs, all over the hills proved how plentiful they had been.... Dikeman shot the last cow and calf about 1863, just west of the Sargent ranch on the North Fork of the San Joaquin near Mokelumne River. The rest of the animals, so far as I know, ranged in the tules and willows between Buena Vista and Tulare lakes, and only on the south side of Tulare Lake, ranging also west into the foothills.

Between the delta area and Tulare Lake the elk disappeared early. In 1851 Edgar (1893) traveling south through the San Joaquin Valley first found sign near Fresno, and Grayson (1920) went from Stockton to Woodville in 1853 without finding a sign of elk. Banta (Evermann, 1915) mentioned the population near Fresno, which agrees with Edgar's sighting of a band of about fifty. However, Grayson's (1920) hunt on the Kings River in 1853 with an Indian guide failed to turn up a sign. The elk were probably gone by that time.

In 1855, Grizzly Adams (Hittell, 1911) found elk still present in a small valley in the hills west of Tulare Lake which agrees with Banta's statement given earlier. According to Boutell (Evermann, 1915) elk were still present in San Benito County as late as 1864.

Grayson (1920) tells of hunting elk at Tulare Lake in 1853 and Adams (Hittell, 1911) in 1855. Banta (Evermann, 1915:89) described hunting at Tulare Lake as follows:

I killed elk at Tulare Lake in 1856 and found them the same as those that ranged up as far as Martinez. Antelope, tule elk and wild horses were plentiful in the Tulare Lake country and in the vicinity of the present site of Fresno at this time.... We hunted in the tules with a sloop, using a ladder lashed to the mast for a lookout. When elk were sighted we would break our way through the tules to them, usually finding them on grass land between sloughs. In one instance in Whisky Slough I cleaned up a band of eight single-handed, keeping out of sight.

For a time it was thought the elk could never be hunted out of the marshes of Tulare and Buena Vista lakes. But in the late 1860's agricultural development was well underway, and ditching and diking began to dry up the marshes and expose the elk to hunting (Van Dyke, 1902). By 1870 the tule elk was nearly extinct.

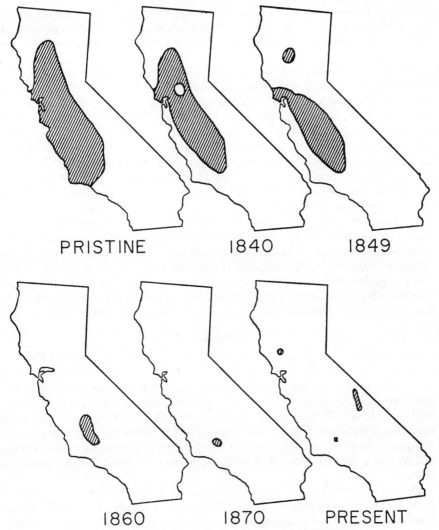

PRISTINE   1840   1849

1860   1870   PRESENT

Fig. 4. Approximate decline in the distribution of tule elk with time.

DECLINE OF ELK DISTRIBUTION AND NUMBERS

The accounts of early travelers are not so precise that an estimate of pristine elk numbers can be derived, other than to say that they were extremely abundant. But, on the basis of data given by Burcham (1957) on range areas and grazing capacity, and taking into account drought and other native competitors, a rough estimate of 500,000 tule elk seems reasonable.

From the historic records it is possible to follow relatively accurately the decline of the tule elk with passing time (fig. 4). The pristine range was retained until approximately 1800. The local removal of elk from the immediate area of the

Spanish settlements had little influence on the total range. Elk were extirpated from specific areas between 1800 and 1840. Hide and tallow hunters killed them from the accessible ranges along the south coast and the San Francisco Bay and fur brigades exhausted the population in the Sacramento Valley in the Woodland region. The period from 1840 to 1849 saw further range reduction in the southern Sacramento due to settlement, and also reduction by settlement of the more accessible south coast valleys. The period immediately following the gold rush in 1849 saw a great decline in elk distribution. By 1860, market hunters had exterminated elk from all but the large marshes of the delta and Suisun Bay, Tulare and Buena Vista lakes, and also in the hills on the west side of San Joaquin Valley. By 1870 only a few elk survived in the Buena Vista Lake area.

If the market hunter had not reduced the tule elk to the point of extinction, the farmer and rancher would have. It was doomed by the very fact that it occupied prime agricultural land.

The hopelessness of legal protection without proper enforcement is well demonstrated by the tule elk. As early as 1852 the California state legislature passed a law setting up six-months closed season on elk in twelve counties, and it was extended to the entire state in 1854 (California Fish and Game, 1928b). There was no regulation of take during the open season, and no evidence that the law had any effect whatsoever. In 1873 a law was passed which gave the elk in the state complete protection—legally. By this time there was doubt if there were any tule elk left.

RECOVERY

According to A. C. Tibbets, a deputy warden for the Department of Fish and Game, whose reputation for veracity was excellent (Grinnell, Field Notes for 1912 on file in the Museum of Vertebrate Zoology), a single pair of elk was found in the tule marshes when the drainage canal from Buena Vista Lake was put in during 1874 or 1875. This was on the ranch of Miller and Lux, the largest cattle operation in California. Henry Miller recognized the desirability of trying to save this last remnant of tule elk. He gave strict orders to his men to protect the elk, and offered a standing reward of $500 for information about anyone disturbing them.

Tibbets believed that all of the tule elk descended from this single pair. While it is impossible to prove this, the precise knowledge of the elk that Tibbets demonstrated to Grinnell would suggest that it was close to the truth. In 1912 Grinnell also interviewed W. S. Tevis, owner of another large holding in the area, the Kern County Land Company. Mr. Tevis disagreed with Tibbets, saying that the Buttonwillow area was an impenetrable willow thicket where hundreds of elk could have found cover. In addition to the fact that Tevis was not so well informed about the elk, there remains the certainty that hundreds of elk did not emerge from the willow thickets as the land was drained and developed for farming. In 1895 Van Dyke (1902) visited the herd, near Buttonwillow, which twenty years after its protection numbered only 28 head.

The buildup of the Buttonwillow herd is shown in figure 5. The initial buildup was extremely slow, but after 1895 the herd began to increase rapidly. By 1905, when the population was about 145, agricultural damage caused by the elk was becoming severe (Merriam, 1921) and in 1912 Grinnell (Field Notes) noted damage to grain, alfalfa and corn, and destruction of fences. In 1914, damage to the Miller and Lux property was estimated at $5,000 to $10,000 each year. Mr. Miller continued to protect the herd during this time, but sought to have the number reduced. Transplants were made during this time but population numbers continued to fluctuate around 400 until 1923.

Between 1923 and 1927, however, the population dropped drastically. In late 1927, Ainsworth (1932), the local game warden, conducted elk counts with the help of two or three men, and could count only 72 head. I could not locate any specific reference as to the cause of this decline. However, this was during the time

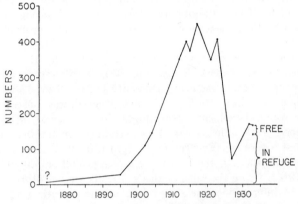

Fig. 5. Recovery of the Buttonwillow herd of tule elk.

that the Miller and Lux land was being subdivided into 40 to 160 acre blocks and sold for small farms. Probably the small operators applied their own brand of damage control.

TRANSPLANTATION

Between 1904 and 1934 a series of transplants of tule elk was made in an attempt to establish the elk more widely and to relieve the pressure of elk damage in the Buttonwillow area. In 1904, Miller and Lux arranged to turn the herd over to the United States Biological Survey, to be moved to a holding pen on the middle fork of the Kaweah River in Sequoia National Park (Merriam, 1921). The move was attempted on November 12, 1904. The plan was to drive the elk six and one-half miles to a loading corral from which they could be loaded and hauled to Sequoia Park. The drive was to be made by 35 experienced riders who volunteered their help.

When the elk were within the sight of the people at the corral, they turned and charged back through the line of riders. Finally 8 elk were roped and hog-tied. Most of the elk were seriously injured in the capture, and 4 died before reaching the corral. Three others died during the move so that only one calf lived through the ordeal. It was from specimens obtained in this operation that Merriam (1905) named the tule elk as a distinct species.

The following year, on October 15, another transplant was made. No attempt was made to drive the herd, but rather 30 animals were roped. Again many were badly injured. Three died before shipment, 25 were eventually shipped and 20 reached the park alive. Thus 21 elk were introduced to Sequoia. No further transplants were attempted by the Biological Survey.

At first the herd did well (Evermann, 1915). In 1914 it was estimated that the herd had increased to about 50 head, and already some had escaped from the enclosure (Ferguson, 1914). Again in 1916 about 50 head were reported (Taylor, 1916). Sometime between 1916 and 1920 these animals escaped from the enclosure and spread to the surrounding area. In 1922 Reddington (1922a) reported elk on the Sequoia National Forest and thought they were increasing, but the following year J. R. White (McAllister, 1924) reported only 12 head. By 1926 they were all gone (Grinnell, 1933). Judging from the reports of damage to fences and orchards caused by the free roaming elk (Ferguson, 1914), probably many were shot by landowners.

The next series of transplants was begun in 1914 under the auspices of the California Academy of Sciences (Evermann, 1915). A different method of capture was used to avoid repeating the heavy mortalities of the previous efforts. A large corral (¼ mile by ⅛ mile) with ¼ mile wings attached, was constructed about an alfalfa field to which the elk came every night. On October 11, 1914, 150 head of elk were trapped. Although the corral was strongly constructed, about 100 elk escaped the first afternoon. Eventually 54 were transplanted to seven localities. Heartened by this success, the operation was repeated in the following year (Evermann, 1916). Using the same methods, 100 elk were captured, and 92 were distributed to 14 different localities. The transplanting operations of the California Academy of Sciences were terminated at that time. Evermann (1916) summarized the project: 146 elk distributed to 19 places; 25 died; 3 fawns born in 1915; 124 left at the time of writing.

Nearly all of these transplants failed. Of the parks receiving elk, only Griffith Park in Los Angeles and Roeding Park in Fresno still maintain tule elk. The only truly successful transplant arising from this period was the Del Monte Park plant near Monterey.

Del Monte Park, Monterey herd.—In 1914, five male and five females were introduced to Del Monte Park (Evermann, 1915), but one female died and another wandered away and was lost. One calf was born in 1915 (Evermann, 1916). In several years the herd built up to a point where damage to gardens was common, and the bulls became a threat to golfers in the park. Animals were removed over a period of years. The first attempt to trap elk was made in 1920, but it was unsuccessful. Twenty-one elk were moved in 1922 to Colusa County, and they gave rise to the present-day Cache Creek herd. In 1923 the Del Monte population was estimated at 30 head (McAllister, 1924). By 1936, at least 48 head had been removed, 22 of which went to the Hearst Ranch. About 15 were still at Del Monte at that time (W. C. Russell, Field Notes for 1936 on file in the Museum of Vertebrate Zoology). In the following years the Del Monte herd was completely eliminated.

The subsequent fate of the tule elk which went to the Hearst Ranch at San Simeon is unknown. Rocky Mountain elk were introduced to the Hearst Ranch from Jackson Hole, Wyoming, and the free-roaming elk herd in the Santa Lucia Mountains at present are said to have been derived from the Jackson Hole stock (Barrett, 1966). Whether or not these animals have hybridized with the tule elk is not known at present.

Cache Creek herd.—In the spring of 1922, 21 elk from the Del Monte herd were placed on private property in Colusa County (near the junction of Highways 16 and 20) with the landowner's approval (California Fish and Game, 1930a). At least four calves were born in 1922 (California Fish and Game, 1922). One large bull wandered off to near Santa Rosa where it was killed by a hunter (California Fish and Game, 1922). By January, 1923, there were only 13 in the herd according to the landowner (McAllister, 1924). However the herd apparently built up rapidly thereafter, for by 1930, the population was estimated at 80 head (California Fish and Game, 1930b). At that time the property was sold, and the new owner felt that damage was excessive, and wished to have the elk removed (California Fish and Game, 1930a). No published records of populations have come to my attention thereafter, but apparently the population increased to perhaps 150 animals in the thirties then dropped again to the more-or-less stable population of about 80 head at present.

The Yosemite Park herd.—Mainly through the efforts of Mr. C. H. McAllister of the California Academy of Sciences, an agreement was reached with the National Park Service on March 20, 1920, to establish a herd of tule elk in Yosemite National Park. Moffitt (1934) gives a complete account of the history of this herd.

By July, 1920, a 28-acre enclosure had been erected on the valley floor near the Sentinel Hotel. Attempts to obtain elk from the rapidly expanding Del Monte herd failed when they could not be captured. However, on May 23, 1921, 3 cows and 1 calf were introduced from Del Paso Park in Sacramento. One cow died during the move. On August 20, 1921, 9 elk from Buttonwillow were introduced but two of these died, leaving 10 elk in the enclosure. The winter of 1921–1922 was unusually severe, and five of the Yosemite elk died, leaving only four cows and a spike bull on May 2, 1922. On May 12, 1922, another spike bull was brought in from Del Paso Park. Thereafter the herd built up gradually to 27 in 1933 (see Moffitt, 1934, for a complete record of numbers). They were turned out of the enclosure during the summer and fall of 1927, but because of damage and the danger to visitors of the bulls during the rut, they were rounded up and returned to the enclosure in November 1927. By 1928, National Park policy opposed the display of caged animals, and Yosemite officials began to consider moving the elk to another area. Finally in 1933, the entire herd was transplanted to Owens Valley.

The Owens Valley herd.—By the late 1920's, it was apparent that the elk in Yosemite Park would have to be moved, and a suitable situation for their transfer was sought. G. Walter Dow, hotel owner and prominent resident of Lone Pine, suggested Owens Valley as a suitable location for the elk, since the Los Angeles Department of Water and Power had purchased the bottomlands for water rights, and agriculture was no longer an important factor in the valley. Shortly afterwards Dow interested the Los Angeles Water and Power board in the introduction and secured their agreement.

The Park Service sent G. M. Wright, Chief of the Wildlife Division, to study the proposed transfer. He recommended that the transfer be contingent upon the approval of all interested parties, including the Owens Valley residents, and that there should be no danger of conflict with economic interests in the valley. This point was supposedly satisfied by Los Angeles ownership of the land. However, it is clear from Grinnell's field notes (1934) that the cattlemen who leased grazing rights from the City of Los Angeles objected strongly to the introduction from the start. Mr. Dow agreed to finance the transfer.

On October 10, 1933, the elk were crated individually and loaded on trucks; 27 head (7 bulls, 3 yearlings, 11 cows, and 6 calves) were released in a small enclosure on Owens River near the now-dismantled Aberdeen Station. One bull died later, leaving 26 animals successfully transferred. Nine days later the herd was released from the enclosure and allowed to roam freely (Moffitt, 1934).

On February 10 to 13, 1934, another group of 28 elk (3 bulls, 19 cows, 6 calves) was brought in from Buttonwillow enclosure. All of these animals survived. Thus a total of 54 elk were included in the Owens Valley transplant (Dow, 1934). According to Dow, the original animals stayed around the enclosure for about two months before moving off. However, within a year one bull wandered into an alfalfa field near Lone Pine, and Grinnell (Field Notes, 1934) reported that bulls had been seen 40 miles both north and south in the valley. At least 9 calves were dropped the first summer (Dow, 1934).

By 1937, the population was estimated at 100 head (W. W. Richardson, Field Notes, 1937), and in 1943 the first Fish and Game Department aerial census recorded 189 animals. Aerial censuses have been conducted yearly since. The buildup of the Owens Valley population is shown in figure 36.

The Buttonwillow Refuge (Tupman Reserve).—Heavy damage to agricultural crops in the Buttonwillow area continued in spite of the removal of many animals for transplantation. As long as the land was in the hands of Miller and Lux, the heavy damages could be absorbed by the sheer size of the operation. However, the small individual farm enterprises which followed the subdivision of the Miller and Lux Ranch could not stand the financial burden imposed by elk damage.

As early as 1912, Grinnell (Field Notes, 1912) recognized that a refuge would probably be the only possible recourse. In a letter to the Fish and Game Commission dated June 13, 1912 (quoted in full by Hunter, 1913), he recommended that land be acquired before subdivision made it impossible. He suggested that one section of land in the Buena Vista Lake area be purchased from Miller and Lux at a cost of about $100 per acre, and two adjoining sections to the west into Elk Hills be secured from the Federal Government; that the three sections be enclosed by an elk-proof fence; and finally that 250 acres of the bottomland be grown to alfalfa. No action was taken on this proposal. In 1928, E. A. Goldman of the Biological Survey found that the four sections, which he felt were needed for an elk refuge, were no longer available in Kern County (California Fish and Game, 1928a.) He suggested that the refuge be obtained in the Los Banos area where Miller and Lux had another very large ranch. Again, no action was taken.

Finally, in 1929, the farmers took the elk damage problem to the Kern County Agricultural Commissioner's Office, which referred it to the Fish and Game Commission (Burtch, 1934). The Fish and Game Commission developed a plan to remove all of the elk to parks and reserves, but this brought such a storm of protest from the Elks Lodge, Fish and Game Protective Association of Kern County, and conservation-minded persons that the plan was quickly abandoned. A refuge again appeared to be the only alternative. A cost study showed that it would require $100,000 to purchase and fence 1,000 acres (Burtch, 1934). Kern County agreed to put up $35,000 toward this end.

Again Miller and Lux acted while the official agencies procrastinated. They made available 600 acres a short distance southwest of the present refuge site for a temporary enclosure until a refuge could be established (Grinnell, Field Notes, 1932). In 1930 the fence was complete, and a drive like that held in 1904 was attempted with the same dismal result (Burtch, 1934). According to Burtch, a single rider with dogs managed to get 75 head into the enclosure. Grinnell (1932, Field Notes) observed that there were three riders with dogs, and that they got 31 elk in on the first attempt and small groups thereafter. When he visited the enclosure in February, 1932, there were 63 elk in the enclosure, and approximately 100 still roaming free. These latter animals persisted in damaging crops and the Fish and Game Commission put on a four-man night patrol to chase the elk from the agricultural areas until the harvests were completed.

On March 15, 1932, the State Park Commission purchased 953 acres on the present site of the Tupman Reserve, and the fence was completed by the end of August, 1932 (Burtch, 1934). The elk in the temporary enclosure were then transferred to the permanent refuge. The Department of Fish and Game managed to round up more animals, so that about 140 were finally enclosed.

By February, 1933, only about 25 head of elk were at large (E. R. Hall, Field Notes, 1933). Of these about 10 were bulls. It was hoped that removal of the bulls would result in the cows moving to the other elk in the refuge where they could be captured (W. C. Russell, 1933, Field Notes). Nine bulls were removed at that time. Elk remained outside of the enclosure until at least July, 1938, when four were taken from China Grade Bluffs, northeast of Bakersfield (specimens in Museum of Vertebrate Zoology).

From the beginning, the elk in the enclosure did not do well. In 1932 Grinnell (Field Notes, 1932) observed that the 63 elk in the temporary enclosure were generally in poor condition, and things were little better in the permanent refuge. Artificial feeding of alfalfa hay was soon begun, which, because of the abrasions of the gums caused by the coarse stems, led to a high incidence of the disease necrotic stomatitis. Construction of the Miller Canal across the middle of the refuge split it into two parts, and dried up the only natural watercourse.

Of the original 140 head in the enclosure, 28 were transplanted to Owens Valley, bringing the population down to 112. Population numbers thereafter are not available, but apparently the population rose gradually, and then declined. By 1947 there were 122 head, and only 13 calves survived in that year. In 1948, 7 calves survived and in 1949 only 2 calves survived. By 1950 the population was 73 head. Finally in 1951 the number of elk was reduced to about 35 head, and generally better conditions resulted. The development of pelleted alfalfa solved the major disease problem.

In 1954 the refuge was transferred to the State Park system, and renamed the

Tupman Elk Reserve. The present management system calls for a population of 32 head. Around 12 calves are born each season and nearly all survive.

In summary, there are about 32 head of tule elk in the Tupman Reserve, and about 80 free in the Cache Creek herd. The Owens Valley population, also free-roaming, is the largest at about 300. My biological studies were conducted mainly in the latter area, and the results obtained are presented in the following pages.

DESCRIPTION OF OWENS VALLEY
TOPOGRAPHY

Owens Valley is a deep narrow trough approximately 75 miles long and 10 miles wide (fig. 6). It is bordered on the west by the massive southern Sierra Nevada range, the eastern slope of which forms a steep escarpment culminating in a series of peaks, the highest, Mount Whitney, reaching 14,495 feet. The White-Inyo chain forms the eastern side of the valley, and although less abrupt and imposing, the highest point, White Mountain peak, also exceeds 14,000 feet. The floor of Owens Valley lies some two miles below these towering peaks at about 4,100 feet at the northern end and slopes gradually to about 3,600 at the southern end. Dry Owens Lake marks the southern end while the northern end is formed by a large volcanic tableland.

Geologically, Owens Valley was formed by the downward slipping of a block along faults on either side of the valley. The original surface lies deep below the present ground level; at some places along the eastern edge of the valley, bedrock is some 4,000 feet below sea level (Bateman, 1962).

The floor of the valley was formed by alluvium deposited in a former lake bed modified by minor stream cutting, flooding, and wind erosion. Owens River runs the length of the valley and all streams from the Sierra are tributary to it. No permanent streams flow from the White-Inyo range. Owens River formerly drained into Owens Lake. Now the water is diverted to the City of Los Angeles aqueduct.

The west side of the valley is covered by a large alluvial slope created by coalescence of the fans and glacial outwash plains. In some places this alluvial plain is eight miles wide. On the eastern side of the valley is a much less developed alluvial slope which forms distinct fans outside of the larger canyons.

Isolated groups of hills—Alabama Hills (near Lone Pine) and Poverty Hills (by Tinemaha Reservoir)—which were formed by secondary faulting, break the general level of the valley. In addition, volcanic fields with cinder cones and lava flows lie in the vicinity of Tinemaha Reservoir. The most prominent extinct volcano is Crater Mountain, south of Big Pine, which rises 2,000 feet above the valley floor.

LAND OWNERSHIP

Virtually all of the bottomland is owned by the City of Los Angeles. It was purchased in the early 1900's to obtain water rights. There is a narrow strip owned by the Bureau of Land Management on the lower alluvial fans on either side of the valley adjacent to the city lands. This strip is usually a mile or two wide. The higher alluvial fans and mountains are in the Inyo National Forest.

There are only a few small scattered privately-owned properties, other than in the towns.

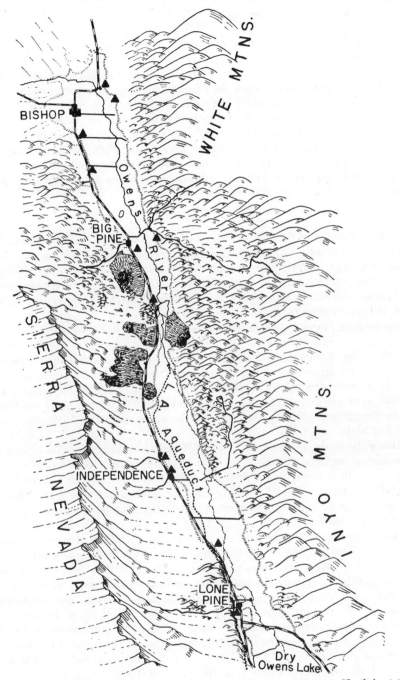

Fig. 6. Map of Owens Valley showing topography and important features. North is at the top of the figure. Triangles indicate location of alfalfa fields.

SOILS

The soils of the northern part of the valley have been surveyed by Watson and Storie (1928). As they point out, all of the soils have been formed from waterborne materials, and none have been derived in place. Most of the soils are young and have differentiated little since the time of deposition. However, locally in the bottomlands there are soils which have differentiated and formed quite distinct horizons. There are wind deposited soils in many parts of the valley.

At least four separate parent materials are present. The alluvial slope on the Sierra side of the valley is practically all granitic in origin, while the east side alluvial fans are sedimentary. The plateau north of Bishop and outcrops in the Alabama Hills are metamorphosed volcanic rock. Some local soils have been derived from volcanic lava and cinders.

CLIMATE

Owens Valley lies in the rain shadow of the Sierra Nevada, and this in conjunction with its southerly latitude predicates an arid climate. Long-term records of temperature and rainfall were available from Bishop, and shorter term records from the Los Angeles aqueduct intake. In addition, I maintained a constant-recording hygrothermograph in the heart of the Independence herd summer range, and a maximum-minimum thermometer at Big Pine.

Precipitation normally occurs during the winter months (fig. 7), and at Bishop the average for 82 years is 5.38 inches annually. Heavy rains are usually general over the valley. Summer thunderstorms are common, but rainfall then is usually light except for an occasional local cloudburst. Drought years are common. Below average rainfall occurred in 57 percent of the last 82 years. Small variations in rainfall occur locally in the valley, with clouds tending to hang along the Sierra slopes. Similarly the hills extending into the valley near Big Pine result in a pocket of higher rainfall.

During the study, the amount of rainfall varied considerably. Above average precipitation occurred in 1962–1963 when 9.44 inches were recorded at the Los Angeles aqueduct intake near Aberdeen; 1963–1964 was a drought year (fig. 7) with only 2.6 inches, most of which fell in May, 1964. Rainfall in 1964–1965 was 3.11 inches, but plant growth was only a little below average because of the early and favorable spring.

Temperatures vary widely with the seasons (fig. 7). Winter temperatures are often below freezing, and snowfall occurs in the bottomlands nearly every year. Usually it is of short duration as warm daytime temperatures accelerate melting, and the snowline recedes up the mountainsides. Heavy snows occur occasionally.

Summers are hot, with readings over 100°F being common in July and August. The diurnal fluctuation, typically wide for desert areas, is about 30 degrees in the winter and 40 degrees during the summer (fig. 7). Temperatures during the study were more or less normal with the exception of the unusually warm late winter and early spring of 1965. Highest temperature recorded was 106°F on July 24, 1964, and lowest was 9°F on December 13, 1961.

Long-term relative humidity records are not available, but the essential nature

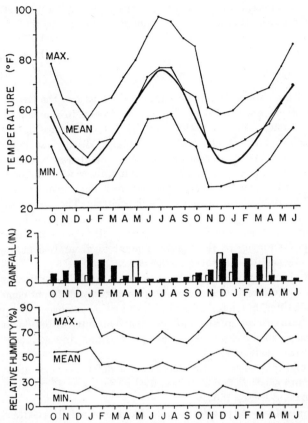

Fig. 7. Climatic data for Owens Valley. For temperature, the heavy dark curve is the long-time mean. The light curves are data recorded during the study. For rainfall, the dark bars are the long-time mean. Open bars are the two years of the study. All humidity data are from this study.

of this factor is shown by the recordings obtained during the study (fig. 7). Minimum humidities, which occur in the afternoon, are quite low throughout the year. Lowest value recorded was 2 percent. Maximum relative humidity shows greater variation, generally correlated with rainfall, and is thus high in the winters and low in the dry summer periods.

Although detailed measurements of winds were not made, daily notes were taken on relative velocity and direction. Typical valley winds occur through most of the summer. Thus during the morning there is a gentle breeze from the north as the cool air moves down the valley because of gravitational pull. With the warming of the air, a lull occurs at about 11:00 to 12:00 noon. Within an hour the warmed air begins to rise, resulting in a gentle breeze from the south which continues until evening. Eddies result in the almost continuous presence of dust-devils during the hot part of the day. Summer thunderstorms are frequently accompanied by sudden west winds as cold air sweeps down from the Sierra.

Regional winds prevail during the rest of the year, coming more often from the north than the south. Dust storms are very common during the winter months, when winds are strongest, and come from either north or south. Dust storm winds occasionally occur during the summertime, invariably from the south.

VEGETATION

Elements of the Owens Valley flora are characteristic of the Great Basin to the north, while others are typical of the Mohave Desert to the south. The diverse topographic, climatic, and soil patterns of the valley influence the interdigitation of these floras both latitudinally and elevationally. Although some mixing occurs, for the most part relatively distinct groupings of plants can be distinguished.

From prior groundwork, a number of communities were defined, and a preliminary map was drawn from aerial photographs. The various communities were then sampled on the ground to reevaluate the criteria. The single most important criterion was the use of key plant species which were characteristic of assemblages of plants, and would serve to delineate a community. Other useful criteria were the general physiognomy of the plants, amount of ground cover, degree of soil alkalinity, coarseness of the soil, and the parent material.

Ten communities were settled upon as giving a good description of the vegetation with relatively few discrepancies. Borders between different communities are occasionally distinct, but more often are intergradations over varying distances. Similarly, certain groupings of plants may have an intermediate character which does not fit the defined categories, yet are too marginal in occurrence to warrant erecting a separate category.

Aerial photographs were used to delineate the defined communities (fig. 8). An extensive ground check of the map boundaries was made. Plant names used here are from Munz and Keck (1963).

Agricultural lands.—Agricultural lands include primarily alfalfa fields, with a smattering of other cultivated crops, and a few highly developed pastures which have been leveled, reseeded, and carefully managed.

The intensive agricultural lands are highly localized and limited in extent (fig. 6). The best fields are on deep soils with high organic matter and are located on the edge of the valley bottom near the mouths of large Sierra creeks. The continuous deposition of relatively fine particles has built terraces of well watered soils with good drainage where harmful alkali has not accumulated. Some agricultural fields are located on deep sandy soils which originally supported robust stands of big sagebrush. The fields in the vicinity of Laws are on the lower edge of the alluvial fans of the White Mountains.

Abandoned agricultural lands.—These lands are those which were formerly farmed, but have been allowed to revert to a natural state. They are still in early stages of succession. Typical dominants are annual *Eriogonum* spp. and Russian thistle (*Salsola Kali*) with brush species slowly invading the edges of the fields. Most of these lands are situated on the deep sandy soils occupied originally by sagebrush, but some are on the east-side alluvial fans. They are on soils of relatively low productivity and high irrigation water debt where cropping was a marginal enterprise. Most of these lands support little grazing.

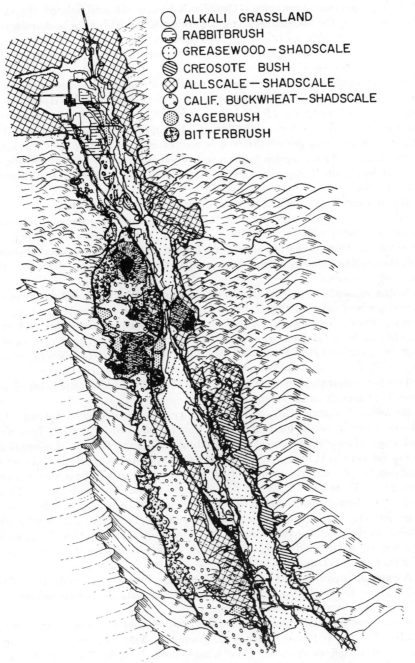

ALKALI GRASSLAND
RABBITBRUSH
GREASEWOOD – SHADSCALE
CREOSOTE BUSH
ALLSCALE – SHADSCALE
CALIF. BUCKWHEAT – SHADSCALE
SAGEBRUSH
BITTERBRUSH

Fig. 8. Natural vegetation types of Owens Valley bottomlands and foothills.

Alkali grassland community.—Grasslands occupy the lowlands on the valley floor, including the floodplains along the Owens River. This type is characterized by a high water table, a distinct hardpan, and poor drainage. These factors result in the accumulation of high alakline concentrations which preclude the development of agriculture.

Further subdivisions of this type are possible, although they were not mapped. In the low boggy areas, spike rushes of the genera *Juncus* and *Heleocharis* are associated with saltgrass (*Distichlis spicata*). Foxtail (*Hordeum jubatum*) is scattered sparsely and slender wheatgrass (*Agropyron trachycaulum*) forms occasional colonies. Forbs include *Nitrophila occidentalis* and mallow (*Sidalcea* spp.).

On the drier flats, saltgrass forms a nearly pure stand. But in local patches, encrusted black alkali deposits are devoid of vegetation other than pickleweed (*Allenrolfea*).

Alkali sacaton (*Sporobolus airoides*), an alkali-tolerant bunch grass, becomes dominant on the higher ground with saltgrass as a common associate. Occasional bunches of giant wildrye (*Elymus cinereus*) are found in this community. Big rabbitbrush (*Chrysothamnus nauseosus*) is a persistent invader in sacaton stands, and the grazing value of much of the grassland is reduced by the density of this aggressive species.

In the grassland type, mechanical disturbance results in the establishment of dense stands of the robust annual *Bassia hyssopifolia*. In the parched and cracked earth of dried-up water courses and ponds, *Bassia* is not so successful, and gives way to sunflower (*Helianthus annuus*), heliotrope (*Heliotropium curassavicum*), and alkali mallow (*Sida hederacea*). Wild licorice (*Glycyrrhiza lepidota*) is common in disturbed areas in the sacaton sites, particularly in burned areas.

This is the most important grazing type in the valley for domestic livestock and is used extensively in the summer by elk.

Rabbitbrush community.—This community was distinguished by the overwhelming dominance of big rabbitbrush, which forms a cover of about 70 percent and which gives every evidence of controlling the site indefinitely. It is restricted to the northern part of the valley where it occurs on the very edges of the grasslands on fine, moderately alkaline soils, and where saltgrass forms a very sparse understory. From here the soil grades into coarser sandy soils with low alkalinity, and the understory is composed of annual *Eriogonum* spp. and Russian thistle. Some formerly agricultural lands which are now taken over by rabbitbrush are included. In the alkaline extremities of the type, an occasional quailbush (*Atriplex lentiformis*) occurs, and on the non-alkaline fringes, four-winged saltbush (*Atriplex canescens*) is found sparingly.

A common environmental factor throughout the type is extreme dryness of the soil surface. Except in the brief period of plant growth during the spring, this type is virtually without grazing value.

Greasewood-shadscale community.—This type occupies the extensive bottomland alkaline flats on the level just above the grasslands. The site is characterized by a fine, alkaline soil overlain by loose wind-deposited sands. These factors have created an undulating surface of sandy hummocks interspersed with small alkaline depressions.

This type supports an alkali-tolerant community dominated by greasewood (*Sarcobatus vermiculatus*) but with shadscale (*Atriplex confertifolia*) as a common associate. Other species which are encountered frequently include *Dalea polyadenia*, little leaf horsebrush (*Tetradymia glabrata*), Parry saltbush (*Atriplex Parryi*), ink plant (*Suaeda Torreyana*), Nevada ephedra (*Ephedra nevadensis*), big rabbitbrush, and burro bush (*Franseria dumosa*). Spiny menodora (*Menodora spinescens*) is locally common. Quailbush is occasional on the grassland edges while four-winged saltbush occurs on the higher parts.

Herbaceous cover is very sparse in this community. Sacaton bunches are widely distributed but only occasionally common. Saltgrass is sparse. Russian thistle is the most common annual. Total plant cover is 30 to 40 percent.

This type is grazed in the winter by elk and in the spring by elk and cattle.

Sagebrush community.—The sagebrush community is characterized by the presence of big sagebrush (*Artemisia tridentata*) which is by far the dominant species. It is typically found on loose, deep sandy soils. At the north end of the valley in the bottomlands, sage occurs where wind-deposited sands have formed substantial dunes. Sage is occasionally found on dunes in other parts of the bottomlands, but these areas are too small to map. In certain areas (for example, one mile north of Big Pine) sand dunes in the greasewood-shadscale community are deep enough that sagebrush is present. These have been mapped as greasewood-shadscale because it is felt that type more accurately reflects the nature of the site.

On the Sierra side of the valley, sagebrush is most common where deep granitic soils have accumulated above glacial moraines and cinder cones, and also at the foot of the alluvial fans in the Aberdeen area. Sagebrush is also well established on lava flows where favorable moisture relations are present.

Other species in the community vary considerably depending upon site. In the bottomlands big rabbitbrush, four-winged saltbush, shadscale, spiny hopsage (*Grayia spinosa*), Nevada ephedra, blue dalea (*Dalea Fremontii*), and spiny horse brush (*Tetradymia axillaris*) are common. On the Sierra slopes big rabbitbrush, four-winged saltbush, spiny hopsage, and shadscale are replaced by California buckwheat (*Eriogonum fasciculatum*), rabbitbrush (*Chrysothamnus viscidiflorus*), and others.

Vegetation cover in the sagebrush type is relatively high (about 50 percent). Annuals are sparse in the bottomland areas, but there is a fair production on the Sierra slopes. Also in the latter area, desert needlegrass (*Stipa speciosa*) is locally abundant.

This type is used year-long by elk and the spring growth of forbs and grasses furnish early spring forage for cattle also.

Creosote bush community.—This vegetation type occupies the extremely xeric Inyo alluvial fans at the south end of the valley. It is the most clearly associated with the Mohave Desert of any of the communities mapped. It occurs on moderate slopes with a gravelly-pavement soil. Washes from rapid precipitation runoff are found throughout the type.

Vegetation cover is extremely low, probably less than 10 percent, and is composed predominantly of widely spaced creosote bush (*Larrea divaricata*). Associated are a scattering of shadscale, burro brush, and blue dalea. Occasionally

Stephanomeria, wishbone plant (*Mirabilis*), *Hymenoclea Salsola,* and allscale (*Atriplex polycarpa*) are found.

Herbaceous cover is extremely sparse, but Russian thistle, desert trumpet (*Eriogonum inflatum*), and various *Chorizanthe* species are present.

This community has no grazing value.

Allscale-shadscale community.—This community occurs mainly along the east-side alluvial fans, but it is also found on some of the lower drier Sierra fans. Allscale is one species that is found through most of this type, and it is usually dominant. However, the relative abundance of the associated species varies greatly from place to place dependent upon the site. Shadscale is probably the most frequently found associate, but *Dalea polyadenia,* winterfat (*Eurotia lanata*), Nevada ephedra, *Hymenoclea,* burro brush, spiny hopsage, rabbitbrush, spiny mendora, and desert thorn (*Lycium Andersonii*) are locally abundant. Blue dalea and spiny horsebrush are found throughout the type. Total plant cover is about 20 percent.

Herbaceous growth is very sparse. Desert trumpet and Russian thistle are fairly common, with a scattering of saucer plant (*Oxytheca perfoliata*), ricegrass (*Oryzopsis hymenoides*) and others.

The lava flows south of Poverty Hills and in the bottomlands west of Black Rock Springs differ somewhat from the typical allscale-shadscale community. Allscale is not present, but most of the associated species are found there. Thus a close affinity to this community was apparent, and the one discrepancy did not warrant naming another type. Also, typical of drier lava soils, these areas support a growth of the annual grasses, red brome (*Bromus rubens*), and to a lesser degree cheatgrass (*Bromus tectorum*).

Both elk and cattle use this community moderately, primarily as winter browse; there is some use of spring forage also.

California buckwheat-blackbrush community.—Located on the Sierra alluvial fans in an intermediate moisture situation, this type is characterized by the presence of either California buckwheat or blackbrush (*Coleogyne ramosissima*). Blackbrush, which strongly dominates certain areas, is not tolerant of burning, and it is replaced by buckwheat following a fire. Presumably succession leads back to a blackbrush stand, but change is extremely slow, and the available evidence is inconclusive. Other areas are known to have been dominated by California buckwheat for long periods of time.

A number of species are associated with this community, including Nevada ephedra, Cooper goldenbush (*Haplopappus Cooperi*), rabbitbrush, *Hymenoclea Salsola,* spiny horse brush, spiny hopsage, winterfat, and occasionally blue dalea. Brush cover is about 30 percent.

This type has a relatively high herbaceous cover. *Stipa speciosa* is common, particularly on southern exposures. In good rainfall years, annual forbs and grasses blanket the ground.

Because of the high production of spring herbaceous growth, this type has a relatively high grazing value for both elk and cattle. In addition, several of the browse species are good winter elk foods.

Bitterbrush community.—Presence of bitterbrush (Owens Valley is a zone of transition between *Purshia tridentata* and *P. glandulosa*) is the sole criterion for the recognition of this type. It occurs mainly at the head of the Sierra alluvial fans on coarse rocky soils of granitic origin. Big sagebrush is the most common associate, but Nevada ephedra, big rabbitbrush, rabbitbrush, Cooper goldenbush, and spiny horse brush are common. In areas green ephedra (*Ephedra viridis*), lupine (*Lupinus excubitus*), desert peach (*Prunus fasciculata*), blackbrush, Gregg ceanothus (*Ceanothus Greggii*), blue dalea, and white sage (*Salvia carnosa*) occur. Shrub cover is approximately 40 to 50 percent.

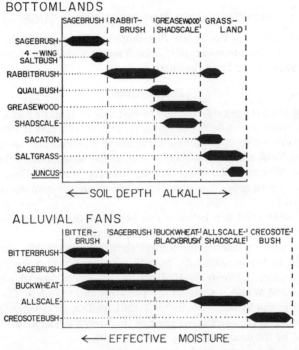

Fig. 9. Relationship of environmental factors to distribution of vegetation communities.

Herbaceous cover is again dominated by *Stipa speciosa*, squirreltail (*Sitanion Hystrix*), pine bluegrass (*Poa scabrella*), and globe mallow (*Sphaeralcea*), and a number of annual forbs and grasses are represented.

This community has the highest grazing value of any brush community in the valley. Elk use of the area year-long and deer depend heavily upon the bitterbrush for winter forage. The good herbaceous cover is used by cattle, and they also will take considerable amounts of the highly palatable bitterbrush.

RELATIONSHIP AMONG THE COMMUNITIES

The relations among the described natural communities are shown schematically in figure 9. It can be seen that in the bottomlands, degree of alkalinity is by far the most significant factor in the distribution of vegetation. Where the loose, sandy soils are deeper, alkalinity is modified and allows establishment of species with relatively low tolerance.

On the alluvial fans, good drainage has prevented the accumulation of alkali deposits and the primary ecologic factor is moisture availability. Because the moisture gradient tends to be continuously variable, the ecotone between the communities is broad, and the borders are more difficult to delineate than in the bottomland communities. The lines were drawn near the lower edge of the indicator species. This would seem to be the most meaningful place from an ecological standpoint.

DISTRIBUTION AND MOVEMENTS OF TULE ELK

The tule elk in Owens Valley are distributed in five main herds, each with its own more or less separate geographic area. These are shown in figure 10, and are described below, starting from the north.

BISHOP HERD

The Bishop herd ranges entirely on the east side of Highway 395. To the north it extends to about one mile north of Laws, and on the east it extends into the White Mountains up to approximately the lower treeline. The town of Big Pine and Westgard Road mark the southern part of the range, but to the southeast it extends across Westgard Road and well up into the Waucoba Pass area. The elk moving into this area cross Westgard Road just where it intersects the lower edge of the foothills.

There is a substantial gap between this herd and the next one south. There is almost no interchange except by bulls during the rut.

During the summer months when good forage was available, the Bishop cow herd remained in the bottomlands, mainly between Warm Springs and Collins roads. Occasionally, particularly if disturbed, the herd moved onto the lower alluvial fans of the White Mountains for relatively short periods. The Bishop herd cows wintered in the bottomlands in 1963–1964 feeding on the stands of big sagebrush. In 1964–1965 the cows spent most of the winter in the foothills where they were attracted by the unusually early green growth.

In spring the cow group split into groups of two to ten, and began moving into the higher canyons in the Whites from Laws south to Waucoba. In drought years green forage is quite limited, and elk frequently come down to various springs or to Owens River for water, then return to the hills. In good years adequate water is obtained from green feed. Calving occurs while the cows are in the rough canyons. Cows do not regroup into a herd until midsummer when they return to the bottomlands prior to the rut.

The Bishop bull group spent the summer and winter of 1963–1964 in the frequently used bull area adjacent to Highway 395 by the Hot Springs turnoff. During 1964–1965 the group was very much more scattered, and many bulls moved up into the foothills. Every year some bulls use the high country in the White-Inyo Mountains. Some large old bulls tend to be solitary until the rut.

When the rut approaches, the bull groups join the cow groups. While the smaller bulls remain near the cow herd there is considerable wandering by the

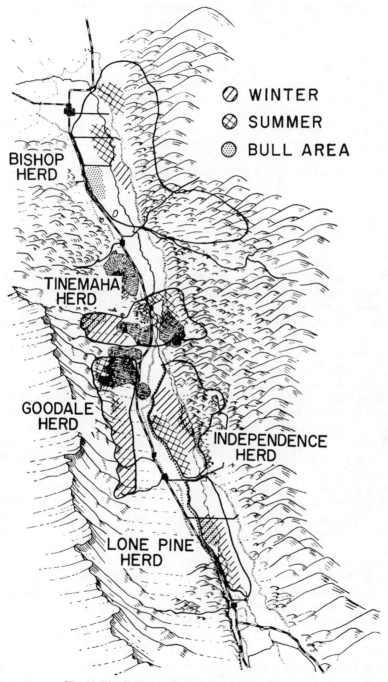

Fig. 10. Distribution of five tule elk herds in Owens Valley.

largest bulls. It is common to observe one coming across country in the distance, only to pass by and move out of sight without stopping. Tracks of bulls can be found crossing many areas where herds are not normally found.

An example of this kind of movement was furnished by "Snag," a bull with the Bishop group with peculiar antlers. He was seen in the Bishop area on July 17, 1963. On July 30, he appeared at the Independence herd as I was observing it. This was an airline distance of about 35 miles. He got my scent, wheeled, and returned the way he had come. On August 31 he was seen near the Tinemaha Reservoir and on October 29 he was with the reconstituted Bishop bull herd. On February 15 he was found in the Inyo Mountains above Soldier Canyon at 6,800 feet.

"Notch," a large bull identified by swallowtail cropping of both ears, was observed in the Independence herd during the rut in 1963. After the rut he disappeared and was not seen until the 1964 rut was underway, when he suddenly showed up again at the Independence herd. It is apparent that some bulls are acquainted with large portions of the valley.

Tinemaha Herd

The Tinemaha group summers in the bottomlands about the Tinemaha Reservoir and on the alluvial fans and lava flow immediately to the east. In the autumn, this herd crosses Highway 395 and winters on the large alluvial plain about Red Mountain, a volcanic cinder cone. In the spring the herd again returns to the bottomlands.

The crossing of the highway usually occurs adjacent to Charlie's Butte at the south edge of the range. The highway to the north is four-lane freeway, and is so strongly fenced that the elk prefer to go around the south end where the fences are weaker. I have varified crossing at this place on three occasions, and three permanent residents told of seeing elk at this place, once when they were actually on the road. Two elk were killed by cars along this stretch in 1964. While this is the most common area of crossing, in the fall of 1964 most of the herd crossed on the north side of Poverty Hills from the alfalfa fields east of the highway to the field on the west side.

In the fall of 1963, the herd crossed the highway between December 7 and 10. A few bulls still remained by the reservoir. Except for a pair of bulls which stayed on the alluvial fans on the northwest part of the area by Red Mountain Creek, these were the first elk found in the Red Mountain area after the beginning of the study in July.

The herd remained on the alluvial plain through the winter and calved there in the spring. Movements were characterized by the herd foraging back and forth between the available water sources, Tinemaha and Red Mountain creeks on the north and Taboose Creek on the south. The bulls tended to localize in the northwest corner of the plain and water at Red Mountain Creek.

During this time the ranges of the Tinemaha herd and the Goodale herd approached each other, but no satisfactory evidence of interchange was found. First, the Goodale cows are on the south end of their range at this time. Second, insofar as naturally marked animals were available, they remained specific to their areas.

Third, no cow group tracks were found moving from one area to the other. There is a buffer zone of lava flow between the two herds, and while this in no way constitutes a true barrier, there seems to be little inducement to cross. A tongue of granitic soils extends up through the lava flow behind Aberdeen to a series of cinder cones at the top. It was along this avenue that tracks were searched for, as well as in the saddle above the uppermost cone. Bull tracks were occasionally found crossing during the rut, but rarely at other seasons.

In mid-May, 1964, the cows began to cross back to the east side of the highway by Charlie's Butte. By May 29 most of the herd had made the crossing, and a reconstituted herd of 38 was sighted east of the reservoir. As in the previous season, two large bulls remained on the northwest part of the alluvial plain throughout the summer. These were probably the same individuals, but no permanent marks were present to confirm this supposition.

At the beginning of the study in the summer of 1963 this herd moved to the higher country for the new green growth, and were not required to come down for water. After they returned to the bottomlands, they began to come into the alfalfa field northwest of the reservoir. After moving to the bottomlands in 1964, the year of poor forb growth, the herd did not go to the higher country, but rather began foraging in the alfalfa immediately.

Some evidence of elk movements from the areas utilized by domestic cattle had been observed previously, but the relationship had been too subtle to assess. However a clear demonstration of this influence on elk distribution occurred in the Tinemaha herd in March, 1965. The livestock were placed on the range with the opening of the allotment on March 1. The elk cows moved back across Highway 395 near Charlie's Butte shortly afterward, and the bulls toward the end of the month. In the previous season when the livestock permittee did not stock the range because of lack of forage, the elk did not leave until calving was completed in May, even though forage conditions were very much poorer in that drought year. This response of elk had been observed by stockmen on the valley floor, and particularly in the Bishop bull herd. Turning cattle into pastures being used by elk resulted in a shift to other areas. Another example will be given with the Goodale herd below.

GOODALE HERD

The range of the Goodale herd lies entirely west of Highway 395, from Taboose Creek south to the south fork of Oak Creek. It is limited to the west by the steep scarp of the Sierra Nevada.

During the summer this herd occupies the bitterbrush area at the head of the alluvial fan between Goodale Creek on the north and Division Creek on the south. A twenty-acre burn near Goodale Creek is a favored area. Bitterbrush is the primary forage species, although a number of other plants are used. In late November, 1963, the herd shifted downhill, and occupied the low edges of the alluvial fans and lava flow behind Aberdeen Resort. They still used Goodale Creek on the north and another water source near Highway 395 on the south. Division Creek is piped from the head of the alluvial fan, but a steady leak by the old power house near the highway furnishes adequate water, and allows better utilization of the southern part of the lava.

While most of the bulls remained in this area through the winter, the cows shifted to the south, and occupied the upper part of alluvial fans as far south as the south fork of Oak Creek. This movement occurred in February, 1964.

There was some movement onto the higher benches and open areas of the Sierra scarp in the spring of 1964, but use was sporadic. Most of the animals remained on the lower fans, and calved there. By June, the herd had regrouped in the bitter-brush areas of the summer range, and particularly at Division Creek. However, in late summer, use was heaviest about the Goodale burn, which is a favored rutting place.

The fall shift downhill in 1964 occurred in September, approximately two months earlier than in 1963. This was no doubt due to the drought and very poor production of bitterbrush. Similarly the winter shift of the cows to the south was begun already in December, and most of the cow herd had shifted by January, 1965. Nearly all of the cow herd could be found in the southern area until March 1, 1965, when domestic livestock were placed on the range. The number of elk present declined rapidly, and by the end of March only a few scattered small groups could be found there. There was a substantial shift to the higher country, and a general scattering during the calving period. Regrouping on the summer range on Goodale began in late May.

INDEPENDENCE HERD

The Independence herd ranges entirely east of the Los Angeles aqueduct from the aqueduct intake on the north to Kearsarge Road on the south. Seasonally the range extends east into the Inyo Mountains. The southern boundary between this herd and the Lone Pine herd is not well defined and is arbitrarily set at Kearsarge Road. Bulls particularly move back and forth between the Independence herd range and the large bull area just south of Manzanar Road of the Lone Pine herd range. Several small groups of cows were also known to have crossed to the south. But on a total population basis this interchange is so small that for practical purposes the two herds can be considered as separate entities.

The Independence herd summers in the large grassland adjacent to the aqueduct from Thibaut Creek south to Kearsarge Road. In January, 1964, the herd shifted to the large bottomland brushfields to the northeast, where they wintered.

By late March, 1964, the cow herd began drifting back to the west, mainly between Black Rock Springs and Thibaut Creek. Calving occurred in that area. In late April, 1964, the herd returned to the grasslands of the summer range. There was virtually no movement into the Inyo foothills by the cows in 1964. A few tracks of large bulls were found about hillside springs, but total use of the high country was negligible.

The summer range was abandoned in the last few days of October, 1964, and the herd shifted more or less directly to the brushlands used the previous winter. In the spring of 1965 virtually the entire herd moved into the Inyo hills. Santa Rita Flat and the large flat to the southwest were used heavily; nearly every water supply showed fresh tracks of cow groups as well as bulls. By March, only occasional small groups of elk could be found in the bottomlands. Tracks of small groups could be found coming out of the canyons to intermittent waterholes along the Owens River channel, then returning.

It was late May, 1965, before the herd began moving back to the bottomland and late June before they came into the large grasslands for the summer.

Lone Pine Herd

The Lone Pine herd, the most southerly, is found entirely east of the Los Angeles aqueduct and Highway 395. The northern boundary, as previously discussed, borders on the Independence herd range, and is set at Kearsarge Road. To the south, the herd extends to about the railroad station, although a small group of cows was seen as far south along the dry Owens River channel as Highway 136, and a lone bull was seen at the edge of dry Owens Lake.

In the summer of 1963, the Lone Pine herd concentrated in the willows of the "island" where dry Owens River splits into two branches just east of the northern edge of Alabama Hills. Here a rank growth of *Bassia hyssopifolia* furnished a major source of food. The herd remained in this area until January, 1964, when there were frequent forays into the brushlands to the east. There was also a concurrent spreading up and down the river channel from the Manzanar area south to the railroad station. The bulls congregated in the bull area about the grassland southeast of the old Manzanar sewage treatment plant.

The Inyo alluvial fans to the east of this herd support a creosote bush community (fig. 8) which is almost worthless for grazing. The Lone Pine herd rarely uses the alluvial fans. The only exceptions are occasional lone bulls which move up into the higher country above the creosote bush zone.

In the drought summer of 1964, use of the island was greatly reduced. There was virtually no *Bassia* growth on the island that year. Alfalfa damage to the fields northeast of Alabama Hills was heavy during the 1964 season.

This herd again wintered mainly around the island and the brushlands to the east. Spring and summer found the herd again in the river bottom from the island to Locust. Natural forage conditions were improved over 1964, and the availability of native summer forage decreased the alfalfa damage.

Factors Causing Movements

Seasonal movements are not regarded as migrations. The areas used during the summer are not inaccessible because of weather during the winter. The movements are not consistent from herd to herd; at the time the Tinemaha herd is moving to higher country, the Goodale herd is shifting to the low elevations. The Lone Pine herd stays in the bottom all year. There is little synchrony in the timing of movements from herd to herd; they are local shifts in response to local conditions.

Several factors have sufficient influence upon the movements of various herds to warrant generalization. Foremost is the availability of sufficient forage of a high quality. There is a general shift from herbaceous forage during the summer to browse during the winter, although both are taken at all seasons. The Goodale herd departs somewhat from this pattern in that browse is quite important during the summer also. The extent to which the high country on both the Sierra and White-Inyo sides of the valley is used is clearly dependent upon the availability of early spring green growth of mainly herbaceous species. This, in turn, is dependent upon the amount of seasonal precipitation. In good years there is a heavy use of the high country, while in poor rainfall years this use is reduced or absent.

A second factor is use by domestic livestock. Pasturing of domestic cattle influences not only the spatial distribution of elk, but also the timing of seasonal shifts. The impact of this factor is dependent upon the availability of suitable habitat to which the elk can shift. In the winter, for example, when most of the stock is on the valley floor, there are few alternatives open to the elk. Yet, even in this situation, there tends to be a local separation of the two species.

A third factor is human activity. Human interference can cause a change in habits of the elk, and a number of instances will be given in later sections. But in general, the herds tend to occupy areas with the least disturbance. The Bishop herd, when it occupies the bottomlands, is constantly shifting from place to place because of human disturbance. In areas where the elk are rarely disturbed, their patterns of movement become fixed.

The extent to which habits of elk are altered by human disturbance is again dependent upon available options. Harassment will move them from an area provided there are adequate resources available elsewhere. When they are dependent upon a particular area, harassment will have only a temporary effect. Thus, in years of very low rainfall some herds can find no nutritious late summer food except cultivated alfalfa. Under those conditions, harassment is largely ineffective.

Long Term Changes in Herd Range

The herd areas are largely in traditional areas that the elk have occupied for a number of years. Many of them were apparently established following the first buildup of the population after introduction.

Yet some changes in the herd ranges have occurred recently. There seems to have been a general shift northward of the Bishop herd. According to local observers, the area about Klondike Lake was formerly heavily used. Now bulls are only occasionally found in that area. Also the damage to alfalfa near Laws is a recent development. Noticeable damage first occurred in 1964. Movement of this herd even farther north is unlikely because of the poor forage resources in that direction.

The Goodale herd is a recent development. Formerly elk moved back and forth between the Independence herd and the lower edges of the Goodale range. According to Harold Gates, who patrolled the aqueduct for the City of Los Angeles daily for years, there were two main crossings on the aqueduct. One was near Thibaut Creek and the other a short distance south of Black Rock Springs. The herd used to cross Highway 395 near Aberdeen Resort, and elk were frequently hit by cars along this stretch. Jones (1954) who studied the Goodale deer herd in the early 1950's, barely mentioned the tule elk. He observed that some elk came onto the lower slopes below the deer range in the winter months, and that there was no competition between the two species. Now deer-elk competition on Goodale is a serious problem (see Range Relationships section, below).

In the late 1950's this crossing by elk stopped. According to Harold Gates, elk have not crossed the aqueduct since about 1958. During the two years of this study the aqueduct road from Black Rock Springs south to Kearsarge Road was traveled at least weekly and sometimes daily. Tracks were carefully watched for and checked out. During this time only a single cow elk track was found on the aqueduct road. This cow came from the east, drank in the aqueduct, and returned to the east. No elk have been killed on the highway near Aberdeen for a number of years. Although the Goodale elk came down to the flat near the highway, no tracks were found crossing the highway, nor were any tracks or droppings found in the area between the highway and the aqueduct. Nor is there a time when a large portion of the Goodale herd cannot be located in the range described.

Another line of evidence is the presence of droppings on permanent transects on Goodale. The California Department of Fish and Game maintained pellet group plots on the Goodale deer range from the winter of 1950–1951 until 1956–1957. No elk use was recorded during this period. The United States Forest Service established pellet group transects on Goodale in 1961–1962. Although elk sign was observed, no pellet groups were tallied on the transects. In 1962–1963, 2.2 elk days per acre of use on the Goodale range was recorded. Studies of the area by this project were begun in August, 1963, and a substantial use by elk of the Goodale range was found. The pellet group transects gave 26 elk days per acre of use for the 1963–1964 season.

This boom is partly the result of a shift in use pattern due to the twenty-acre burn of 1962. Besides producing a tremendous amount of herbaceous forage during the 1962–1963 high rainfall season (9.44 inches), the burn also furnished an open area which is favored for rutting activities. But concurrently there was probably a rapid increase in the Goodale elk population which continued during the course of the study. And, along with the population increase there has been an increase in the use of the southern portions of the Goodale herd range, and a continuing expansion in that direction.

Because of the herd organization, colonization is performed by small groups rather than by individuals. Pressure to colonize new areas results from a shortage of resources, a condition under which elk readily move. In original times this was probably accomplished by buildup in population, and in the unhunted Goodale herd, this appears to be occurring at present. In the bottomlands, the periodic hunts have more or less stabilized the population, and there is little pressure for expansion.

DAILY MOVEMENTS

The elk is a highly social animal, and the herd is the focal point of its existence. The herd is a flexible entity which allows easy shifting about to obtain the most favorable environmental circumstances without disrupting the social organization of the group. Still, the herd is not truly nomadic since the previously described herd ranges are adhered to persistently in what might be described as a herd "home range." Presumably, familiarity with the range is a herd tradition passed on continuously to the young.

In any locale, elk establish a daily pattern suitable for exploiting the local resources. It soon became apparent that movements of the herd rarely involved pioneering new ground. The habit patterns suitable for exploiting each particular site within the herd range were a part of the common experience of the herd. Indeed, a herd range is nothing more than a geographic area encompassing a mosaic of such sites.

The summer range of the Independence cow herd can be used as an example. In 1963, water was abundant, and the cow group might be found in a number of places in the summer range, and would move but little from day to day. However, limited sources of water in 1964 resulted in localization of the Independence herd in small groups about sources of water. From the water the herd would feed out about one-half to one mile and back, performing the same circuit from day to day.

Although the same general route was followed, a specific trail was not formed. A herd advances on a broad front which results in a maze of individual tracks. The many and well-developed trails found in the bottomlands are maintained by livestock. During the summer, when most of the livestock is removed, the trails fall into disuse.

A certain amount of trailing occurs in other areas, such as the Goodale range where the elk come to Goodale Creek to water through quite rough terrain and tall brush. The best travel routes are used and a particular path may be beaten several inches into the substrate. When use ceases, these trails are quickly obliterated by the elements.

Elk using alfalfa fields show a systematic movement pattern of feeding at night and retreating to a safe area by day. The Tinemaha herd, for example, spends the day on the lava flow east of the Tinemaha Reservoir. At about 4:00 P.M. they are up and begin moving. By dusk, they are at the Owens River where they water and feed upon native foods along the watercourse. They then cross the river at about dark, and move into the alfalfa northwest of the reservoir by Highway 395. At times they go north of the reservoir, and then at times south and up between the caretaker's house and the highway.

Usually they leave the fields by dawn, but sometimes they can be seen in the fields at first light. They retrace their paths of the previous evening, reaching the lava by late morning. Although the details differ from area to area, the use of alfalfa fields follows the same general pattern throughout the valley.

Agricultural damage will be covered in detail in a later section.

TULE ELK LIFE HISTORY AND THE ANNUAL CYCLE
SIGNS

Tracks of elk can be distinguished from those of domestic cattle, the only animal with which they might be confused. Adult cattle tracks are usually larger, broader, and blunter-tipped than those of elk, but young cow prints are virtually identical to elk, and other characters are needed to distinguish them. In overall pattern the tracks of elk are arranged in two parallel rows, while cattle tracks have a zigzag pattern (fig. 11). Both animals place the hind foot in the print of the forefoot when walking so that the tracks are superimposed. The stride of elk is precise, and the print appears as a single track, while those of cattle are invariably offset slightly. The typical drag mark an elk makes in lifting the hoof from the print is straight forward. Drag marks are often present in cow tracks, but are frequently curved rather than straight, particularly in young animals whose tracks might be confused with those of elk. The drag mark allows determination of the animal's direction even when the imprint is not distinct.

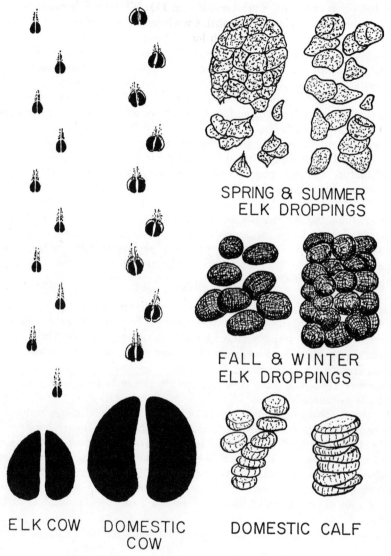

SPRING & SUMMER
ELK DROPPINGS

FALL & WINTER
ELK DROPPINGS

ELK COW   DOMESTIC   DOMESTIC CALF
COW

Fig. 11. Sign of tule elk as compared to domestic cow.

The tracks of elk calves are distinguishable from those of adults on the basis of size through their first winter. Calf tracks are broader than deer tracks of the same length. Yearling bull tracks are quite similar to those of cows, but older males have a track wider toward the front than females as has been reported for deer (McCullough, 1965b). Also the tracks of bulls increase in size with age. Very old bulls have tracks which approach those of young domestic cows in size and shape, and can be confused with them if observed casually.

The droppings of elk are characteristic (fig. 11). When on green succulent feed they are amorphous and often congealed. On winter dry feed the pellets are oblong, dark and hard, approximately ¾ inch long. Pellets from herds wintering in the brush fields of the bottomlands are frequently congealed in large tubular masses (fig. 11). The droppings of domestic calves are often mistaken for those of elk, but they can be distinguished by their characteristic shape, often being linked one to another in bead fashion, or stacked like poker chips if in amorphous condition. During the summer, elk calf droppings cannot be reliably distinguished from those of deer. By fall, they are larger than those of deer and are easily recognizable.

Other signs of elk include the characteristic appearance of antler polishing activities. The bushes with stripped bark are typical of those frequently reported in the literature. On fence posts, the wear occurs about three feet from the ground, and well-used posts taper inward at that level. Several posts were found completely worn through, and with the tops broken off. The ground is often raked with the antlers, and occasionally areas ten to twenty feet across will be ripped up.

Cast antlers are frequently encountered, and they persist for a long time. Rodent gnawing is rarely apparent, and they are reduced entirely by normal weathering. Patches of hair are found on the ground or on bushes during the period of the spring molt.

GROUPINGS

Group sizes and seasonal changes are shown in figure 12 based on the Independence herd. Other herds differ in absolute numbers, but the patterns are similar.

During most of the year the larger bulls form separate groups. These range in size from about thirty down to one, and average about six. As mentioned earlier, old bulls are often solitary. Even during this time, however, a few bulls remain with the cow herds (fig. 12). These are mainly the spike bulls, but often young adult bulls are included.

With the approach of the rutting season, the bull groups disperse and join the cow herds. For example, the Hot Springs bull group of the Bishop herd declined from 18 on July 19 to 15 on July 22, 11 on July 31, 9 on August 10, 2 on August 15, and all were dispersed by September 1. As the rut begins, one bull assumes command of the cow group and drives the other bulls out of the herd. The bachelor bulls form a retinue which remains in the vicinity of the cow herds throughout the rut. Bulls do not form geographically separate groups again until the end of the rut.

Changes in the size of the bull groups are frequent due to the loose social structure.

Several cases were observed of male yearlings just beginning their first antler growth joining the bull groups during the spring calving period. Usually the yearling males remain with the cow groups until they are driven out by the herd bull during the rut at which time they join the bull retinue. After the rut some remain with bull groups but many return to the cow groups and do not join bull groups until the following season.

Many changes in the size of cow groups are also due to happenstance. Still, several seasonal changes are apparent in figure 12. Groups are large during the pre-rut and early rut period. As the rut progresses, the cow herd is broken into subunits and the average group size declines. At the end of the rut, the herd regroups and most of the cows will be in a large herd.

In winter, mean group size declines, particularly if there is movement into the higher country. The absence of data in the spring of 1965 is due to the virtual disbanding of the Independence herd in the foothills where observation was difficult. Small group size continues during the spring calving period. When the calves are able to follow the herd, the cows again aggregate.

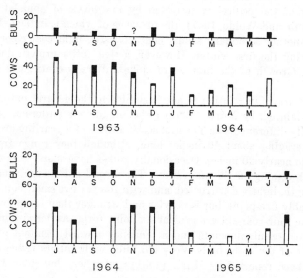

Fig. 12. Changes in group size and composition seasonally, based on observations of the Independence herd. Bulls in cow groups are indicated by black at the top of the white bars.

DAILY ACTIVITIES

During the many extended periods of observation, the number of animals active was recorded at five-minute intervals. Mean values calculated from this mass of data showed a statistically demonstratable decline in midday activity. Nevertheless, a pattern of alternating periods of rest with active periods better describes what is observed on a day-to-day basis. The length of these periods varied considerably, but were usually about two hours of feeding followed by two hours of resting. Limited nighttime observations, and following of paths taken by herds during the night, show that a similar rhythm is maintained around the clock.

Frequent disturbances alter this pattern. If a herd has just bedded, and is only momentarily disturbed, they will usually bed again. However, if the disturbance occurs after having been bedded for a longer period, the herd will begin feeding. Bulls during the rut often will herd the cows up and will continually disrupt the usual pattern. On the other hand, the bull serves to coordinate the activity of a large cow group by keeping them bunched, and engaged in the same activity. In large groups at other seasons, sometimes one part of the group will be bedding down as another is just getting up to feed, so that opposite ends of the strung-out herd are out of phase. Even in a bedded group, animals frequently stand up, turn about, look around, and bed down again.

Antler Development with Age

At birth, male calves give no indication of the pedicel sites on the frontal bones which will give rise to the pedicel (Goss, Severinghaus and Free, 1964). By the first winter, the pedicel site is clearly visible on the five- to six-month-old calf. Development of the pedicel is activated by low levels of gonadal testosterone (Wislocki, Aub, and Waldo, 1947), the presence of which is indicated in the male elk calf by another secondary sexual characteristic, light coat color, which also develops during the first winter. However, active antler growth does not begin until spring. Growth of the first set of spike antlers is continuous with pedicel growth.

The size of antler in relation to age is similar to the general pattern given for Rocky Mountain elk by Murie (1951) although tule elk antlers are smaller, and show a slightly different form. The first set of antlers of a yearling are a simple set of spikes averaging about 10 inches long, although they range from virtually nothing up to nearly 20 inches. Occasionally spikes have simple prongs an inch or two in length coming off the main beam. The second antlers are usually 25 to 30 inches in length, lightly constructed, and with four or five small points. The third set is invariably five-point, but is heavier and stronger than the previous set. The antlers of the four-year-old are typical six-point form. Antler size increases with age, and extra terminal points and a tendency toward terminal palmation are characteristic of the older bulls. Very old bulls with antlers reduced to clublike spikes have been reported by Murie (1951) and others, but none were observed in this study.

Antler Casting

Antlers are usually cast in March, but cast bulls have been observed as early as February 6, and as late as May 5 (fig. 13). With only a few exceptions, the largest bulls cast earliest and the smaller ones later as is general among cervids (Goss, 1963). Generally last to cast are the yearlings. An exception is that occasionally a few yearlings cast first (fig. 13), as was observed by Murie (1951).

This anomaly is probably correlated with the near absence of antler growth in some yearlings, and is probably related to body size and to testicular influence. Following good rainfall years, the crop of calves shows a marked difference in body size. The larger calves, which predominate, constitute a group of animals of more or less the same size born at the typical season. The smaller calves are late born. Consequently, the late born grow only the pedicel or spikes several inches high (these small yearlings are referred to in this paper as "nubbins") while normal yearlings grow typical spikes before the rising testosterone level of sexual development inhibits further growth, its normal role in maturation of antlers (Wislocki, 1943).

Casting of antlers in the spring is due to falling testosterone levels with regression of the gonads. The situation in the small spikes is not clear, but it seems probable that they undergo sexual regression early, perhaps because they were barely mature in the first place.

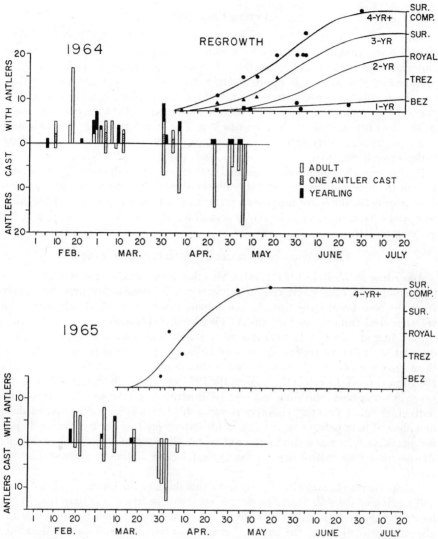

Fig. 13. Comparison of antler casting and regrowth by year. Note the variation in timing between years. The late retention of antlers by yearlings also occurred in 1965, but was not adequately quantified.

The base of the newly cast antler is usually pure white, although occasionally bits of dried blood are present in the porous bone. Bleeding is usually slight, but one case of substantial bleeding was observed. This animal was surprised in his bed, and as he fled, he left an easily followed blood trail for about three-quarters of a mile. Several days later I had an opportunity to observe him carefully at about 15 yards distance, and verified that he had no body wound, and had only recently cast antlers.

ANTLER REGROWTH

Since antler casting itself is a process of regrowth (Waldo and Wislocki, 1951), elaborate reorganization occurs over a considerable period of time before visible appearance of the new antler. In the tule elk, the period from casting until appearance of new growth is approximately a month (fig. 13). As with casting, the oldest bulls begin regrowth earliest, and the smallest last. It is interesting that the new yearlings begin growth of their first spikes earlier than the previous year's spikes, now two-year-olds, which cast so late. The antler growth curve is sigmoid in shape, with the exception of the yearlings, which show a more or less linear antler growth (fig. 13).

During growth, the antlers are carried carefully to avoid damage. Rings of bone around the hard antlers are commonly observed, and these mark sites of fractures during growth. Bulls are often seen scratching the velvet gingerly with a hind foot, and even more commonly gently scratching their flanks with the tips of the growing antlers.

MATURATION OF ANTLERS AND SHEDDING OF VELVET

According to Wislocki (1943), mineralization is initiated by the reactivation of the gonads and consequent rise in testosterone. Mineralization proceeds slowly from the base toward the tips. As the gonads reach their full development, the velvet is shed from the mature antlers (Wislocki, 1943; Robinson et al., 1965).

Shedding of velvet by tule elk is a precipitous event. Figure 14 shows the shedding schedule for the Independence herd bulls, two years or older in age. Most of them shed in a matter of ten days. Spikes shed velvet later than the older bulls in 1963, but carried the velvet throughout the 1964 rut, although some shed late in the year. The process of shedding can best be illustrated by relating the course of an individual bull. "Tritops," a clearly recognizable bull which was the first to shed, first showed bare patches on the tips of his antlers on July 28. By August 1, just four days later, he was virtually clear of velvet. Observations on other known bulls showed that four to five days is the typical length of time for removal of the velvet.

This period is characterized by rigorous thrashing of the herbage and prodding and tearing of the soil. Shedding progresses from the tips of the tines toward the base. As the velvet is stripped away, it hangs in tattered ribbons, revealing the glistening white bone of the antler. Considerable bleeding accompanies shedding.

Wislocki (1942) felt that dried blood was responsible for staining the antlers, but this overlooks the pure white color of the newly exposed antler. Furthermore, it fails to explain why the antlers show essentially the same pigmentation as the teeth. Undoubtedly, most of the staining comes from the normal chemical constituents of damaged plant tissues. Exactly what components are responsible is unknown, but they are apparently associated with climatic patterns. Antlers of animals living in xeric environments show lightest pigmentation, while those in very wet areas are generally darkest.

While fence posts, woody bushes, and tree limbs are used to some extent by tule elk, most rubbing is done on low-growing herbaceous vegetation and on the ground.

Antler Abnormalities

Minor abnormalities in the placement of tines, form, number of points, etc. are quite common in these elk, and have little bearing on the functional purposes of the antlers. That these may be genetic in origin is suggested by the work of Linsdale and Tomich (1953) and Winans (1913). However, abornmalities of antlers which are permanent because they reflect pedicel deformation are also common. This kind of deformation occurs in approximately 5 percent of the bulls in Owens Valley. In some cases the antler fails to develop at all. In others it has

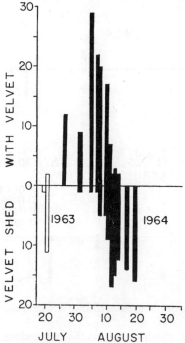

Fig. 14. Shedding of velvet in the Independence herd. Data for 1963 are limited since the study had just begun, but the marked difference in timing between years is readily apparent.

a stunted and imperfect form, typically an outward curved club-form with a single upward projecting tine near the base. Occasionally multiple tines arise from the single deformed pedicel. Having the antler cocked downward along the cheek is also a common variation. Almost without exception, the opposite antler is typical for the age class.

Since these bulls are ineffectual as herd bulls, it does not seem that these abnormalities are likely to be genetic in basis. Also the fact that only one antler is deformed would seem to argue for an environmental cause. Goss (1961) has shown experimentally that damage to the lateral part of the pedicel results in permanent deformation of the antler. The antlers of the tule elk are extremely fragile, and this factor may be related to abnormalities. The problems involving mineral metabolism will be discussed later in the section on food habits.

A final aspect of the antler cycle, and also of all other life cycle events, is the pronounced influence of plane of nutrition upon the timing of events. This influence will be considered below under a single heading for all life cycle data.

MOLT

The spring molt varies between animals in the same manner as antler casting. Oldest animals are earliest, with the previous year's calves being latest. An exception is adult cows with nursing calves, which are delayed in shedding and coincide more or less in timing with the yearlings.

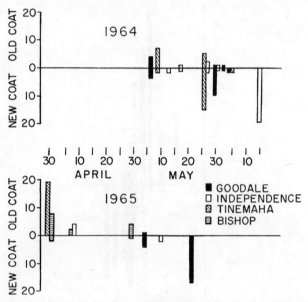

Fig. 15. Timing of spring molt, based on observations of four Owens Valley herds.

The period of molting, which also shows the tremendous influence of nutrition, is shown in figure 15. The molt begins on the forelegs and lower shoulder, followed shortly by the hind legs. It then spreads along the sides and to the neck. The molt line then moves rearward along the back of the neck, over the back and flanks, and finally to the rump. This pattern probably is simply a function of abrasion on grass and brush which scrapes the old hair as the animal moves. Clumps of hair caught on bushes are a routine sight during the molt.

The new summer coat is short, smooth, sleek and rufous reddish in color, and stands out in sharp contrast with the faded shaggy winter coat. Bulls at this time become the same reddish color as the cows and lack the characteristic dark neck mane. This, plus the absence of prominent antlers, gives them an appearance similar to that of the cows. The old hair clings together, and animals in the process of molting often trail banners of old coat along the sides and back.

Examination of museum skins shows that there is no fall molt, but that the changes in color and length are due to continued growth and fading of the same

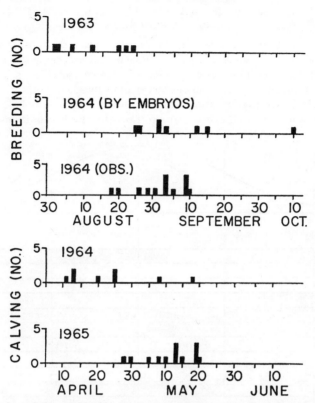

Fig. 16. Timing of the rut based upon observed copulations in the Independence herd and birth of calves for the same herd. The observed copulations for 1964 are compared with estimated breeding dates from embryos collected from cows taken in the legal hunt. Birth of calves in 1965 is projected from the dates of copulation based on a 250-day gestation period.

coat which began growth in the spring. By late October and November the coat has completed the gradual change to the heavy, light-colored pelage of winter.

BREEDING SEASON

Many physical and behavioral changes in the bulls herald the approach of the rut in late July and early August. These are presented in detail in the section on behavior, where a full discussion of the breeding season is given. However, it is the receptivity of the cows which ultimately determines the timing of the actual breeding. The breeding dates based on observations of copulation are shown in figure 16 for the Independence herd. Once again, the nutritional influence is obvious between years.

BIRTH OF CALVES

The time of birth of calves in the Independence herd as observed in 1964 is shown in figure 16. For 1965, the dates of birth are projected from the dates of observed copulations on the basis of a 250-day gestation period (see section on reproduction).

TIMING OF THE ANNUAL CYCLE

One of the most important proximal timing factors is the level of nutrition of the food available to the elk. Nutrition influences all aspects of the annual cycle (fig. 17). On a season-to-season basis, events in the year of 1963, a high rain fall year, were approximately two weeks earlier than in 1964, a drought year. Although 1965 was a below-average rainfall year, the spring was exceptionally early, and forage production was well above average. These favorable conditions resulted in

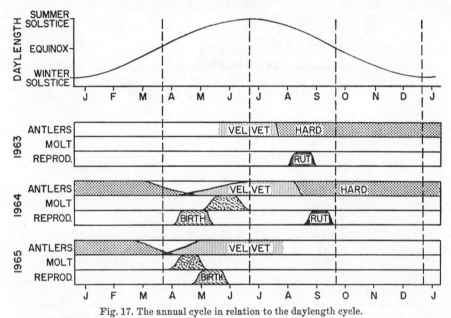

Fig. 17. The annual cycle in relation to the daylength cycle.

a remarkable advance of the cycle to a timing more or less comparable to that of the 1963 season.

This relationship is further apparent on a herd-by-herd basis. The habitat occupied varies to a greater or lesser degree between herds, and these differences are reflected in their nutritional status. Thus the Goodale herd was clearly the one on the best feed, and hence the most advanced in the life cycle during the good year of 1963. Cow groups were observed unaccompanied by bulls at a time when the rut in the bottomland herds was still on. Calves in the Goodale herd were dropped at least as early as March 20, while the earliest in the Independence herd were born in April. In the bottomlands, the southern herds (Independence and Lone Pine) were ahead of those in the northern part of the valley. Many bulls were still in velvet in the Bishop herd when the Independence bulls had polished antlers. The rut was well along, and a copulation was observed in the Lone Pine herd on July 23 when all of the Bishop herd bulls were in velvet.

Significant shifts in this pattern occurred in the poor season of 1964. The

Goodale herd was again earliest in the spring, having shed antlers and undergone molt in advance of the bottomland herds. The advantage in nutritional status was due to a carryover of forage from the previous season. By summer, this resource had been used and the timing of later events was like that in the more advanced bottomland herds.

In the bottomlands, the pattern of the previous season had been reversed. The Bishop and Tinemaha herds were earlier in the cycle than the Lone Pine and Independence herds. The success of the southern herds in 1963 was due to the tremendous production of *Bassia*. In 1964, by contrast, there was almost no *Bassia*. The Independence herd was the worst off and the latest in the annual cycle; the other bottomland herds turned to heavy depredations upon alfalfa, but the Independence herd had no alfalfa available. Antler polishing activities were observed in the Tinemaha herd on July 24, while it was August 1 before the first bull at Independence began antler polishing. On August 5, five Bishop herd bulls were completely out of velvet, and on August 7, fourteen Bishop bulls were moslty out. This was approximatley a week ahead of the Independence herd (fig. 14). In the good spring of 1965, antler casting and molting of the northern herds were still slightly ahead of the southern herds, but the greatly improved conditions in the latter area may have allowed them to close the gap by late summer and the breeding season. The completion of the study at the end of June precluded these observations.

These results demonstrate the necessity of an adequate supply of nutritious forage throughout the year. The decline of the Independence herd came because of the failure of spring and early summer forage. Winter forage for this herd remaining from the previous favorable season was at least as good, and probably better, than for the northern herds. Similarly, the advantage of the Goodale herd over the bottomland herds declined late in 1964 because of poor late summer to early winter forage. Condition of all herds improved greatly with the good spring of 1965.

Not only is the timing of events altered by nutrition, but also the rate. This is particularly noticeable in casting and regrowth of antlers (fig. 13). In the good seasons these processes were completed in a much shorter time than in the poor year, indicating that availability of nutrients plays a major role in the rate of those phenomena involving growth. It is also significant that these events coincide with the period of first active vegetation growth in the spring when nutrients are most available (fig. 17).

While nutrition has an important local influence upon the annual cycle, the ultimate factor in setting the cycle is no doubt photoperiod. As observed by many authors, the breeding season of most north temperate ungulates is associated with declining daylength, and this is true of the tule elk (fig. 17).

Bissonnette (1941) found that keeping goats in a darkened situation hastened the breeding time, thus adding experimental support to the idea that declining light serves as the clock for the rut, and Goss (1963, 1967) has shown experimentally with sika deer (*Cervus nippon*) that it is, indeed, the decrease in daylength in the fall which regulates the antler cycle in cervids.

REPRODUCTION IN TULE ELK

This section will cover primarily the role of the female in reproduction, including birth, care, and development of the calf. The role of the male in reproduction will be presented in the section on behavior.

AGE AT MATURITY

The females of most subspecies of elk typically first breed as two-year-olds. However, breeding of yearling females is not uncommon under good food conditions (Buechner and Swanson, 1955; Kröning and Vorreyer, 1957; and others). Yearling cow tule elk reach adult size by midsummer of the yearling year at which time they are indistinguishable from adult cows. In most other elk, yearlings can be recognized through their second summer.

The reproductive tracts of four female yearlings taken in legal hunts since 1961 were examined by Oscar Brunetti of the Fish and Game Laboratory, and three were gravid. The fourth apparently had a corpus luteum in one ovary, but no fetus could be found. One copulation observed in this study involved a cow which appeared to be a yearling. This was in the Independence herd in the poor year of 1964, as was one of the above known cases of yearling breeding. It seems the yearling females of the tule elk commonly breed.

Murie (1951) pointed out that yearling male Rocky Mountain elk show behavior which would suggest maturity; and the same has been observed in tule elk. Conaway (1952) has shown that yearling Rocky Mountain elk produce live sperm. While spikes are not able to compete successfully with the older bulls for females, the observation that cows in an enclosure were bred when only yearling males were present (Moffitt, 1934) demonstrates that tule elk yearlings are physically capable of breeding.

CONCEPTION AND GESTATION PERIOD

Breeding is not accomplished until the cow becomes receptive and will allow mounting by the bull. Collection of a receptive cow from the Tupman Enclosure herd during the annual reduction showed that receptivity may occur prior to ovulation, since the distended follicle still had not ruptured. Morrison (1960a) reported a 21-day estrous cycle in Rocky Mountain elk, should the cow fail to breed in the first receptive period.

The gestation period of the tule elk was not determined on known individual cows. However the intensive observations of the Independence herd allow a fairly close estimation of gestation. From the earliest copulations in 1963 to the earliest births in the following spring gives a period of about 250 days (fig. 16). This agrees closely with the 247-day gestation period reported for the Rocky Mountain elk by Morrison et al. (1959).

In figure 16 it can be seen that estimation of breeding dates derived from embryos taken from Independence herd females during the 1964 hunt differ slightly from the observed breeding dates. These estimates, performed by the California Fish and Game Laboratory, were based on information on embryo growth in the Rocky Mountain elk (Morrison et al., 1959). However if a small correction in the growth curve is made to offset the smaller size of the tule elk and lower calf weights at birth, the estimated and the actual breeding dates agree closely.

BIRTH

Normally a single calf is born, but one cow taken in the 1964 hunt was carrying twin fetuses. Twins, though unusual, have been previously reported by Murie (1951), Kittams (1953), and Kröning and Vorreyer (1957).

The expectant cow leaves the herd just prior to birth and selects a place removed from the area normally used by the grouped herd. I have not observed an actual birth, but I have come upon a newborn calf. On April 13, 1964, at about 10:00 AM I flushed a lone cow. On searching the area I found a newborn calf, umbilical cord still wet and a trace of moisture still on the pelage (pl. 1). It had probably been born just that morning, since things dry rapidly in the low humidity (22 percent at 10:00 AM) and intense sunlight. The calf was able to stand, but could barely hobble about, with arched back, hunched shoulders, and wide-spread, partially flexed legs. It would go to the next bush and lie down in the typical pose shown in plate 1. The coat of the calf is a very light rufous color, much lighter than that of the newly-shed adult animals. It is only faintly spotted. Compare the pattern of the calf in plate 1 with photographs of prominently spotted Rocky Mountain elk calves (Johnson, 1951). The generally dull pattern of the tule elk calf is appropriate to the light tones and little contrast of the desert. While the calves' neutral shades do not attract notice, they are by no means cryptically colored, and are easily recognized once the eye falls on them.

WEIGHT AT BIRTH

In 1964 I managed to catch and weigh six calves (not counting recaptures). Although the mean for the six is 28.7 pounds (range, 18 to 42), this is too high for newborn weight since some of the calves were older. The three youngest calves showed a newborn weight of approximately 20 pounds. However, a 38-pound male was a relatively young calf, suggesting that he weighed considerably more than 20 pounds at birth. Probably the average of all newborn calves would be between 20 and 25 pounds, with a range of about 18 to 30 pounds. Johnson (1951) found that twenty-three newborn to one-day-old Rocky Mountain elk calves weighed from 19 to 45 pounds with an average of 32.5.

Three recaptures of marked calves gave a growth rate for tule elk calves of approximately one pound per day. This is lower than the two pounds per day obtained for Rocky Mountain elk by Johnson (1951). However, when his greater number of older calves and their larger initial size is taken into consideration, the gain in relation to body weight is probably similar for both forms.

PRIMARY SEX RATIO

Of the six calves caught four were females and two males. This sample is obviously too small to be meaningful, but when it is added to the sexed embryos examined by the Department of Fish and Game, a total sample of 42 is obtained, with 21 males and 21 females. The balanced primary sex ratio agrees with reports of Johnson (1951), Kittams (1953), and Murie (1951), for Rocky Mountain elk, and Kröning and Vorreyer (1957) for red deer.

BEHAVIOR OF THE COW AND CALF

During the day the cow beds and feeds near the calf. I have found cows as near as 30 yards and as far as about 300 yards from the hidden calf. The calf, rather than the cow, selects the hiding place by wandering off some 20 yards or so and bedding down under a bush. Several hiding places are usually examined before one is finally decided upon. Most Independence herd calves bedded under grease-wood (*Sarcobatus*) bushes (pl. 1), but rabbitbrush, quailbush, and dried *Phragmites* patches were also used. Availability seems to be the determining factor; entirely different sets of plants were used in other herd areas.

The cow will come to the defense of the calf against predators, with the exception of man. When a calf is caught or chased, it squeals loudly and frequently. If the cow has not already discovered that a human is involved, she will come back to the calf until she indentifies the intruder as a human. She then will leave the area, usually joining other groups of elk. I have waited until dark trying to see the disturbed cow return to the calf, but always without success. However, examination of the tracks next morning always showed that the cow returned during the night and found the calf.

When undisturbed, the calf often sits with its head up and looks around. It flops its ears to chase away flies, and often lifts its nose into the wind and tests the air for scents. Occasionally an older calf will stand up and shift positions, or even move to a nearby hiding place, but at the slightest sign of danger it lowers its head to the ground and remains motionless.

When the cow returns for the calf, she gives a nasal whine which is described by Murie (1951) and Harper et al. (1967). She gives the call as she approaches the location of the calf, and the calf returns the call and comes to meet the mother. Even the first night after birth, the calf joins the cow during the dark hours, and follows her on her feeding route. The cow remains in the same vicinity all night, often crossing and recrossing her trail. This amounts to a substantial workout for the calf since a linear distance of several miles is common for these nightly forays, and the calf follows all the way. The resulting tracks are so confusing and the distance so great that tracking was found to be a poor method of calf location. In only one case was a calf located when its tracks were found to leave those of the cow, and it was trailed to its bedding place.

EARLY DEVELOPMENT OF THE CALF

The course of development of the calf can best be presented by the history of Female No. 2, the newborn previously described (pl. 1).

DAY ONE: Calf, a female, was born in the morning, caught, and earmarked at 10:00 AM. It could barely stand, and walked poorly. Weight 18 pounds.

DAY TWO: At 6:00 AM the cow and calf were found together about 300 yards north of the birthplace. The cow began to move at a trot and the calf was unable to keep up and fell behind slowly. It soon dropped down and hid. I ran it down easily. Weight 19 pounds.

DAY FIVE: Located calf about ½ mile west of where she had been caught on day two. Caught her before she got up. Weight 22 pounds, and she seemed very strong and in good condition. When released she headed southwest, but after travelling about 100 yards she swung north, then proceeded in a large circle and bedded down in a *Phragmites* patch about 100 yards from where

I had caught her. The run covered about 700 yards. I thought I could have run her down in a fair chase but it would have been a close race.

DAY THIRTEEN: As I drove through the area where the calf had been last seen, I jumped the calf and cow. They ran parallel to the road so that I was able to time them with the car. With the cow running at normal herd speed (22–24 mph), the calf kept up. When the cow was forced to full speed (about 28 mph) the calf fell behind and soon stopped and hid. As I approached her on foot, she jumped up and easily escaped. I later jumped her again where she had hidden about 300 yards from the first site, and she headed back to the area where I had seen her with the cow in the morning.

DAY SIXTEEN: Walked the area in search of Female No. 2. Found the fresh moist remains of an elk calf cranium and parts of the lower jaw where a coyote (*Canis latrans*) had lain under a bush and chewed them up just that morning. The cranium showed signs of hemorrhaging, suggesting that the coyote had made the kill, rather than finding the calf dead. There was only one other elk calf in this area, and I jumped him later in the morning. So while there is no absolute certainty that this was Female No. 2, it probably was, for she was never seen again.

The observations on this calf show the relatively rapid development of the motor responses of the calf, growth rate, and reliance on hiding as a means of avoiding enemies. By two weeks of age, the calf is able to keep up with most of the movements of a herd, but it is probably about three weeks that the cow normally brings the calf into the herd.

Another important fact is that the calf remains in the same general area throughout its early development. The entire travels of Female No. 2 occurred within an area of about three-quarters of a mile in diameter. In other cases I have repeatedly tried without success to chase a calf away from its home area. It will circle back when it gets very far from where it was found, and when chased in the opposite direction does the same thing.

TEMPERATURE REGULATION

While air temperatures are not excessive during the calving period, the direct sun, lack of shade, and white alkaline substrate result in relatively intense heat near the ground where the calves remain through the day. On the other hand, temperatures at night are fairly low, and occasionally skiffs of snow occur during the calving season. In 1964, cold rain and snow occurred on April 19. The calf must be able to adapt to these extremes.

On April 17, 1964, I had an opportunity to observe the means used. I approached a calf without its detecting me at 11:25 AM and watched it with binoculars and spotting scope at a distance of about 20 yards. At 11:30 AM the temperature was 79°F and the relative humidity 14 percent. The calf was lying on its ventral surface with its forelegs out from the body and extended forward. Its back was elevated. It was exposing itself to the air as well as it could. In addition it was panting continuously. At 11:30 I counted 144 pants per minute. At 11:56 clouds obscured the sun and the mild south breeze suddenly shifted to the west. I counted 100 pants per minute shortly afterwards. With the cold wind coming down from the Sierra the air turned cold. At 12:05 I made two successive counts of 24 and 25 pants per minute. These came during short periods, with rests in between. They soon stopped entirely and I became uncomfortably chilly in a heavy khaki shirt. The calf settled down to the ground almost out of view of my position, shifted to its side, folded in its forelegs and curled its head around to its side. In about 15 minutes it had shifted from trying to dissipate heat to trying to conserve it. At 12:30 the sun came out and the rest of the day was comfortable with a steady cool breeze. I observed until 5:00 pm, but the calf did not resume panting.

NURSING

Normally a cow will allow only her own calf to nurse, although other calves try to join in. Only one case was observed where another calf approached from the rear while the cow's own calf was nursing and was able to nurse for about 20 seconds. Most nursing is initiated by the cow with a signal that is obvious to the calf, since it leaves what it is doing and immediately runs to the mother and is never rejected. I have not been able to determine precisely what the signal is, although it is probably auditory. Harper et al. (1967) refer to Roosevelt elk cows calling their calves for nursing using the cohesion call. If the same call is used by tule elk, it must be given very quietly. Calves often try to initiate nursing, but they are only occasionally succesful.

Nursing usually occurs following a bedding period, but I have observed a calf nursing a bedded cow. The calf butts vigorously, and continues until the cow terminates the feeding by unceremoniously walking away. Twenty nursings were timed and ranged from 15 to 120 seconds with a mean of 40.3. In general the length of nursing depends upon the time since the previous feeding.

The calf begins to take tender green shoots several days after birth. A recently dead calf, about one day old, was examined and there was only curdled milk in its stomach. However a calf four to five days old was observed actively feeding on new grass, and this is commonly observed in calves of a week or two. The persistence of these calves in feeding suggests that a fair amount of material is ingested; but obviously the calf is primarily dependent upon milk. By several months of age the calves are feeding routinely with the rest of the herd.

Weaning begins in September as the cows are often observed rejecting the attempts of calves to nurse. In 1963 the last observed nursing was September 14, while in 1964 it was September 11. Some nursing continues after this period since two cows taken in the 1964 hunt in late October were still lactating. However most cows are dry at that time.

MOLT OF CALF COAT

The calves molt the spotted coat in late July and August when they are approximately four months old. The molt is very obvious as the calf's new pelage is the same short red coat as that of the adults in their spring molt. As the coat grows in length, the reddish tint is lost and the calves become the same color as the cows.

MORTALITY OF CALVES

When the calf is old enough to be brought into the herd, it is virtually secure against predation. There are no predatory animals in the tule elk range today which are effective against the herd. The ratio of calves to cows remains the same from the time the herds reconstitute following the calving until December (see Population Dynamics section, below).

It is during the period from birth until the calf can be brought into the herd that it is vulnerable. Coyotes are extremely abundant in Owens Valley. They were seen almost daily, and their tracks were encountered everywhere. This sheer number, hunting in a random fashion, would constitute a considerable hazard to the defenseless calves.

Johnson (1951) believed that new calves were scentless, which would serve as a means of avoidance of predation. Murie (1951) discussed this subject at length and gave conflicting evidence. He concluded that there is probably some scent, but that it is slight. My observations agree with this conclusion. Certainly the mother is easily able to distinguish her own calf from all the others, probably by scent. A totally neutral-scented living organism is hard to imagine. Yet, the scent of the new calf cannot be great. The cow's use of calls to locate the calf, and the reluctance of the calf to leave a particular area, argue against a developed scent. The sort of scent trail which would allow a cow to follow the calf to a far-removed place would also give predators a fool-proof hunting cue. I have observed a coyote pass less than 100 yards downwind of a hidden calf on a day with a steady medium wind. It passed without a sign of having detected the scent of the calf, although it bolted when it struck my trail from earlier in the day.

The second line of defense is the presence of the watchful cow nearby. She investigates any disturbance, and routs the coyote in most cases before it has an opportunity to come upon the calf. And if the calf is jumped, she comes to its rescue.

In 1964, I attempted to mark as many calves as possible in the Independence herd. To this end I spent most of the daylight hours six days a week working in the herd area to locate calves. The routine usually followed was to drive the road system in the early morning trying to jump lone cows. After the road system was covered, I selected the more promising areas to cruise on foot for the rest of the day.

The behavior of elk is quite flexible, and can be altered by human interference. Spotting of lone cows early in the morning was very fruitful for locating calves the first few days, but this soon changed. Lone cows were encountered only occasionally as most joined small groups before daybreak, apparently in reaction to my activities. The calves were left alone during the day. That the cows returned at night was apparent from the numerous calf and cow tracks together.

The calf crop of the Independence herd failed that year. Only 3 calves joined the herd of 55 cows (5.5:100 ratio) and yearling cows (which cannot be distinguished reliably by mid-summer). By comparison, the Tinemaha herd to the north had 9 calves for 28 cows (33:100) and the Lone Pine herd to the south 8 calves for 23 cows (35:100). None of the 5 calves I marked survived.

It is my belief that the Independence calves were lost to coyotes, primarily due to the removal of the protection of the cows by my activities.

Documenting the predation of coyotes on calves is extremely difficult, since the calves are devoured completely, bones, hair and all. There were two known coyote kills. The one involving Female No. 2 has already been mentioned. The bone fragments probably remained only because I disturbed the coyote. The second known kill occurred May 8. In the morning I observed a lone cow in a grassland, and decided to check for a calf later. When I returned in the early afternoon I found the cow by a ditch about 500 yards from where she had been in the morning.

She acted strangely and I suspected she had a calf, but decided to wait to see if she might give some indication of its location. She kept looking toward the ditch, and soon I saw a coyote peering over its edge. When she went over into the ditch the coyote disappeared. While she was out of sight in the bottom of the ditch, I came up on the downwind side and got to within about 30 yards before she heard me. I froze when she came back over the edge of the ditch. She watched me for about five minutes, then advanced about 10 yards. She then turned and walked away from the ditch to where she had been when the coyote appeared at the ditch. She licked something and I could see it was the calf. She then started back toward the ditch, but the wind shifted and she got my scent and went out of sight without stopping. I went over and found the calf dead. It was still warm and had doubt-lessly been killed only an hour or two earlier. It had been bitten in many places, including the legs (one was broken), hind-quarters, stomach and base of the skull. The cow had torn up the ground for about 25 feet all around the carcass with her hooves. Most of the coyote tracks had been obliterated. Apparently the coyote had come upon the calf while the cow was still some distance away. If she had remained where she had been seen in the morning, the calf would have been out of her view behind the ditch bank. The cow probably came when the calf squealed, but arrived too late to save it, although she continued to defend the carcass from the coyote.

During the time of calving, all recent coyote scats found in the Independence herd area were examined. Of 33 scats found, 5 (15 percent) contained calf remains.

The possibility that my handling of calves had some influence on their survival rate also must be considered, but the fact that all recaptured calves were growing rapidly and appeared to be in fine health argues against this. They clearly were not abandoned by the mothers. Also, this would not explain the mortality of the other calves not handled. On the basis of a 33:100 calf-cow ratio, there must have been at least 18 calves in this herd, and probably more, since the calf ratios given for the other herds are after early mortality too.

The 1964 season was a poor one, but the Independence herd was still in fairly good shape by calving time. Although the Tinemaha and Lone Pine herds main-tained better health through the season because of alfalfa depredations, alfalfa was just beginning to grow this early in the season. Also, the Tinemaha herd calved on the Sierra alluvial plain where there is no alfalfa. Thus, nutrition of the cows does not adequately account for the failure of the Independence herd calves.

As a check, in 1965 I stayed out of all of the calving areas. Significantly, the Independence herd calf production was as good as that of the Tinemaha and Lone Pine herds. Consequently, coyote predation in the abnormal situation created by my activities seems the probable explanation for the 1964 failure of the Indepen-dence herd calf crop.

BEHAVIOR OF TULE ELK

THE HERD: COMMUNICATION AND INTEGRATION

Senses.—Olfaction is highly developed in elk, and it is probably the most dis-criminatory sense. There is little doubt that elk are able to recognize other elk individually, and also the other species in the ecosystem, solely on the basis of scent. Elk do not hesitate when a scent is detected. The scent of a human at close range will cause immediate flight.

The sense of hearing is extremely sensitive. I had an unusual opportunity to observe this on one occasion while attempting to catch a calf. It was escaping me through a heavy stand of rabbitbrush. When it stopped, I stopped about 12 yards away, hoping to sneak several yards closer before it started to run again. I could barely see its head and ears facing away from me, over the top of the brush. However, I had stopped with my pants leg pressed against the tip of a dry rabbitbrush twig, and every time I attempted to move it away, the calf's ears came to attention. It could hear the muffled scratch on cloth despite the fact that there was a strong wind blowing in my favor, and the rabbitbrush all around was waving to and fro. I checked this calf's hearing a number of times by waiting until his ears relaxed, then again moving my leg. There was absolutely no doubt that it was hearing this sound, which I could barely detect. This demonstrates that not only do elk possess highly developed auditory receptors, but also that they are able to filter background noises and detect sounds which are foreign.

Elk apparently lack visual acuity. A human can be in plain sight only 10 yards away, and as long as no motion is made, they will watch for awhile, then go on about their business. Clearly their attention is more readily attracted by a person standing upright than crouched. The upright position obviously focuses attention, for such objects are not common in the normal environment. The most obvious object in the environment that a crouched person might be taken for is a bush. At various times in strong winds I have waved my torso in imitation of the bushes about me. The herd was no more bothered by such movements than by my remaining still.

Still another curious aspect of elk vision relates to motion. They are very perceptive of motion within certain limits. It was discovered early that the herd could be approached directly at a moderate walk to within about 200 yards. Under the same conditions and distances, walking at a tangent to the herd usually attracted their attention. I also discovered that when an elk was alerted at close range and was looking directly at me, I could very slowly lower myself behind a bush, and the elk would soon resume its activities as though nothing had happened. Thereafter, this technique became a routine part of my stalking. I could work close to the herd, and when I made a mistake and was spotted, I could correct it, so to speak, by this maneuver.

The closer to the herd, the slower the movement had to be. The rate of movement had to be less than about one minute of arc per second. Movements faster than this would alert the herd. This explained why walking directly toward a herd from a distance was less likely to attract attention than walking at a tangent. When I kept my rate on tangential moves below this speed, I had no trouble. Thus there is a "zone" of elk vision where neither visual acuity nor motion detection are very effective. This suggests the possibility that the slow fluid motion of a stalking predator may be adapted to such "blind zones." This kind of stalking is particularly characteristic of felids, from housecats stalking mice to lions stalking African antelope as described by Wright (1960).

The visual mechanism underlying this behavior is a matter of speculation. The discovery of several different kinds of motion receptive units in the retina of the frog (Maturana et al., 1960), the rabbit (Barlow et al., 1964; Barlow and Levick,

1965), and the ground squirrel (Michael, 1966) may be pertinent. These workers have shown that much of the integration of visual stimuli involving motion occurs at the level of the retina rather than in the brain. These results suggest that a similar situation may exist in the elk retina, which is apparently oriented toward detection of movements. Discrimination at the level of the retina would explain why the elk responded as though they truly could not see slow movements.

These characteristics of elk hearing and vision are probably responsible for the fact that elk are very calm on quiet days and extremely nervous on windy days. On quiet days, people can walk in plain view to within about 100 yards without a herd taking flight; it is impossible to stalk closer than around 60 yards without being heard. On windy days, elk are unapproachable except by stalking. The stronger the wind, the more excitable the herd is. In winter, when strong winds are the rule, the elk are generally wild. On windy days, it is possible to stalk much closer before being discovered; but once the elk discover the stalker, they run precipitously. This may be explained by the fact that on windy days, the rustling of brush masks sounds and the motion of brush masks movements; the elk run rather than trust their senses. On quiet days, elk rely upon their receptors to detect and locate intruders before they are close.

Auditory communication.—Elk make a number of sounds which convey information to the other members of the aggregation. Some of these have been previously described by Murie (1932). Best known is the bugling of adult bulls during the rut. It has several properties that are not discussed in Murie's (1932) paper. Heard close by, the bugle has a distinct throaty roar, with a pronounced tin horn quality. This element is the most impressive part of the bugle, but its carrying qualities are poor, and it cannot be heard much beyond 60 or 70 yards. The other element is a whistle which carries very well, and is the only part of the call heard at a distance. The bugle is often followed by a series of grunts as described by Murie (1932). This call is not at all specific, and the poorest sort of imitation will elicit a response. See Struhsaker (1967) for sonagrams of elk bugles.

The cow-calf location call described by Murie (1932) has been previously discussed. The call is primarily a cohesion signal, and is used even after the cow and calf join the herd but are separated in the group. After weaning, it is heard only infrequently.

The calf squeal has already been described.

The alarm bark described by Murie (1932) is an explosive call given when an unidentified movement has been seen, and occasionally when an unknown sound is heard. See Struhsaker (1967) for sonagrams of this call. It is produced by a forceful expulsion of air by the diaphragm, and is accompanied by a sudden contraction of the abdominal region. The same animal usually repeats the call as all of the herd watches in the general direction in which the alarmed animal is staring. Occasionally another animal will repeat it, but usually not. Barking is continued only as long as the cause of the disturbance is unknown. If the intruder is exposed, barking ceases. Flight is never precipitated by the bark, unless the disturbance is confirmed. It takes a long time for the herd to relax following the barking of one of its members. I have imitated this call to groups unaware of my presence, and they responded as expected by coming to full alert, but not taking flight. I have also found the call useful in delaying incipient flight in alarmed groups. It seems that the typical response is to attempt to identify the intrusion rather than to flee.

Grinding of teeth is very common, but the observer must be very close to detect it. It is clearly antagonistic in nature, and plays an important role in maintaining individual distance or the individual's living space. It is also associated with aggressive interactions between individuals involved in hierarchical disputes as will be described further below.

Of a different nature from the above call is the whistling exhalation through the nostrils sometimes given by seriously fighting bulls. This sound is much less subtle, and can be heard up to 50 or 60 yards away.

On several occasions I have heard threatening bulls give a guttural "rattle" that is apparently produced by a panting sort of respiration. The significance of this sound is not known. Elk also occasionally snort, but this seems to have no overt communicatory function.

Several involuntary sounds are produced which have a definite integration value. The first is caused by the foot bones which on all movements produce a creaking sound much like that produced by a leather saddle. In a running herd this is audible 60 to 80 yards away, and in normally feeding animals it can be heard with each step when at very close range. Second is the noise produced by the digestive tract, probably caused by the quantities of gases produced in rumen digestion. There is little question that these sounds coordinate the herd. Each individual is aware of the surrounding individuals due to this nearly constant output of auditory signals. In the normal feeding of a herd there was a continuous snapping and crunching of vegetation associated with feeding; yet if I happened to cause a similar sound the herd was immediately alerted, which puzzled me at first. This ability to discriminate foreign sounds is probably based on the fact that an elk is aware of the positions of its herd-mates, and sounds coming from other quarters are suspect.

When the herd is viewed from a distance, one gets the impression that communication and interaction between individuals of a herd is sporadic and based on isolated individual acts. But on those rare occasions when one gets very close to the herd, it is discovered that there is a continuous array of sounds—foot bone creaking, stomach rumbling, teeth grinding, and others. To the keen hearing of an elk, this must be a virtual din. The integrative signals of a herd, far from being sporadic, are essentially continuous.

Visual communication.—In a real sense, every act of an elk conveys information to the other members of the herd. Like auditory signals, the flow of visual signals is essentially continuous. There is not only a large number of identifiable visual signals, but also a tendency for them to be graduated rather than simply on or off. These acts will be discussed under functional headings. Those occurring specifically during the rutting period will be described in the major section on this topic.

Alert-alarm behavior.—If an animal becomes suspicious, it scrutinizes the source of suspicion in a head-high ears-out posture (pl. 2, *a* and *b*). This is the posture from which barking is given when it occurs. If the elk confirms its suspicion it lifts its head above the horizontal, places its ears back, and starts moving away (pl. 2, *c*). If unsure of itself, it moves slowly in a stiff-legged gait with the head kept high and ears back. As it moves it turns its head slowly from side to side (pl. 3, *a* and *b*). In this position the visual field is unobstructed, and the blind spot immediately to the rear is covered by the head movements. The ears are oriented to pick up sounds from the rear. The stilted gait and slow rhythmic movements of the body are probably related to the need to maintain the head in a stable situation, so that motion detection is effective. Even when the animal breaks into a trot, the head is maintained on a steady horizontal plane (see illustration in Murie, 1951:- 112). In flight, a "rocking horse" gait is used, and observation of the intruder is curtailed until the herd draws to a halt, usually on high ground, and watches its back trail.

If an elk is sure of an intruder, it will take flight and the rest of the herd will follow. If less sure, it will move and stop. The rest of the group congregates about it, and stares at the source of disturbance. When there is indecision about whether to continue watching or take flight, many individuals will hold their mouths open (pl. 3, *c*). This is a signal of incipient flight. The animals in flight often run with their mouths open even when not winded, and opening the mouth before flight is probably a ritualization of this response. The tail is held erect by the alert animals and defecation and urination are usually accomplished before flight.

Flight behavior.—Once a herd is alarmed it aggregates. In an unalarmed cow herd, the calves tend to be grouped closer than the older animals, and they form the "nucleus" or rallying point for aggregation. The herd moves in an elliptical-shaped formation. Elk usually hold a fairly straight course, the objective seemingly being to put distance between themselves and the disturbance. They do not look about while they are running—their heads are held in the direction of travel.

The speed of the running herd is paced. Any individual in the herd can run much faster. The paced speed has been clocked on many occasions at about 22 to 24 miles per hour. Elk can run at a top speed of about 28 or 30 miles per hour, but they cannot maintain the herd formation at full speed. The faster animals pull ahead while the slower ones stretch out behind. Certain individuals break from the string and lead separate groups in various directions. Confusion results, with small groups scattering about, sometimes racing back and forth and attempting to join other groups.

The safety of the herd consists of the cohesive mass of animals running in an organized manner. The animals exposed are only those on the outside, and even these are protected by the number of flying hooves and the ebbs and surges within the group. The vast array of movement in a running herd has a disorienting effect on the observer's vision.

The tendency of the animals to open their mouths in flight often gives the impression that they are winded from a long run, even though they may have just begun. When they pause to look about they concentrate their attention on their back trail, even when they are clearly aware of your presence to the side. This often gives the impression that they were alarmed by something else.

Another response which is common to many ungulates that escape by running is to attempt to cross in front of a moving car. Presumably this behavior evolved long ago as a response to pursuing predators, and clearly must have a distinct selective advantage to have developed in such remotely related species as elk and antelope (*Antilocapra americana*). It is characteristic of open country ungulates; forest ungulates escape to the nearest cover. A possible explanation is that it evolved under the pressure of hunting by large team-hunting predators, where one animal attempts to drive the prey toward a hidden partner. Tule elk are notably hard to drive. Crossing in front nearly always occurs when the herd is approached at an angle, as though to turn them in a desired direction. Perhaps related is the fact that a disturbed herd will often stand and watch a person in plain view walk directly, or nearly so, away; they almost always take flight if one walks at a tangent.

While herds escape by direct flight, solitary elk sometimes assume elusive behavior. On two occasions during aerial censuses individual bulls were observed to bed down and remain still. Also a lone cow was spotted where she was bedded in a shallow draw, and when we circled around a second time to confirm the sex, she was found with her head stretched out on the ground in the posture of a hiding calf. During one hunt an apparently dead bull was sighted from the air. When a ground crew was directed to it by radio, it jumped up and ran away.

I have not observed such attempts to hide when lone elk are encountered on the ground, but escape maneuvers are occasionally evasive. I once jumped a very large bull which ran over a rise out of sight, then circled around and escaped behind me. Such cases are rare.

Aggressive-submissive behavior.—The elk social structure is based on a hierarchy. This system manifests itself in maintenance of individual distance in a herd, squabbles over resources, and rivalry of bulls during the rut. The latter topic will be taken up in the section on rutting behavior.

Young calves are exempt from the adult hierarchies. When a calf gets in the path of an older elk, it is unceremoniously pushed aside with a foreleg, or occasionally with a nose. Even adult rutting bulls, which show aggression toward a number of innocuous animals, do not seem to be annoyed by the calves. They shove them aside in the same casual manner as cows do. The calves themselves form the most cohesive class in the herd. Yet even they have a hierarchy among themselves, and it is based on the same mannerisms as used by the adults. By one month of age, just shortly after they have joined the herd, the dominance of certain calves over others is apparent.

The hierarchy in adult males is strictly linear, and is based on body size and antler development which are correlated with each other and with age. The dominance of a bull with mature antlers is asserted by an act which I shall call "antler threat." This is accomplished by snapping the head downward, displaying the antlers, while at the same time laying the ears back. This bold assertion of dominance is not used with other bulls of about the same rank, but rather is given to clearly subordinate bulls, which promptly move away.

Bulls of nearly equal rank do not use the antler threat, but bring their heads down slowly, often twisting them from one side to the other. This is often followed by "sparring" or "mock sparring." In the latter, the two bulls stand with their antlers separated by several feet, and twist them about at each other while making body gyrations as if their antlers were engaged. Often they will mock spar on opposite sides of a bush, each thrashing the bush with his antlers. In sparring, bulls engage their antlers and push. This is a test of strength, rather than an antagonistic combat. One partner may turn and look at something in the distance, or brush flies from his back; the other patiently waits until he is ready to resume the test. Sometimes these bouts consist of merely knocking antlers together, first on one side, then the other.

Almost all sparring and mock sparring occurs between individuals of nearly the same age and size as previously reported by Struhsaker (1967) for Rocky Mountain elk. Occasionally mismatched bulls spar or mock spar, but latent aggressiveness on the part of the dominant animal usually begins to emerge, and the subordinate quickly retreats.

Bulls with a rudimentary or deformed antler on one side are low in the hierarchy even though the opposite antler may be perfectly developed. During sparring the antlers are engaged at the tips and the lack of engagement on the deformed side allows the opponent's antler to strike the neck or shoulder of an animal with a deformed antler.

The hierarchy among females is also well developed. I did not have enough known individual cows to analyze the exact nature of the hierarchy, but limited evidence suggests that it is basically a linear ranking.

In encounters between antagonistic cows, the aggressor approaches the opponent with head and neck extended and ears depressed. In conjunction with this act, which I have called "charge," are the tooth-grinding sound and a display of the upper canine teeth. The latter is performed by pulling the lips upward to expose the canine teeth against the contrasting black patches on either side of the lower lip. This act has not been previously reported though the threatening action of the head, neck, and ears has been observed by numerous authors. This also explains the role of the upper canine tooth, which lacks an opposing tooth and serves a minor function in gathering and masticating food.

If the animal approached by the aggressor is clearly subordinate, it retreats rapidly, an act I have referred to as "decamp." The aggressor places her muzzle along the flank of the subordinate animal, and stamps the near foreleg on the ground. This stamp or kick terminates the encounter. The kick is not directed at the body of the subordinate animal, and involves no physical blow. This action is apparently a ritualized signal of what was originally an offensive blow.

If the hierarchical relationship is not clearly established, the opponents face each other in the same manner—neck out, ears depressed, tooth grinding, and displaying canines with their muzzles about a yard apart. If the encounter continues, both cows elevate their muzzles, and begin to rear on their hind legs (see Struhsaker, 1967, for illustration). The contestants begin to flail with both forelegs, an act I have called "boxing." Few blows are actually struck, and these, because of the spacing of the combatants, land on the forelegs where little harm is done. On one occasion a cow was struck on the jaw by an upward swing of the opponent's foot. This accidental blow immediately ended the bout in favor of the animal which delivered it. Of 129 encounters recorded in detail, and many others observed casually, this was the only occurrence of this kind.

The sequence from initial threats through charge (with grinding and canine display), rear, and box represents a continuum which may be terminated at any stage by submission of one animal.

The victor is always the animal which does not turn away. The direct look as an aggressive posture, well known among mammals and birds, is clearly apparent in elk. The hesitancy of an antagonist is manifested by a wavering of the direct look and a tendency to look away briefly. In many cases, the elk which was most aggressive in terms of initiating the encounter, rearing the highest, boxing the hardest, or even forcing the other reared cow to back up, lost the encounter for being unable to maintain the direct look.

These encounters between cows are a mechanism for spacing the individuals in the herd, and the frequency of encounters increases with crowding. Following

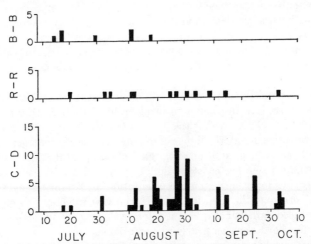

Fig. 18. Fighting among females. Histogram C–D shows encounters which consisted of only a charge by one animal and decamp by the other. Histogram R–R shows encounters in which both animals reared on the hind legs. Rearing is followed by charge-decamp, but these are not included in the C–D histogram. Histogram B–B shows encounters which led to boxing. Here again the rear–rear preceding and the charge-decamp following are not included in the other histograms.

flight, when the animals are closely bunched, encounters are more common than when the herd is relaxed and assumes normal spacing. An important factor in the frequency of encounters is close herding of cows by master bulls during the rut. In the rut of 1964, a total of 95 cow encounters were recorded in detail (fig. 18). Eighty percent were resolved by charge-decamp because the dominance was clearly established; 12.6 percent led to rearing, and 7.4 percent to boxing. The frequency of these encounters in relation to the rutting season in the Independence herd is shown in figure 18. The greatest frequency occurred during the peak of the rut when bulls were herding the closest. But boxing, the most aggressive stage, was most common at the beginning of the rutting season when the herd first came under control of a bull. As the hierarchy became well established, boxing diminished rapidly, and the outcome of most encounters was a foregone conclusion. However, a low level of rearing persisted, indicating that hierarchical relationships were still being tested.

During the period after the bulls have cast antlers and while they are growing new ones, they also use the cow system of maintaining the hierarchy. The hierarchy does not break down during the casting period (old dominant bulls cast first) because the aggressive animal which initiates the encounter also selects the mode by which it is settled. Thus an aggressive bull will threaten a subordinate with an antler threat when he has antlers, but with a neck out charge if he has cast. The opponent responds in the same manner, even though he may still have his antlers and could defeat the unantlered bull if he would use them.

Cows maintain their dominance over the antlered spikes and often two-year-olds by the same means. In general, adult cows are dominant over young cows, spikes, and most two-year-old bulls. The bulls become dominant over cows when they have developed sexually to the stage where they are adequately aggressive and initiate encounters with cows based on an antler threat. I have observed cows defeat three-year-old bulls by rearing and boxing. Yearling bulls are dominant over yearling cows. Adult bulls are dominant over cows and younger bulls. As previously mentioned, calves are exempt from the hierarchical system but maintain a hierarchy among themselves.

The head is extremely important in elk communication, and the fact that the head and neck are dark in color is probably related to attracting attention. One cannot escape the conclusion that the eye is attracted by the erect heads of attentive elk. On the other hand, the light rump patch is a sharp contrast with the dark head and neck, and the orientation of the animal is apparent even when it is barely visible. The rump patch is a constant signal, since piloerection is virtually absent. Besides conveying information on the orientation of distant animals, it may also function to coordinate the herd in flight. In contrast to many mammals, elk have a greatly reduced tail, which plays a minor role in communication, except for erection during herd alert as previously mentioned.

The herd.—The habit of herding is related to the need for protection from predators in open country. Forest herbivores can rely upon the concealing vegetation to avoid discovery by predators. Living solitarily or in small groups is appropriate to such an environment. In open habitats, cooperation of individuals in forming herds which are much less vulnerable to attack is a necessity for survival.

The hierarchy serves as a framework within which intraspecific competition can be exerted without disruption of the herd. Sociality, resulting from the cooperation of the individual members, conveys survival benefits to all members of the herd, and is a distinct advantage to the species. Yet, within the herd, the hierarchy allows intraspecific competition to continue to favor those individuals which are best adapted.

It is interesting that handicapped animals do not stay with the herd. Badly wounded animals will veer away from the running herd, or move off from a standing herd.

That the herd itself may cull the handicapped from its ranks is demonstrated by the following observations. On May 29, 1964, a crippled cow was observed straggling along some 10 yards behind the Tinemaha herd. She had a broken bone just below the left hock and the leg was totally useless. She moved along by hopping on the right hind leg. She was in good condition, but was still straggling along behind the herd on June 5. As I watched, two different cows in succession walked from the herd and drove the cripple away. It was apparent that the cow was straggling behind not because she was unable to keep up with the feeding herd, but because they would not let her join it. On June 8, the herd was sighted again, with the cripple following along behind. She apparently left the herd shortly afterward for she was not seen in observations of the Tinemaha herd on June 9, 15, 20, and 22. She was not seen again for so long that I assumed that she had died. But on May 27, 1965, I jumped her all alone on the lava near where she had been last seen a year before. The leg was still totally useless, but she was still in good shape. She apparently assumed a completely solitary life.

Three other elk with crippled legs were observed, two bulls and a cow. All were solitary. Some handicaps not related to ability to move do not seem to be discriminated against by the herd. For example, an earless cow was with the Tinemaha herd all through the period when the cripple was being kept out.

Leadership.—Leadership among the loosely organized bull groups is quite variable. More often than not a spike or two-year-old will take the lead when alarmed. Large bulls, whether in a bull group or cow group, tend to run in the middle of the herd.

In cow groups or mixed groups an adult cow is the leader. However, leadership is quite fluid in the tule elk, and never approaches the rigidity described for red deer by Darling (1937).

In small groups of about ten or less, one cow often emerges as a consistent leader. Leadership in tule elk depends primarily upon taking the initiative. The spike with the lowest status in the group can initiate flight and set the direction to be taken if he is the animal which has been alarmed.

Even a small group will not blindly follow the cow which is usually the leader. While catching calves, I caught the offspring of a cow that was clearly the leader of a small group. The cow came toward me, and was followed by the rest of the group. But at about 80 yards the followers stopped, then turned and ran away, even though the leader continued toward me without hesitation until I yelled at her.

In large groups, a number of cows may assume leadership by taking the initiative. Several cows may end a bedding period by feeding off in opposite directions. Sometimes part of the herd follows each and the group splits in two. Sometimes no cows, or only one or two, will follow one leader, yet they may continue as a very small group.

In running herds I have observed leadership change many times with the ebb and flow of the herd. Yet a consistent direction is maintained. On many occasions I observed master bulls during the rut attempt to hold herds of cows in areas where they did not want to stay. The direction in which the cows wanted to go was abundantly clear, and any number of cows might have assumed leadership. As the front cows started off, the bull would turn them and drive them to the rear of the group. The cows then in the front would attempt to move until the bull turned them. The next rank would then assume the leadership. In some cases the cows would finally break into a run which the bull could not stop, and the herd would move away, with the bull following along.

Thus leadership is not a static position. It involves first of all an animal which takes the initiative, and second a group of animals who are willing to follow. There is nothing rigid about following, either, except in the case of calves.

Play.—Cavorting is the most commonly observed kind of play, and is indulged in by all ages and both sexes. Cavorting includes chasing, bucking, spinning, dodging, and a number of related movements. The entire herd may engage in these activities. Often this kind of play occurs as the herd is coming into water, and they seem to enjoy cavorting in shallow water as reported by Murie (1951).

Two kinds of individual play were observed. The first involved splashing of water. This was observed only among cows. They would stand in water a foot or more deep an slap the water mainly with their forefeet, but occasionally with their hind feet also. Commonly the head was turned away from the slapping forefoot to avoid the flying water. Some cows engaged in these activities for several minutes at a time.

The second kind of individual play was engaged in by both adult bulls and cows. It involved picking objects up in the mouth, lifting them high, and dropping them. This was repeated a number of times. This play was first observed when a small bull was playing with an old rag. He would hook it on his antlers and flip it up in the air, then lift it with his mouth. Subsequently, adult cows were observed lifting and dropping a piece of fish net, a small clump of dried rabbitbrush, and an old elk bone. The bone was not chewed as was reported by Harper et al. (1967) for Roosevelt elk.

Beds.—Tule elk do not prepare beds beyond an occasional scratch with a forefoot. Most beds are not prepared at all. Sometimes a subordinate animal is driven from a bed which is then taken by the dominant animal. Occasionally the displaced animal displaces another over which it is dominant. Struhsaker (1967) reported similar behavior for the Rocky Mountain elk. During a bedding period, individuals often stand up, turn around, void, and bed down again.

Sleep.—Elk are occasionally found sound asleep. The eyes are closed and the head rocks slowly to and fro so that antlers of sleeping bulls sway gently. The ears are relaxed, but if noises are picked up, the ears become erect and the head stops swaying, even though the eyes may not open. If no further disturbance occurs, the ears relax and the head begins swaying again.

Bulls with large antlers sometimes put their heads to the ground, but cows rarely do. Most elk rest with the head held erect.

Rumination.—A large portion of time bedded is spent in rumination. At any one time, 50 to 60 percent of the bedded herd will usually be ruminating.

Voiding.—Voiding of both urine and feces is performed by both sexes in the normal standing position. On only one occasion was a bull observed to squat to urinate. Feces are often voided while walking, so that the pellets are strung out.

Stretching and yawning.—Following a bedded period, elk typically yawn and stretch. Stretching involves placing the fore- and hind feet far apart, stretching the back and neck, and depressing the muzzle downward against the neck.

RESPONSES TO VEHICLES

Aircraft.—Both light planes and helicopters have been observed circling the elk herds, in addition to the usual Department of Fish and Game census planes. Elk bunch and watch the aircraft, but usually do not run. It is extremely difficult to drive tule elk with an airplane.

Sonic booms from jet aircraft are an almost daily occurrence in Owens Valley. Some are extremely strong and are felt as well as heard. The elk come to alert immediately after a boom and listen until the jet sound is heard. They then resume their normal activities. Nearby gunshots also alert them, and they do not relax quickly. While there are many other clues to distinguish gunshots from sonic booms, there is little question that the elk recognizes the jet sound as associated with a boom of a harmless kind.

Automobiles.—Elk become accustomed to certain vehicles that they see and hear regularly. Traffic along the aqueduct is a common part of the Independence herd's environment in the summer. With any given set of conditions, elk were more tolerant of my jeep or the pickup of the aqueduct patrol. Strange vehicles have alarmed the elk only minutes after a familiar one passed. But the velocity of the wind and of the vehicle is a far more important factor in their response than the kind of vehicle.

RESPONSES TO WEATHER

Wind.—The remarkable influence of wind upon the response of tule elk to intrusion has already been mentioned. The casual observer who encounters elk on a calm day concludes that they are tame, while a person encountering them on a windy day assumes that people must be harassing them to cause them to be so wild. For example, on one occasion a herd took flight at three-quarters of a mile from a single vehicle when I was attempting to show the herd to people from the Bureau of Land Management; yet on another occasion 32 elk calmly went about their business a few hundred yards from Highway 395 when I showed them to a group from the California Section of the Range Society of about eighty people, with two buses and six or eight cars.

Temperature.—There appears to be little change in response to temperature by tule elk. That they are active through the day, and that the rut is carried on in the heat of summer when temperatures are often over 100°F, shows that they can tolerate rather intense heat. Winter temperatures are not severe and the elk do not seem to be adversely affected.

Relative humidity.—Darling (1937) attributed irritability in red deer to changes in relative humidity. In *Odocoileus*, Hahn (1949) and Linsdale and Tomich (1953) found that humidity influenced activities, and McCullough (1964) correlated movement responses with changes in humidity.

In tule elk, relative humidity was found to be inconsequential in influencing behavior. The marked response of elk to wind was independent of relative humidity. Perhaps the desert situation where humidities are typically low results in this factor being relatively less important as an environmental cue compared to the more mesic environments where the above cited studies were conducted.

Rain.—Light rains apparently have little effect upon tule elk behavior. They carry on their activities in a normal manner. After a bedding period the animals shake their coats vigorously, then begin feeding as usual. Heavy rains appear to cause discomfort; the elk tend to stand with head and ears drooped, much as domestic cattle do. Activities are curtailed somewhat.

Snow.—Tule elk show no particular response to snowfall. They carry on their usual activities as best they can. Elk were observed to eat snow and scratch it away to get at grasses. Sometimes they bedded on top of the snow, and at other times they scraped it away to form a bed. No particular shifts occurred in elk distribution following snowfall, although the movements of the Tinemaha herd suggested that in still deeper snows, they would move into the bottomlands.

INTERSPECIFIC BEHAVIOR

Rabbits.—Black-tailed jackrabbits (*Lepus californicus*) are extremely abundant, but they and the elk ignore each other. The only interaction I observed was when a rabbit bursting out of a form under a rabbitbrush plant startled the elk feeding close by.

Antelope ground squirrel.—This rodent (*Citellus leucurus*) is common in the valley in good rainfall years. Elk are alerted by its alarm call. The ground squirrels were breaking apart elk droppings for undigested sweetclover seeds in the fall of 1963.

Deer.—Elk pay little attention to deer (*Odocoileus hemionus inyoensis*). Their ranges overlap, particularly in the Goodale area, but there are also a few scattered deer in the bottomlands, mainly along the river. On February 22, 1964, while stalking a small group of elk of the Goodale herd, I jumped two buck deer, which moved away past the elk. The mild alarm of the deer had little influence on the elk, which continued to feed. Probably elk would be alerted by rapid flight by deer.

Cattle.—The strong tendency of elk to abandon areas where domestic cattle are grazed has already been discussed. The mechanism by which this segregation is accomplished is apparently quite subtle. On occasions, scattered herds of elk and cattle would intermingle. This always occurred on quiet days when the elk were calm. Yet the cattle and elk do not actually join in a single herd. There is a certain edginess during these contacts, and the individuals of each species keep their distance.

On one occasion a black domestic calf came near a rutting master bull. The bull snapped his antlers down in the "antler threat" posture. The domestic calf quickly retreated and the bull ignored him. But the distressed calf and another domestic calf began to bawl. The domestic cow, mother of the black calf, became disturbed but was separated from the calves by a string of feeding elk cows. The mother hesitated to pass through the elk group until it split. The domestic cow quickly moved through the space and joined the calves. Both species resumed feeding with no further incidents.

On another occasion a cow elk began cautiously approaching a domestic cow, which began to watch her. When the elk cow was several yards away, the domestic cow snapped her muzzle outward with her neck extended as if to push something away. The elk cow retreated a step, turned, and hesitantly watched the cow, then moved off with minced steps. Soon both were feeding again.

These low level mutually aggressive tendencies probably result in the elk leaving any area occupied by cattle on windy days when the elk are nervous.

Elk are alarmed when cattle run, and usually take flight themselves. Domestic cattle are much less influenced by alarmed elk.

Horses and mules.—The relationship between elk and horses is similar to that between elk and cattle. Elk are greatly alarmed by running horses, and horses tend to run much more than cattle. Elk and horses are sometimes found in close proximity, but again, the elk are watchful and keep their distance. On one occasion when two horses walked through a herd some of the elk acted giddy, suggesting play.

Horses and particularly mules are quite curious. My presence in the area was frequently inspected by them. Once a mule walked directly toward a herd and they began to be alarmed and started to move away. The mule was joined by three horses and they ran in a circle around the herd, which began to take flight but settled down again as the mule and horses left. On several other occasions I observed mules inspecting nervous elk herds, and mules often would stand all alone a short distance from elk.

Coyotes.—Incidents involving coyotes during the calving season have already been given in the reproduction section. Seventeen other elk-coyote interactions were recorded. Generally, a coyote pays little attention to the herd as it goes about its hunting. In ten of the observed cases the elk watched the coyote until he moved away. In one instance a coyote caught a small mammal which squealed, and the herd was immediatley alerted. In six observations of a coyote coming close to a herd, some elk moved out and ran it off. This is more frequent during the early summer when the calves are still small. Cows usually do the chasing, but once several spikes chased a coyote away.

The coyote never seems harried but usually keeps a good distance between itself and the elk, and does not hesitate to move when an elk starts towards it. Once two cows left the herd to chase a coyote until he was about 40 yards away. One cow stopped, but the other continued to move him away, starting toward him again whenever he stopped to look back. When he was about 80 yards away she gave up the chase.

Once, a coyote run off by a cow passed within ten yards of a bedded adult bull which did not even get up. During a coyote chorus, a small group of bedded bulls was observed to get up and look about, but there was no particular alarm.

Birds.—Most contacts between elk and various birds in the environment are uneventful. Several birds—Brewer blackbirds, starlings, and magpies—land on the backs of elk. Usually they are chased off by a toss of the head, but sometimes they are tolerated. Ducks on the water within the herd ranges usually come and go with no notice taken by the elk. Once a flight of ducks swooped low over a herd and startled them, and a similar reaction occurred with several ravens. A flock of Canada geese calling high overhead aroused the curiosity of a herd. Other large birds such as vultures and golden eagles passing low overhead attract only passing attention. The alarm call of chukars alerts the herd, but usually not for long if the disturbance is not confirmed.

Elk sometimes appear annoyed by birds nearby. I have observed cow elk chasing away ravens, magpies, and in one case a small flock of teal. One rutting master bull was observed to stamp with a forefoot at some starlings on the ground, and another chased starlings on three different occasions, including giving an antler threat, a ludicrous scene.

RUTTING BEHAVIOR

Bull advertising acts.—The most characteristic act of rutting bulls is bugling. This call is given while extending the neck and muzzle outward and slightly upward (pl. 4, *b* and 5, *a, b*). Before the rut begins bulls often assume this posture, but without producing any sound.

Two other acts are advertising in that they indicate sexual readiness. One is "grimacing," in which the head is held in a position similar to bugling, but the nostrils are widely expanded and the lips drawn back so that the lower incisors and dental pad are exposed. The act is probably related to scent detection since it is always directed into the wind, and the head is moved slowly in an arc on the windward side. In most cases it is given in relation to a cow group.

The third act is "thrash-urinate." The bull rakes the ground and low herbage with his antlers while releasing spurts of urine upon the long dark hair of the brisket and neck. The penis is projected and the muscles of the sheath contract, causing the penis to swirl from side to side and up and down, spattering the urine all over the underparts. The orifice of the urethra is directed upward, further assuring that the urine is directed onto the body. This act has been observed in studies of *elaphus* behavior in many parts of the world (see Darling, 1937; Graf, 1955; Kiddie, 1962; Struhsaker, 1967; Harper et al., 1967, and others). The various elements of the act correspond so closely, that there is little doubt but what the act is virtually identical in all races. There has been question concerning the identity of the fluid released. Darling (1937) considered this act to be masturbation, and the fluid to be semen. This interpretation is quite widespread among workers in the field. Certainly the palpitations of the penis superficially suggest masturbation. But Graf (1955) calls the fluid urine. I can unequivocally state that it is urine, having been just yards away on the other side of the fence when a bull gave this act a number of times at the Tupman Enclosure. In the two rutting seasons this act was observed more than 350 times, perhaps a third of them at close enough range to determine the nature of the fluid. In all cases it was urine.

The thrash-urinate act develops early in the rut, first as thrash alone, associated with clearing of velvet from the antlers. As the bull's rutting condition progresses, the palpitation of the penis sheath and urination begin to be shown weakly. In full rutting behavior urine in large amounts is released onto the underparts. In fact, I have not seen a rutting bull urinate in the normal manner. Frequently the bull beds down in the spot where he thrashed and urinated.

This act is also related to wallowing activities of bulls. Wallowing is not so pronounced in Owens Valley, probably due to the low availability of suitable boggy areas. But where there is water, the bulls will thrash-urinate, gouge chunks of sod with their antlers, throw them into the air, and splash water on their sides and bellies with a forefoot. They usually bed in the place, often rolling on their sides and hooking with their antlers. Some bulls (pl. 5, *a, b*) are caked with mud, while others always remain clean. The breeding success of bulls seems to be unrelated to the presence of mud on the body. Many bulls have debris hanging from their antlers while they are wallowing.

Antler polishing activities are commonly observed. Wooden posts are preferred.

The bull rubs the antlers up and down on one side, then the other, to cover all the antler surface. In between rubbings, the bull swings the lower jaw to one side and scrapes upward on the post with the incisors. This action appears similar to that described by Graf (1955) for Roosevelt elk. However, I did not observe the head rubbing or smelling he described. Only the incisors and antlers were used. After scraping with the incisors for awhile, the bull again begins rubbing the antlers. I timed the lengths of eight rubbing sessions of three master bulls. They ranged from 2 to 15 minutes with a mean of 8.4.

Bull-bull acts.—As the tempo of the rut increases, the master bulls begin to drive other bulls away from the cow herds. Antler threats are no longer used by the master bulls. Instead, the act I called "charge" is used. The head and neck are extended and held about parallel with the body axis, but with the head tilted slightly upward. The herd bull runs at the intruder with a stiff-legged jog, and gives the "canine display" and tooth grinding sound.

If a contender does not give in, a serious fight will ensue. The rivals walk side by side, separated by approximately three or four yards ("parallel walk"). They bugle frequently, and twist their antlers toward each other. Suddenly one bull wheels to face the opponent and brings his antlers down to touch the ground. Almost simultaneously, the opponent does likewise ("thrash-thrash"). Sometimes the bulls back away while raking the ground with their antlers. Other times they whip their antlers about in a horizontal figure 8 pattern with the circles to each side, the antlers striking the ground at the center. If the head-on stance is maintained, they will then smash together ("clash") with their antlers tip-to-tip (pl. 5, c). If one bull turns away, a parallel walk will be repeated. Sometimes they avoid the clash by stopping with their antlers just inches apart.

When the antlers are engaged, a rapid and deadly serious contest of strength follows, with advantage shifting back and forth as the contestants struggle for balance and footing. The bulls twist their necks from side to side trying to take the opponent off-balance. Sometimes disengagement is followed immediately by another clash, but usually they go through another parallel walk.

Bull-cow acts.—The act used to maintain a harem is "herding." Herding is virtually identical to the "charge" used against bulls, except that it is usually directed at cows. Cows often do not respond until the herding bull gives the tooth grinding noise, and several times I have seen the cows and spikes jump at the same instant, the spikes moving away from and the cows back to the herd. There is obviously a difference in response by the sexes to the same act.

Yearling males are last to be driven from the harems, partially due to the fact that they are just maturing, and are seasonally later to come into breeding condition. But also, there is a change in response of the maturing male to the herding act. As calves they respond to herding by the master bull as cows do. In fact, rutting bulls prevent their leaving the harem just as if they were cows. As yearling bulls, they continue to respond with cow-like behavior until the master bull is so persistent that they finally leave the harem. However, in 1963, the Independence herd included several nubbins which never did leave the herd. No matter how many times the herd bull chased them, they circled back into the cow group. Sexual immaturity apparently resulted in their retention of cow behavior.

And because the stiff-legged gait of the "charge" is slower, the master bulls were
ineffective against the free-running nubbins, which would not give the response
appropriate to bulls.

Master bulls make sexual approaches to the cows by coming up to them from
the rear ("approach"), running the tongue in and out ("tongue lapping"), and
occasionally by attempting to mount ("attempted mount"). Nasal-perineal contacts and licking of the perineum occur only occasionally because the cow usually
retreats quickly. The cow uses several behavioral acts in rejecting the bull's
advances. One is an apparently ritualized kick with the hind leg. Although it was
observed often, it was never given completely so as to deliver a blow. Besides
retreating from the bull, cows will occasionally turn about sharply and brush
past the bull in the opposite direction. A bull will often try to stop a cow by
moving beside her or nudging her with his head, or by placing his head and neck
over the back of her neck. In some cases, a cow pursued persistently will trot with
her head high, snapping her muzzle upward a number of times in quick succession.
This is a signal of incipient flight. The bull apparently recognizes this signal, since
his pursuit of the cow is curtailed. If one cow runs the herd will follow, and the
bull cannot retain control of a running herd, but must wait until they stop to
reassert his domination. I have seen cows give head bobbing of this sort in response
to harassment by large flies, perhaps nose-bot flies. The ritualization of this behavior is a possible origin for rejection of bull advances.

Another bull-cow act occurs when the cows are bedded down. The bull goes
around smelling them ("smell") mainly on the back over the shoulders and on the
rump just at the top of the rump patch. It is interesting that here too, cows react
with fly-chasing behavior, tossing the head and flopping the ears. If the bull
persists, the cow often gets up and moves away.

Copulatory behavior.—Until a cow is receptive and will stand for mounting,
the bull will be unsuccessful. I have not observed receptive cows seeking out the
bull as reported by Morrison (1960a) in his observations of penned Rocky Mountain elk. In all of my observations cows were passive toward the bull and did not
initiate sexual encounters. There was no need for a cow to seek out a bull because
bulls were always present. Perhaps Morrison's results were influenced by the
penned condition, the cows having no means of escape, and only one bull being
present and that one only during daytime. The head bobbing of cows (described
above) he reports as performed by the cow while running around the bull during
courtship; yet my observations in open herds showed that such behavior preceded
bolting from the herd.

Several stimuli alert the bull to a receptive cow. Scent is obviously involved,
and also the manner in which a cow stands. A cow standing to allow a calf to
nurse greatly excites a bull, and he will rush over and attempt to mount. Subtle
sounds may also be involved, but I have not been able to detect them. Morrison
(1960a) reported lordosis in Rocky Mountain elk cows but it was not pronounced
in tule elk. The only difference from normal standing position was the slight hump-
ing of the back and spreading of the hindlegs.

Receptive cows will stand to allow mounting. Often they will lick first one flank,
then the other. The bull stands motionless some three to five yards behind the cow.

He then walks up to the cow, carefully places his chin on her rump, and literally slides his forequarters onto her rump. He does not grasp with his forelegs, which are splayed awkwardly to either side. Apparently the careful placing of the chin and sliding onto the cow accomplishes the correct orientation. As the bull slides up on the cow's rump, his penis is projected, and he continues to mount until the penis contacts the cow. Usually after several seconds he will slide down off the cow, or she will walk forward. She often licks her flanks, and the mounting sequence is repeated. This behavior is quite similar to that reported for Roosevelt elk by Graf (1955) and Rocky Mountain elk by Struhsaker (1967).

The number of mounts is highly variable. In the 20 copulations I observed, the number of mounts before ejaculation ranged from one to 33 with a mean of 5.8. Probably ejaculation is stimulated by successful intromission as has been reported by Morrison (1960*a*) and Struhsaker (1967). Pelvic thrusts are not performed prior to ejaculation. Ejaculation is accomplished in one violent thrust during which the bull literally leaps upward. The force of the thrust drives the cow forward, and in one instance a cow was knocked to her knees. The bull's hind feet completely leave the ground, and often he lands off balance. One bull went so far off balance that he fell down on his side. The bull then pays no more attention to the serviced cow and resumes herd tending. The cow stands with her back humped for several minutes, sometimes again licking her flank. She then resumes her normal activities. The pronounced post-copulatory behavior of cows reported by Morrison (1960*a*) was not observed.

The 1963 rut.—The Independence herd was observed about every third day during the 1963 breeding season. An attempt was made to locate as many of the cows as possible, and the master bulls were identified.

On July 19 when the herd was first located, all of the cows were in the possession of a large six-point bull, Old Gray (fig. 19). He was out of velvet and showing strong rutting behavior. All of the bachelor bulls nearby were still in velvet or in the process of shedding. Changes in master bulls, and the number of cows they controlled are shown in figure 19. Copulations are shown in figure 26.

Only one serious fight was observed in 1963. On August 24, Forks had 24 cows and 6-5 had 35. At 10:55 AM a cow ran away from Forks' herd and over toward 6-5's herd. Three bulls from near Forks' herd and two from near 6-5's herd ran into the 6-5 herd in pursuit of the cow; 6-5 followed her and mounted her twice in quick succession, ejaculating on the second mount. Then 6-5 began to run the bulls out of the milling herd. A large 5-point would not submit, and after giving a thrash-thrash, the two bulls clashed violently; 6-5 forced the challenger back steadily. They disengaged and 6-5 chased several other bulls. He then came back and the two clashed again and 6-5 forced the 5-point back steadily. They disengaged and 6-5 ran off some smaller bulls. He returned and clashed with the 5-point a third time and drove him backward rapidly. The 5-point disengaged and moved into a parallel walk. The herd bull chased smaller bulls, and when he returned the 5-point retreated. A large 6-point bull came up then, but did not try to enter the herd, which 6-5 now had well under control. The 5-point shortly afterward left the bachelor bull cohort and disappeared to the north. Later in the afternoon the bred cow evaded 6-5's herding and moved back to Forks' group. The bachelor bulls and Forks paid little attention to her.

By early October, the rut was essentially over. In fact, the last harems were large in size, mainly by default. Wide-sur began to be quite lax about keeping the bachelor bulls out of the harem, and had no rival until Spike-tip appeared (fig. 19). On October 25 Wide-sur had his left antler broken off just below the

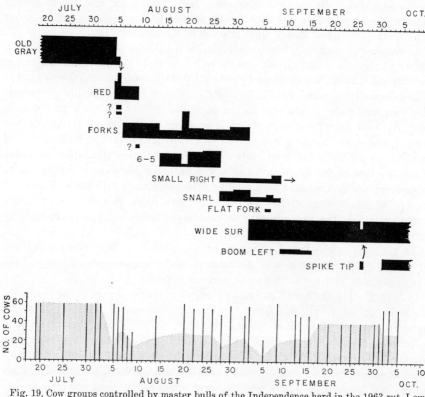

Fig. 19. Cow groups controlled by master bulls of the Independence herd in the 1963 rut. Lower vertical lines indicate numbers of cows and calves accounted for, and the stippled area indicates the mean harem size. Arrows indicate observed harem changes.

surroyals and Spike-tip had all of the cows. So apparently there had been a fight leading to Wide-sur's defeat.

The 1964 rut.—It was possible to observe the development of the rut in 1964 from its earliest stages, and to identify individually the Independence herd bulls and ascertain the hierarchy before the rut got underway. Also I attempted to observe the herd daily once the rut began.

The development of the heavy dark mane and lightening of the body color became apparent as early as the beginning of July. By July 6, a large bull, Tritops, had joined a herd of 36 cows. On July 13 he left the herd to go to water. On July 14 he was back with a herd of cows, and remained with them continuously thereafter, even though he was still in velvet.

Figure 20 shows the onset of various rutting behavioral acts. The first to appear are those related to the maintenance of a harem, followed by acts indicating the rutting condition of the bull. Actual copulation and serious fighting are last to appear. Herding by Tritops was observed first on July 14, and tongue lapping on the same day. The first bugle, an abortive one, was heard July 28.

Tritops was the first bull to assume control of the cow herd because he was the most advanced in sexual preparedness. He was the first to come out of velvet. He began on July 28, and was virtually out of velvet on August 1. The other bulls

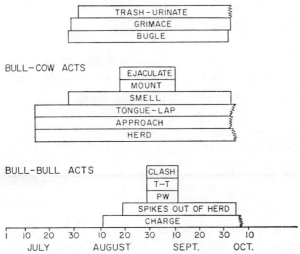

Fig. 20. First appearance and duration of rutting behavioral acts by Independence master bulls in 1964. Broken lines indicate a low level of behavioral act long after the rutting season.

lagged considerably behind (fig. 14). By the time other bulls were physically prepared to contest the control of the herd, Tritops was firmly established as the master bull.

There were markedly more frequent changes in harem size in 1964 than in 1963 as is apparent from a comparison of figures 19 and 21. In 1963, when both water and forage were abundant and distributed widely over the rutting grounds, there was little incentive for the elk to shift about. Thus it was possible for master bulls to hold cow groups continuously in a given area, and reduce the frequency of contact with other master bulls. The 1964 season was a drought year, and both forage and water were limited and spotty in distribution. Coming to water, particularly, resulted in frequent encounters between rival bulls. Furthermore, the moves from one place to another resulted in frequent changes in the size of harems since a moving group is far more difficult for the master bull to maintain than a stationary one. This is apparent in the fluctuations in Tritops' herd during July, when he had no rival (fig. 21).

Serious challenge to Tritops did not come until the end of August. On August 29, I found the entire cohort in the cow herd with both Tritops and Sport present.

Bugling was given only by these two. They finally clashed twice during which Tritops' left royal tine was broken off. The tip of his right trez was already broken, indicating that they had clashed previously. The encounters were a stand-off. Plates 4 and 5 illustrate the herd turmoil on this occasion. They then joined the stampeding herd and ran to water. There Monarch, another large 6-point

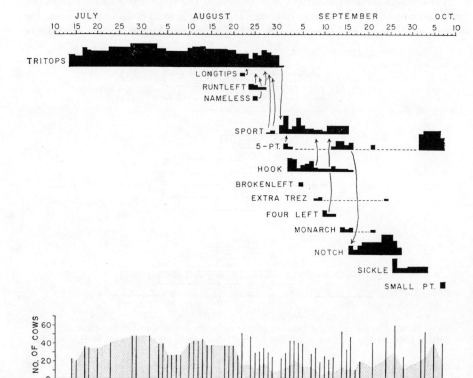

Fig. 21. Cow groups controlled by master bulls of the Independence herd in the 1964 rut. Lower vertical lines indicate number of cows and calves accounted for, and the stippled area indicates the mean harem size. Arrows indicate observed harem changes.

bull, had a receptive cow, Sport had 6, and Tritops had 18. All three of the large bulls were bugling frequently. There were 16 other bachelor bulls on the scene. Monarch mounted the cow 12 times before ejaculation at 12:22. Sport came over to Monarch several times and they parallel walked and thrashed, but did not clash. Bachelor bulls would start running Sport's cows and he would return to them. Sport also came over to Tritops but they did not clash. Sport then returned to Monarch and they continued the psychological battle while Sport's cows came into Tritops' herd. The recently bred cow wandered off through all of the bulls and to Tritops' herd. The bulls paid little attention to her. Monarch and Sport faced off several more times, but did not clash. They were no longer in possession of cows, and they soon moved apart and all three large bulls bedded down shortly afterward, Tritops in possession of the harem.

The herd was not observed on August 30, but on August 31 Sport had 16 cows and Tritops 3. Twenty other bulls were about. Monarch was not present. Tritops had a broken right brow tine and broken surroyals, indicating that he had continued to fight with Sport. Sport acquired Tritops' three cows in a bugling battle. Sport came out to Tritops and they parallel walked and thrashed. Sport came out many times between 9:00 and 11:25 AM but each time the bachelor bulls would move into his harem and he would return. Tritops continued to bugle. There were no more encounters until 2:40 PM when after a series of parallel walks and thrashes, they clashed once, indecisively. At 3:52 they again postured, but did not clash. At 3:58 Sport mounted a cow, and mounted her six times before 4:28 when the cow ran away from him and over to Tritops. Tritops came to meet her and mounted her three times before she began running again, back toward Sport. Tritops and the other bulls followed. Sport and Tritops gave a quick thrash-thrash, then came together hard. They clashed seven times in rapid succession. The first encounters were even matches. Then on the fifth encounter they both had good footing and were locked in stand-off for about five seconds. With a great effort Sport forced Tritops backwards. The next encounter was undecided. In the final encounter Sport forced Tritops backwards rapidly and got his body twisted sideways. Sport pushed relentlessly as Tritops ran sideways with his antlers still engaged for about four seconds, then disengaged and turned and ran. Sport struck him in the side as he was disengaging but caused no visible wound. Tritops ran for all he was worth, Sport just one step behind, for some 30 to 40 yards before Sport stopped and returned to the cow. While Sport and Tritops had been fighting, Extra-trez, the ranking bull of the bachelor cohort, had singled out the cow and mounted her three times. Sport came back and ran Extra-trez off and began mounting the cow. He mounted 20 times before ejaculating at 4:44 PM. The herd was running by this time, but Sport soon brought it under control.

Tritops' defeat was complete. When Sport came his way while chasing the receptive cow, he ran fearfully. His bugling stopped immediately after his defeat. Several loose cows came past him from the milling herd and he paid them no attention. Later, he followed slowly far behind the running herd. On the following days he stayed near the bachelor bulls, but bedded alone a short distance away. He showed absolutely no rutting behavior. On September 1 the bachelor bulls again rushed into the herd, but Tritops stayed off by himself. Twelve free cows came past him and he paid no attention. He left the rutting area on September 3.

It is interesting to follow the decline of Tritops with the progression of the rut. Tritops lasted just one month from the time of coming out of velvet until the day of his defeat. The tremendous demand upon the bull's resources cannot be met indefinitely, and a steady decline in condition is clearly visible as illustrated by photographs of Tritops. Plates 6 and 7 show him early in the rut before activity has become intense, and at various times thereafter, including following his defeat by Sport.

Figure 22 demonstrates the increased demand upon the bull's time to hold a harem and defend it against bachelor bulls. Not only does the percent of time spent bedded decline with the intensity of the rut, but also the average length of bedded periods declines, as the bull is frequently interrupted by rutting chores. Upon defeat, the time bedded increases tremendously.

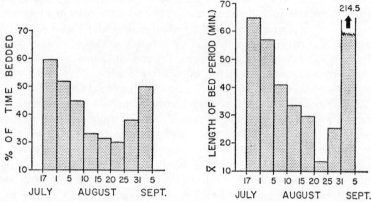

Fig. 22. Change in bedding pattern of Tritops as the rut progressed. He was defeated on August 31.

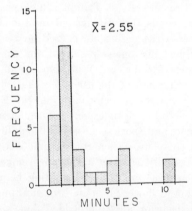

Fig. 23. Length of feeding periods of Tritops on August 21 at an intense rutting stage.

Some authors have stated that rutting bulls give up feeding during this time. Actually they continue to feed, but are unable to keep up with the energy demands of the rut. Before the rut the bull feeding pattern is nearly identical to that of the cows. Approximately 40 percent of Tritops' time was spent feeding in late July. On August 21, every feeding period by Tritops was recorded to the nearest one-half minute (fig. 23). In 425 minutes of observation Tritops fed 76.5 minutes (18 percent of the time). However these feeding periods were continuously interrupted by the need to herd cows, or chase off bachelor bulls. Feeding periods ranged from less than 1 to a high of 10 minutes. The average length of 30 feeding periods was only 2.6 minutes. The inability to maintain a feeding schedule is apparent in the appearance of the abdomen. When the bull is feeding regularly the abdomen is distended. When the bull is unable to feed the abdomen is sleek and drawn up (pl. 7, *a*).

Sport was unable to retain the entire cow group, and lost about half of them to Hook (fig. 21). Although many clashes occurred between these two master bulls, none involved a fight carried on until the defeat of one or the other. Instead the encounters were short, with the cows being divided up again, sometimes to the benefit of one, sometimes the other (fig. 21).

Thereafter the rut followed the general course as in the previous year. The rut was over in early October.

Analysis of rut behavior acts.—In the 1964 rut, behavioral acts of master bulls were recorded on minute-by-minute intervals. Approximately 200 hours of such observation were made. The relationship of the frequency of acts to time of day is shown in table 1. In all cases there is a high in activity during the morning, a lull around noon, and another high in the afternoon. These results are generally related to the frequent bedding of cows and bachelor bulls during midday, even though the master bull is active through the day (table 1). Observe that copulations follow a bimodal curve, with peaks at 11:00 AM and 3:00 PM.

The summary on the right-hand side of table 1 shows that acts related to herding and inspection of cows are most frequent, followed by bull advertising acts. Chasing bachelor bulls is third in frequency, but occurs at a much lower level than the first two categories. Although the number of high intensity fights between master bulls was quite low (8 total) the number of behavior acts shown in these encounters is relatively high. Copulations are the least frequent of the major categories.

Table 2 shows the changes in frequency of the recorded acts with the progression of the rut based upon active hours of the master bulls. Active hours were used since almost no rutting acts are performed while a bull is bedded. Occasionally a bull will bugle while bedded, but these are so infrequent in relation to the total number of bugles that they can be ignored. The number of active hours of observation will vary in different tables and figures depending on how they are tabulated. For example, total observation hours for individual bulls is higher because at times it was possible to observe two master bulls at the same time. In general, 120 to 125 hours of observation of active master bulls were obtained. The number of acts observed during the main part of the rut was six to eight times higher than during the pre- and post-rutting periods. Bull-cow acts as exemplified by herding were relatively more frequent in early and late rut than at the peak. Bugling was the most frequent single act during the peak of the rut, and also for the season (27 percent of all acts).

Bull-cow acts predominate over bull-bull acts in the pre- and post-rut periods. High level sexual and aggressive acts occur only during the active stage of the rut.

Note the relatively infrequent occurrence of attempted mounting and smelling. Attempted mounting rarely occurred since the cows retreated from the bulls before attempts could be made. Only in cases where the cow was detained, as for

TABLE 1

Hourly Totals of Rutting Behavior Acts by Tule Elk Master Bulls of the Independence Herd in 1964

	Hour								Total
	9	10	11	12	1	2	3	4	
Hours observed	13.97	27.0	31.55	29.78	32.0	32.58	26.6	7.17	200.7
Hours active	7.8	14.65	19.48	16.5	20.85	20.43	17.15	4.55	121.41
Percent active	55.8	54.3	61.7	55.4	65.2	62.7	64.5	63.5	60.5
Bull advertising acts									
Number	157	247	223	89	95	147	242	70	1,270
Number per active hour	20.13	16.86	11.45	5.39	4.62	7.20	14.11	15.38	
Bull-cow acts									
Number	171	308	236	140	229	286	348	72	1,790
Number per active hour	21.92	21.02	12.11	8.48	10.98	14.0	20.29	15.82	
Copulatory acts									
Number mounts	9	22	21	10	2	4	14	33	115
Number ejaculations	2	2	7	1	1	2	4	1	20
Bull-bull acts									
Number	34	29	27	13	12	24	39	8	186
Number per active hour	4.36	1.98	1.39	0.79	0.58	1.17	2.27	1.76	
Number parallel walk	2	6	8	11	0	8	2	12	49
Number thrash-thrash	2	8	24	9	0	20	10	24	97
Number clash	1	2	6	2	0	4	0	22	37
Total number acts	378	624	552	275	339	495	659	242	3,564
Number per active hour	48.5	42.6	28.3	16.7	16.3	24.2	38.4	53.2	

TABLE 2

Frequency of Rutting Acts by Periods as Given by Tule Elk Master Bulls in the Independence Herd in 1964

Act	Pre-rut period July 15-Aug. 5			Mid-rut period Aug. 6-Sept. 25			Post-rut period Sept. 25-Oct. 5			Total		
	No.	A/AH*	Percent	No.	A/AH*	Percent	No.	A/AH*	Percent	No.	A/AH*	Percent
Bugle	7	.55	14	968	9.70	27.9	1	.11	2.1	976	8.04	27.4
Thrash-urinate	8	.63	16	200	2.0	5.8	1	.11	2.1	209	1.72	5.9
Grimace	1	.07	2	80	.80	2.3	4	.45	8.3	85	.70	2.4
Herd	12	.94	24	508	5.09	14.7	12	1.36	25.0	532	4.38	14.9
Approach	5	.39	10	597	5.98	17.2	13	1.47	27.1	615	5.07	17.3
Tongue-lap	5	.39	10	588	5.89	17.0	13	1.47	27.1	606	4.99	17.0
Attempted mount	3	.23	6	10	0.10	0.3	0	0.00	0.0	13	.11	.4
Mount	0	.00	0	115	1.15	3.3	0	0.00	0.0	115	.95	3.2
Ejaculate	0	.00	0	20	0.20	0.6	0	0.00	0.0	20	.16	.6
Smell	4	.31	8	17	0.17	0.5	3	.34	6.3	24	1.98	.7
Charge	5	.39	10	180	1.80	5.2	1	.11	2.1	186	1.53	5.2
Parallel walk	0	.00	0	49	0.49	1.4	0	0.00	0.0	49	.40	1.4
Thrash-thrash	0	.00	0	97	0.97	2.8	0	0.00	0.0	97	.80	2.7
Clash	0	.00	0	37	0.37	1.1	0	0.00	0.0	37	.30	1.0
Total	50	3.90	100	3,466	34.73	100.0	48	5.45	100.0	3,564	29.36	100.0
Observation time in active hours	12.8			99.8			8.8			121.4		
Percent of time active	43.4			64.07			76.7			60.5		

* Acts per active hour.

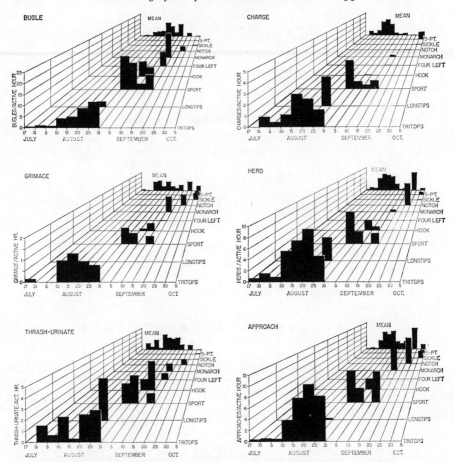

Fig. 24. Behavioral acts by master bulls in the Independence herd in the 1964 rut.

example during nursing a calf, was the bull able to attempt to mount. None of these attempts were successful. Smelling occurred only when cows were bedded, and the bull went around smelling them. Because of their infrequent occurrence, these two acts will not be considered further in this analysis. Observe also, that approach and tongue-lap almost always occurred together. Hereafter only approach will be analyzed, since tongue-lap can be considered as a part of the act of approaching.

The behavior of the individual master bulls with the advance of the rutting season is given in figures 24 and 25. Unfortunately, other project work interfered with observation of rutting behavior in the two periods September 16 to 20 and 25 to 30, and the blanks for these two periods are due to absence of data, rather than to lack of behavior.

There is a considerable amount of variation with the season and between individual bulls (fig. 24). Generally the frequency of the various acts increased until

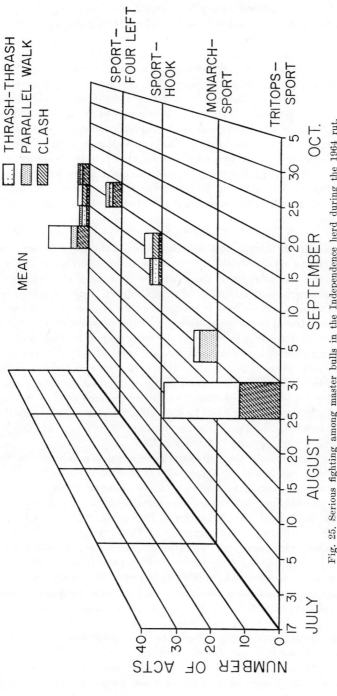

Fig. 25. Serious fighting among master bulls in the Independence herd during the 1964 rut. All three acts are plotted from the base line, rather than accumulatively.

the end of August, remained at a plateau until September 10, then gradually declined. Much of the variation in this general pattern is due to replacement of exhausted bulls by vigorous new bulls. One exception is in the frequency of grimacing which remained relatively low and fluctuated erratically. Another was in the number of charges, which reached a peak earlier than most of the acts. This was due to the driving out of yearling males and other young bulls with the ascendancy of rutting behavior. These young animals soon resign themselves to remaining away from the harems and become a part of the bachelor bull cohorts. I have not seen widely wandering, confused, and harassed spikes such as Altmann (1960) reported in Rocky Mountain elk. These animals merely take their places at the bottom of the bull hierarchy and are integrated into the loose cohort social structure. Another factor influencing the low level of charges in the second half of the rut is the breakup of the large cow group into smaller units. These can be guarded more effectively by the master bulls, so that the opportunity for bachelors to slip into the harems is limited.

Most of the variation in behavior of master bulls is loosely correlated with the number of cows in the harem, but also important is the physiological condition of the bull, and the seriousness of the challenge to his supremacy. For example, bugling arises early in the rut with the sexual development of the bull and declines late in the season with the dropping off of sexual interest. Bugling is most frequent during times when a master bull is being seriously challenged, but varies with time of day, number of cows in the harem, and the presence of a receptive cow. Thus at least five known factors influence the frequency of bugling, and there are probably others. Most of the behavioral acts are controlled by a number of inter-dependent factors. There is also considerable variation in individual bulls, independent of other influences. For example, Sport was an unusually aggressive fighter less given to elaborate gesturing and more inclined to make contact than most master bulls. On the other hand he was rather complacent about maintaining a harem and lackadaisical about keeping younger bulls away. Similar "personality" differences were apparent in other bulls.

Copulations performed by the individual bulls are shown in figure 26. Morrison (1960a) reported copulation occurring more than once in the same heat period, which lasted up to 17 hours in some of the cows he observed. Cows which copulated in a normal manner one day would sometimes allow a second copulation the following day, but would show no interest. In my observations, receptive cows were bred only once during a day's observation. On numerous occasions bred cows came into contact with other bulls immediately following copulation and would not stand to be mounted even though the bull pursued them vigorously. Also, the interest of bulls in recently bred cows waned quickly. I cannot say whether or not individual cows which were observed to be bred were bred again during the night or in following days, due to lack of adequate individual identification of cows.

There is a suggestion that bulls are able to distinguish bred cows from unbred cows, and that master bulls concentrate their efforts upon the latter. Although I spent a considerable amount of time watching harems controlled by lesser bulls, particularly in 1963, I never once observed a cow come into heat in one of these groups. Conversely, in 1964 I concentrated on following dominant bulls until their final defeat. Many copulations by these bulls occurred in very small harems. An outstanding example was September 9 when Sport and Hook contested over 11 cows, 3 of which came into receptive condition and were bred. On the following day, Sport had only 6 cows, one of which was bred, the last observed copulation of the season. The high number of receptive cows in relation to the small total number would seem to be more than chance.

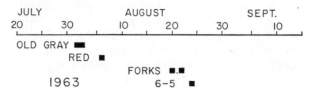

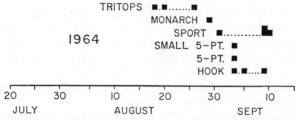

Fig. 26. Copulations observed in the Independence herd in two rutting seasons. Note timing difference between years.

The ability of a bull to service many cows is illustrated by Sport's servicing two cows 13 minutes apart and contesting Hook for another receptive cow 14 minutes later. This was at a time when Sport was nearly spent and in visibly poor condition.

Serious fighting among master bulls is shown in figure 25. No fighting occurred until Sport displaced Tritops at the end of August. A small number of serious encounters occurred in the following three periods. Unfortunately I could not make observations from September 15 to 20 when both Sport and Hook were defeated. However, a considerable increase in fighting probably occurred, presaged by Sport's strong encounter with Four-left on September 11, and indicated by Notch's strong display of breeding behavior in the subsequent period (fig. 24). Also, during the unobserved period, Sport and Notch both broke antler tines.

Discussion of the breeding system.—The individual bulls can be assigned to four main categories based on the evidence presented in figures 19 and 21: (1) the primary bulls; (2) secondary bulls; (3) tertiary bulls; and (4) opportunists.

The primary bull is the one that takes control of the herd first due to his advanced sexual condition. He is the first to come out of velvet, but has established himself with the herd long before that. The secondary bulls are those large bulls which split the herd up upon the defeat of the primary bull. The tertiary bulls take control of the herd following the decline of the secondary bulls. The opportunists engage in contacts with cows when they receive the chance by accident. They join the harems when the master bull's attention is turned elsewhere, or pick up stray cows which have evaded the master bulls. The secondary and tertiary bulls also act as opportunists before they become master bulls in their own right.

The assignment of bulls into the various categories is clearly based upon the hierarchy. As the rut progresses, spent bulls are replaced by bulls of the next lower rank. Even the opportunists function on the basis of the hierarchy; stray cows fall to the highest ranking bull in the bachelor cohort. Thus, if a receptive cow runs away from a master bull, there is no question of which bull will take possession of her. It is always the dominant bull of the cohort, and the other bachelor bulls do not interfere when he is servicing her. But if the master bull has the opportunity, he regains such lost cows without a fight. The fact that largest bulls come out of velvet earliest assures that the bulls highest in the hierarchy have the advantage from the very beginning of the rut.

With age and increased size and strength, bulls move up in the hierarchy and gain status in the breeding order. Red of the 1963 season was probably the bull called Tritops of 1964; this bull was exceptionally reddish in body color, even much more so than the spikes, which retain the darkest (least gray) body color. This bull advanced from being a secondary bull in 1963 to being the primary bull in 1964. Unfortunately Forks, a clearly ear-marked secondary bull in 1963, was killed by a poacher before the rut in 1964. However Notch, another ear-marked bull, was an opportunist in 1963 as a medium sized 5-point. In 1964, as barely a 6-point, he had advanced to being a tertiary bull.

The regular bull complement of a herd is augmented by bulls from other areas, and also contributes some of its own to the wandering bull population. In 1964 3 out of 13 (about 20 percent) of the important bulls in the Independence herd were outsiders. All three were in the tertiary class. This wandering behavior not only insures a constant influx of new genes, but also shifts bulls from herds with a surplus to herds that may have an inadequate supply. Or, more precisely, it assures an optimum allocation of the male breeding stock.

Some authors have questioned the advantages of maintaining a harem, suggesting that old bulls are kept so busy fighting that young bulls do most of the breeding. Table 3 shows the observed copulations of various classes of bulls in the Independence herd. That the largest bulls do most of the breeding is clearly demonstrated. Primary and secondary bulls comprised only 12 percent of the bull population, but they did 84 percent of the breeding. Even when receptive cows ran away from master bulls, the ranking bull in the hierarchy of the bachelor cohort assumed the breeding function. And the cohort is always nearby.

The psychological advantages of the master bull are easily understood once it is recognized that he had previously held a higher position in the hierarchy than his rivals in the cohort. Challenges occur during states of flux when the usual harem control breaks down—at times of alarmed flight and similar disturbances, but most commonly when a receptive cow is present in the harem. The master bull's attention is turned to breeding the cow, and the bachelor bulls become highly excited and often rush into the herd. If the master bull services the cow before the bachelors come into the harem, he immediately increases the tempo of bugling and herding to avert the crisis. If the bulls are already in the herd, there is a milling confusion as the master bull "inventories" the opposition. He soon picks up his bugling, and the dominant bull of the cohort returns the bugling if he is a serious contender. None of the lesser bulls bugle.

Surprisingly, the master bull is not seriously challenged until his strength is nearly spent. Figure 25, which shows when serious fighting occurs during the progression of the rut, demonstrates this phenomenon. In fact, bull cohorts usually do not contain a serious contender while the harem bull is in good condition. For

TABLE 3

SUCCESS OF VARIOUS CATEGORIES OF TULE ELK RUTTING BULLS IN PERFORMING COPULATIONS
(Copulatory numbers are enclosed in parentheses.)

Year	Primary	Secondary	Tertiary	Opportunists
1964	Old Gray (2)	Red (1) Forks (2) 6–5 (1)	Snarl (0) Wide sur (0) Spike-tip (0) Small right (0)	All others 21 (0)
1965	Tritops (3)	Sport (4) Hook (3)	5-pt. (1) Monarch (1) Notch (0) Sickle (0)	All others 22 (1)
Total............2 (5)		5 (11)	8 (2)	43 (1)
Percent............3.4 (26.3)		8.6 (57.9)	13.8 (10.5)	74.1 (5.3)
Copulations per bull.......2.5		2.2	0.25	0.02

12 percent of bulls account for 84 percent of copulations

example, Sport did not join the bachelor cohort until four days before he defeated Tritops. Similarly, neither Sport nor Hook had a serious contender besides each other. However, their fights were brief and indecisive. The purpose seemed not to be the defeat of one or the other, but rather to obtain a more favorable distribution of cows. Apparently two closely matched bulls in good condition cannot do more than maintain a standoff. Yet when Sport and Hook became exhausted they were deposed by the tertiary bulls. Indeed, the assignment of bulls into primary, secondary, and tertiary classes is based upon the length of time it takes for rutting bulls to use up their resources.

Obviously the bulls themselves have a rather precise means of determining the condition of a master bull, since they do not challenge him until the appropriate time. This is probably the underlying function of urinating on the long hair on the underside of the body in the thrash-urinate act. The bull is marking himself with his own metabolic products to advertise his condition. He retains his strength as long as he is metabolizing reserve body fats and dietary energy. When these are exhausted and he starts metabolizing his muscle tissues his strength declines rapidly. It would seem incredible that the extremely sensitive olfaction of elk could not detect the shift in metabolism as reflected in the urine products.

This sort of advertisement of physical condition would have a distinct advantage for the master bull as well as for the total breeding system. It would avoid needless encounters at a time when the master bull is in prime condition and cannot be defeated. Conversely, it facilitates the replacement of spent bulls by fresh ones to carry on the breeding. Still, it is inevitable that fighting will occur, since a change in bulls requires that a bull lower in the hierarchy defeat one which is normally dominant, accustomed to asserting that dominance without challenge, and not willing to give up voluntarily. Thus, while much fighting is avoided by ritualization, fighting ultimately occurs. Ritualization assures that the appropriate bulls fight at the appropriate times. Thus, nearly every tertiary or higher bull engages in serious combat during the normal course of a rutting season.

The thrash-urinate act may also serve another function since bred cows would be "marked" olfactorily much as domestic sheep ewes are marked visually by blue chalk placed on the breasts of rams. This would facilitate the determination by bulls of cows which had already been serviced, since only receptive cows allow mounting.

These observations prompt a comment on the selective pressure for sexual dimorphism and particularly for antlers. The communicatory and combative function of antlers in the male hierarchy is obvious. My evidence is all positive that antlers are indeed useful. The suggestion of some authors that bulls lacking antlers or having short stubs compete successfully for harems is certainly not true of these animals. The burden of proof (i.e., quantitative measure of breeding success) would seem to be on the assumption that the antlerless condition is an advantage. This also requires an explanation of why, if it is an advantage, antlers have not evolved into rudimentary stumps, or have not been lost entirely.

Continued growth in body and antler size allows bulls with superior survival qualities to advance to the head of the hierarchy where there is greater opportunity to pass their genes on to subsequent generations. Nearly every bull has the potential to reach a large size and grow massive antlers; the problem is to live that long. The notion that large antler size is selected for ad infinitum, and that some forms (e.g., the Irish elk) became extinct because their antlers grew too large, is ill-founded. One selective force favors large antlers for behaviorial reasons, but it is balanced by another selective pressure to keep the antler size within the normal growth capacity of the animal. Too much energy diverted to antlers decreases the bull's chances of living long enough to make an important contribution to the gene pool. In the Owens Valley bulls, the general antler growth was very good in the high rainfall season of 1963; nearly all the tertiary bulls (generally four-year-olds) grew good 6 point antlers. In the 1964 drought season, the antlers were much poorer; the tertiary bulls were just barely 6-pointers or large 5-pointers. Clearly antlers are grown with whatever resources can be spared from the needs of the body, which are paramount, as shown by the studies of Cowan and Long (1962) on white-tailed deer.

Females also have a strongly developed hierarchy. Dimorphism, and particularly having antlers, assures that the male can immediately assume dominance over the highest ranking females and thus dominance over the entire cow group. This is a necessary prerequisite to a breeding system based upon harems. Tule elk cows, either among themselves or with bulls, are certainly not selfless as red deer hinds are described by Darling (1937). The cows are quite rebellious and will run away from a bull which is unable to assert his dominance, allowing them to evade a bull's attempts to hold them in unsuitable situations. The independence of the cows, in conjunction with harassment by bachelor bulls, further keeps pressure on the master bull, and creates conditions favorable to displacement of unsuitable bulls. This constant testing of the master bull assures that the strongest bulls control the harems.

In polygamous species, successful males make inordinate contributions to the genetic makeup of the succeeding generations. The ungulate hierarchies based upon age are a means of assuring that appropriate males (i.e., those which have survived over a number of seasons) do most of the breeding. This study showed the importance of hierarchy in harem keeping species. In other species such as the Uganda kob (*Adenota kob*) (Buechner, 1961) and roe deer (*Capreolus capreolus*), the males tend to defend territories. The studies of Hennig (1962) showed that the hierarchy in roe deer is important in maintaining a favorable territory. In still other species, males tend estrus females. Lent (1965) reported this kind of breeding system in caribou (*Rangifer tarandus*), and it serves in a number of other species. Burchardt (1958) describes it in red deer in Switzerland, and copulations by opportunist bulls in this study are probably manifestations of a "tending" response. Yet in all three common types of breeding systems, the hierarchy based upon age favors the most adaptive bulls. Perhaps this is a generalization which can be extended to most ungulates.

RANGE RELATIONSHIPS
Food Habits

Many plant species in Owens Valley are occasionally grazed by elk, but the bulk of forage is obtained from a few important plants. At any one time, the most palatable species are sought out, and the food habits shift with the seasons accordingly. Most of the information on food habits was obtained by direct observation of feeding animals, and by later checking of the exact place to be certain of kinds of plants taken. Much other information was obtained by following tracks of feeding animals to see which plants were visited and cropped. Droppings were routinely crushed and examined for identifiable remains. This approach was particularly useful in the fall and winter when many seeds were passed unaltered. Food habits of domestic stock were observed by the same methods.

Annual forbs.—This group of plants is extremely important as spring and early summer forage. The movement of elk into the canyons and foothills in the spring is primarily influenced by the availability of the new growth of ephemeral annuals. The number of species of annuals is very great, and most are palatable. Important genera are *Eriogonum, Layia, Anisocoma, Mentzelia, Cryptanthus, Gilia, Erodium,* and many others. Typically these plants begin to appear with the first warm period of the spring, grow quickly, flower, seed, and dry up by early summer. Their period of availability is short, but their contribution of forage is great. They come at a time when winter forage is declining, and they produce an abundance of highly palatable and nutritious food at the beginning of calving, molting, and antler regrowth.

The production of ephemeral annual forbs is directly dependent upon the amount of effective precipitation, and the year to year fluctuation is great. This fluctuation is clearly demonstrated by studies on the 20-acre burn on the Goodale range. Two matching pairs of 9.6 square foot plots were selected, and one of each pair designated by a coin flip to be protected from grazing by a wire cone. The cones (pl. 8) were constructed as described by Wood et al. (1960) from half-circles of welded wire fencing, 2 by 4 inch mesh of 11½ gauge wire, rolled into cones with a base diameter of 4.5 feet and securely wired. They were held in place by three 18-inch reinforcing rod stakes. The cones protected a plot of 9.6 square feet with an adequate buffer area. The precise plot was delimited by a plot frame which was a steel rod hoop of 1.75 feet radius with cross reinforcing rods dividing it into quarters. This plot size has the advantage of easy conversion to pounds per acre by simply multiplying the grams of forage clipped from the plot by a factor of 10.

TABLE 4

MEAN PRODUCTION AND TULE ELK AND DEER UTILIZATION OF AIR-DRIED
FORAGE PER ACRE OF TWO PAIRED PLOTS ON THE 20-ACRE GOODALE BURN
(in pounds)

Forage	1964		1965	
	Production	Utilization (elk)	Production	Utilization (deer)
Mallow	261	239 (91.6%)	2716	2035 (74.9%)
Annual forbs	160	74 (46.3%)	637	335 (52.5%)
Total	421	313 (74.3%)	3353	2370 (70.7%)

In 1964, a drought year (2.6 inches of rainfall recorded in the bottomland adjacent to the study area), the average production of the two protected plots was 16.0 of air-dried annual forbs (table 4). While two cones are not an adequate sample for statistical purposes, the figure suggests an annual production on the order of 160 pounds of air-dried forage per acre or about one and one-half tons for the 20-acre area. In 1965 the favorable growing conditions of late winter warm weather for germination and later a cool spring to sustain growth, resulted in production well above what the 3.1 inches of rainfall would have suggested. An average of 63.7g of air-dried forage was obtained from the cones, suggesting a production of 637 pounds per acre or better than six tons for the area. Thus between years there was a fourfold difference in annual forb growth. On a long term basis, there is probably a tenfold fluctuation between the best and poorest years. Production on the burn, where competition from brush was largely removed, was much higher than on surrounding range. Yet it is apparent that substantial amounts of annual forage are available during favorable years. In the 1964 drought year, the elk concentrated on the burn to feed on the annual growth, which was very limited elsewhere. They utilized about 46 percent of the production of annuals (table 4). In the following year when growth was good over the range, elk did not even come to the burn until after the annual growth had dried up. However, the Goodale deer herd concentrated on the area like sheep on a meadow, and utilized about 53 percent of the production of annual forbs.

Over most of the bottomland, ephemeral annual forbs are sparse. However, there are several summer annual forbs which are extremely important producers of forage. By far the most important, and a very significant elk forage plant, is bassia (*Bassia hyssopifolia*), also called five-fingered hysop or five-fingered bassia. This robust, rank annual which grows to three feet in height is an alien plant native to the Caspian Sea region (Robbins, 1940). It occurs locally in Owens Valley bottomlands as an invader of mechanically disturbed soils, where it forms thick stands.

Bassia is the single most important elk summer forage plant in the bottomlands. In the summer of 1963, the Independence and Lone Pine herds virtually existed on the extensive stands of bassia, and it was an important food of the other bottomland herds. The elk were in excellent condition that year. In the 1964 drought year bassia production was very low. There was not a single bassia plant in the Lone Pine herd area where the robust stands had been the previous year. The herd shifted away from this area, and began to cause serious damage to alfalfa fields. In the Independence area the bassia grew to about eight inches in height in the bottoms of a series of shallow dry ponds. The Independence elk dropped to their poorest condition of the two years of the study in June of 1964, when many species such as saltgrass, *Juncus*, and sacaton were readily available, and domestic stock was out of the valley for the summer. What was absent was bassia and other annuals. When the bassia became available in the bottoms of the ponds in late June, the elk fed heavily on it. By late July they had regained much of their condition. Throughout the valley in 1964, isolated patches of bassia were cropped down to the ground, and the plants grew in a mat form.

White sweetclover (*Melilotus albus*) is also sought by elk. It grows mainly along edges of water ditches and banks in the alkaline areas, and where it occurs it furnishes significant amounts of forage.

Another important summer annual is sunflower (*Helianthus annuus*). In this area it rarely grows more than a few feet in height and is taken readily by elk. They pull the plant up by the roots and eat all parts except the root which is clipped off and dropped. Sunflowers grow late in the summer, and reach their peak after bassia. However, they dry up quickly and are then no longer taken.

A number of other summer annuals are common in the bottomland. Annual *Atriplex* species are very common but are quite unpalatable. Others, such as curl-leaf dock (*Rumex cripus*), Russian thistle (*Salsola kail*), milkweed (*Asclepias* spp.), etc. are taken sparingly. In total, the summer annuals play a very important role in the elk diet in the bottomlands. They are heavily used until they dry up in early fall.

Annual grasses.—On the Sierra fans and foothills red brome (*Bromus rubens*) is common in rocky and lava areas. It is particularly abundant on old burns. Elk utilize red brome both during the growth period and as a dry forage in the winter. Cheatgrass (*Bromus tectorum*) is widespread, but much less abundant than red brome. In areas of the Great Basin cheatgrass is a problem species as a strong invader of burned areas, but in Owens Valley it causes no problems. It is a minor forage for elk.

Annual grasses are not common in the bottomlands, but some, such as barnyard grass (*Echinochloa crusgalli*) and rabbitfoot grass (*Polypogon monspeliensis*) occur along water ditches. Nearly all of these grasses are palatable and are used by elk.

Perennial forbs.—On the foothill areas, particularly on the Sierra side, globe mallow (*Sphaeralcea ambigua*) is an important elk food. It is most common in rocky areas, and reaches its greatest abundance following fires. Mallow was a common plant on the Goodale burn, where it was studied in conjunction with the annual forbs previously discussed (table 4). It was higher in production than the annual forbs, and utilization by elk and deer was very high. The production in the better year was about eight times that in the poor year (table 4). Globe mallow is far less common on the White-Inyo side, but where it occurs it is closely cropped.

In the bottomlands, wild licorice (*Glycyrrhiza lepidota*) is a particularly important perennial forb. It grows best in the alkali sacaton grasslands and is an aggressive invader following fire. It declines in abundance as the grasses recover several years after burning and choke it out. It stays green until late in the season, and during the early winter the seed burrs and some of the twigs are utilized. Licorice is second to bassia during the summer in the diet of elk, and becomes more important as the fall approaches and bassia dries.

Alkali mallow (*Sida hederacea*) is commonly taken by elk. It occurs on dry, mud-crusted pond and ditch bottoms. In the winter of 1964–1965, the Independence herd moved into a pond area and fed very heavily on alkali mallow.

A great number of other perennial forbs contribute minor amounts of forage. And, of course, alfalfa is a significant item in the diets of all but the Independence and Goodale herds.

Perennial grasses and grasslike plants.—On the Sierra slopes, desert needlegrass (*Stipa speciosa*) is the most common and abundant perennial grass. Elk use it when green or dry. Often the old dried bunches are pawed apart with a forefoot and the leafage cropped down to the coarse base which is clipped off and falls as small whists. Squirreltail (*Sitanion Hystrix*) is widespread but not abundant. It is cropped by elk, particularly when green. Indian ricegrass (*Oryzopsis hymenoides*) is another quite palatable species, but it is nowhere common. Pine bluegrass (*Poa scabrella*) is fairly common in the higher Sierra foothills, but in poor years it produces almost no forage.

These species also occur on the White-Inyo side and constitute part of the diet of elk using those ranges. In addition galleta (*Hilaria Jamesii*) is found in some of the higher areas.

Saltgrass (*Distichlis spicata*) and alkali sacaton (*Sporobolis airoides*) are by far the two most common grasses in the bottomlands. Neither of these species is very high in palatability to elk, although they prefer sacaton to saltgrass. Some animals will also crop the seeds of sacaton. Use on slender wheatgrass (*Agropyron trachecaulum*) was not observed, but may occur very occasionally. Giant wildrye (*Elymus cinereus*) leafage is sometimes cropped. In the moist lowlands, wirereeds *Juncus* and *Heleocharis* are commonly grazed in the spring. In the same areas wild barley (*Hordeum jubatum*) and sedge (*Carex*) are scattered, and are carefully sought out by the elk. In the marshes, *Phragmites* and alkali bullrush (*Scirpus robustus*) are common, but are utilized only a little in poor years, and almost not at all in good ones.

A number of grasses occur along water ditches, such as knotgrass (*Paspalum distichum*) and bermuda grass (*Cynodon Dactylon*), and most of these are quite palatable to elk.

Browse.—A relatively large number of browse species contributes importantly to the total diet of elk. Browse is particularly important in the winter, although some is taken at all seasons.

On the Sierra foothills, bitterbrush (*Purshia tridentata*) is an important feed for the Goodale elk herd, and this plant will be discussed in detail in the section on deer-elk competition. Other important species on the Sierra fans are sagebrush (*Artemisia tridentata*), California buckwheat (*Eriogonum fasciculatum*), hopsage (*Grayia spinosa*), winterfat (*Eurotia lanata*), ephedra (*Ephedra nevadensis* and *E. viridis*), white sage (*Salvia carnosa*), encelia (*Encelia virginensis*) and others.

In the White-Inyo foothills allscale (*Atriplex polycarpa*), hopsage, winterfat, and Nevada ephedra are taken in quantities. Mojave aster (*Machaeranthera tortifolia*) is highly palatable, and is always grazed very low. Fremont dalea (*Dalea Fremontii*) which is of low palatability to elk, indirectly furnishes forage in the form of dodder (*Cuscuta* sp.) which is parasitic upon it. The dodder is highly relished, and elk seek it out.

In the bottomland, big sagebrush is important as a winter food where it is common in the north part of the valley. The Hot Springs bulls and the Bishop herd use these stands heavily. There is heavy winter and spring use of greasewood (*Sarcobatus vermiculatus*) which is sometimes considered to be a toxic plant. Greasewood is one of the earliest plants to produce new growth in spring and it is used heavily by both elk and cattle. This use also occurs during good years when there are a number of alternate forages available, so it is a matter of preference.

Willows (*Salix* sp.) are a favored elk food, particularly in the summer, but the twigs are also taken in the winter. Young sprouting willows are preferred, but a surprising amount is browsed from the low hanging branches of mature trees. Other trees which are often browsed are cottonwood (*Populus Fremontii*) and locust (*Robinia Pseudo-Acacia*).

Other important bottomland browse species are quailbush (*Atriplex lentiformis*), rose (*Rosa ultramontana*), shadscale (*Atriplex confertifolia*), and four-wing saltbush (*Atriplex canescens*). Also, the first green growth in the spring of big rabbitbrush (*Chrysothamnus nauseosus*) and little-leaf horsebrush (*Tetradymia glabrata*) is grazed to a small extent.

Poisonous plants.—A number of plants that are often poisonous to domestic livestock are eaten by elk. These include greasewood, little-leaf horsebrush, locoweed (*Astragalus*), Mexican whorled milkweed (*Asclepias fascicularis*), and horsetail (*Equisetum* sp.). None of these plants seems to cause any difficulty. Water hemlock (*Cicuta Douglasii*) occurs in Owens Valley, but I have not observed grazing on it.

NUTRITIONAL QUALITY OF FORAGE

An extensive forage sampling program was carried on to establish the nutritional value of the important forage species of Owens Valley and to determine seasonal changes in nutrients. P. Dean Smith, Inyo-Mono County Farm Advisor,

TABLE 5

NUTRIENT COMPOSITION OF OWENS VALLEY FORAGE PLANTS SAMPLED BIMONTHLY

Forage plant	Month	Dry matter	Protein	Ash	Fat	Fiber	NFE*
Saltgrass.................	April	29.9	26.5	15.2	3.8	21.1	33.4
	June	41.5	15.2	16.4	2.6	20.0	45.8
	August	54.2	10.3	20.2	1.9	21.9	45.7
	October	81.5	6.5	19.0	2.2	21.9	50.4
	December	93.7	4.4	9.5	2.3	27.4	56.4
	February	90.0	3.8	6.9	2.2	27.8	59.3
Bassia....................	April	12.1	22.7	28.9	3.3	15.0	30.1
	June	17.5	25.7	21.2	2.1	10.0	41.0
	August	30.5	28.3	12.5	1.7	16.6	40.9
	October	92.6	22.6	13.5	2.9	15.2	45.8
	December	92.4	7.2	5.7	1.0	34.1	52.0
	February	91.8	3.0	2.4	0.5	42.6	51.5
Sweetclover..............	April	18.0	39.8	10.9	3.6	7.5	38.2
	June	18.2	31.5	11.2	3.7	19.5	34.1
	August	21.6	29.1	9.8	3.1	8.9	49.1
	October	22.2	30.4	11.0	2.1	8.5	48.0
	December	92.9	5.7	4.4	0.5	52.7	36.7
	February	91.8	6.0	2.3	0.5	54.8	36.4
Four-wing saltbush.........	April	54.6	14.5	15.3	2.5	13.0	54.7
	June	40.9	16.1	15.8	1.7	14.2	52.2
	August	56.0	13.4	15.1	1.9	12.0	57.6
	October	58.1	14.2	16.5	1.9	11.5	55.9
	December	61.2	13.9	13.5	2.4	15.2	55.0
	February	57.6	12.7	12.3	2.0	20.0	53.0

* NFE = nitrogen free extract.

cooperated in the project, and Extension Technologist John Rible performed the chemical determinations.

Four species were sampled bimonthly to establish in detail the seasonal changes in these representatives of major kinds of forage: bassia (an annual forb), white sweetclover (an annual legume), saltgrass (a perennial grass), and four-wing saltbush (browse). A second group of plants was sampled seasonally in conjunction with the intensive range studies in the Independence herd area: licorice, greasewood, quailbush, sacaton, and saltgrass. A last group of plants, the largest, was sampled only once or twice a year as a broad survey of Owens Valley forages.

All forage samples, including the spiny bushes, were hand picked to simulate as nearly as possible the actual materials ingested by animals. In the bimonthly samples, where the only variable desired was season, all material was collected in a very restricted area. The other samples were collected over broad areas to reflect normal variations in nutrient levels by site, plant phenology, and other factors. These data are presented in tables 5 through 10.

Dry matter.—The amount of moisture in most plants remained high from first growth until about August, when most species dried. In winter, herbaceous species

TABLE 6

Mineral Composition of Owens Valley Forage Plants Sampled Bimonthly

Forage plant	Month	Ca %	P %	Ca/P	Mo ppm	Cu ppm	Mo/Cu	SO₄-S ppm
Saltgrass...........	April	.70	.34	2.1	3.2	10.8	.3	1860
	June	.31	.21	1.5	7.6	3.3	2.3	1745
	August	.30	.10	3.0	10.5	1.2	8.8	3150
	October	.20	.07	2.9	8.0	1.7	4.7	3450
	December	.17	.04	4.3	5.4	2.0	2.7	....
	February	.12	.03	4.0	3.6	4.2	.9	560
Bassia.............	April	1.40	.30	4.7	3.8	14.7	.3	3200
	June	.50	.56	.9	3.8	7.5	.5	1373
	August	.20	.29	.7	3.9	8.3	.5	1500
	October	.20	.41	.5	3.6	12.1	.3	2850
	December	.28	.11	2.5	1.6	9.6	.2	....
	February	.25	.02	12.5	1.0	5.3	.2	110
Sweetclover........	April	1.60	.44	3.6	30.4	17.9	1.7	3840
	June	1.70	.31	5.5	20.8	10.0	2.1	1888
	August	1.60	.26	6.2	32.4	8.7	3.7	1450
	October	2.10	.21	10.0	42.0	11.3	3.7	3600
	December	.48	.04	12.0	28.8	6.7	4.3	....
	February	.53	.03	17.7	18.0	5.6	3.2	160
Four-wing saltbush.	April	2.00	.18	11.1	3.8	14.7	.3	4480
	June	.90	.25	3.6	2.8	9.1	.3	2574
	August	1.30	.10	13.0	6.5	7.5	.9	4300
	October	1.40	.10	14.0	8.8	9.5	.9	4850
	December	1.52	.12	12.7	9.4	7.7	1.2	....
	February	1.47	.12	12.3	8.2	11.7	.7	1920

were around 90 percent dry matter. Browse plants showed much less variation seasonally.

In view of the fact that herbaceous forbs are about 80 percent water in the early growth stages, it is not at all surprising that when total availability of forbs is high in the spring of good years, elk do not need to come to water.

Crude protein.—Crude protein values varied greatly between species. Legumes are known to have high protein levels, and the samples of sweetclover, verified this. Similarly, forbs were high in crude protein, and both they and the legumes held their levels until drying occurred. Grasses (and *Juncus*) were, for the most part, lower in protein initially, and they fell off rapidly. Crude protein levels of grasses in the winter were very low, and dried forbs were little better. Again, browse species were far more stable throughout the year. They tended to be higher in protein in the early growth period, but never declined to the lows reached by grasses and forbs.

Although proteins can be metabolized for energy, their primary function is growth and repair of body tissues. Nearly all growth by elk occurs during the green plant stage when proteins are in good supply. During the winter, elk can survive on a maintenance level of protein intake. This is even markedly noticeable

TABLE 7

NUTRIENT COMPOSITION OF OWENS VALLEY FORAGE PLANTS SAMPLED SEASONALLY

Forage plant	Season	Dry matter	Protein	Ash	Fat	Fiber	NFE†
Sacaton....................	Spring	37.6	13.6	11.3	2.4	29.1	43.6
	Summer	42.4	9.9	11.7	2.1	28.0	48.3
	Fall	55.9	5.4	17.2	1.2	25.6	50.6
	Winter	90.9	2.4	15.0	1.7	30.2	50.7
Licorice....................	Spring	23.0	32.0	7.2	8.2	10.7	41.9
	Summer	25.9	24.2	5.9	9.9	8.9	51.1
	Fall	34.5	17.5	13.1	3.3	6.6	59.5
	Winter	92.2	5.0	5.6	1.3	44.3	43.8
Juncus.....................	Spring	36.5	11.9	6.2	1.7	31.0	49.2
	Summer	40.1	7.4	5.9	1.7	32.7	52.3
	Fall	46.1	5.7	7.4	1.6	34.3	51.0
	Winter	93.4	2.9	7.4	1.8	36.5	51.4
Saltgrass....................	Spring	35.7	14.1	11.2	2.1	26.4	46.2
	Summer	44.3	11.4	12.5	2.1	29.4	44.6
	Fall	67.7	5.0	22.2	1.9	21.7	49.2
	Winter*	90.0	3.8	6.9	2.2	27.8	59.3
Greasewood.................	Spring	17.5	31.3	20.3	1.8	8.4	38.2
	Fall	30.4	6.9	25.9	2.9	15.1	49.2
	Winter	78.1	6.7	8.3	1.5	38.8	44.7
Quailbush....................	Fall	52.6	8.7	21.9	1.9	18.9	48.6
	Winter	57.3	10.2	18.8	1.8	20.3	48.9

* This sample is repeated from the bimonthly samples. All other samples in this table are separate.
† NFE = nitrogen free extract.

in calves. From birth through the first fall they grow rapidly, but growth virtually stops over the winter. With the new spring forage comes a rapid spurt of growth, and by midsummer they are virtually the same size as adult cows, from which most yearling cows cannot be distinguished.

No absolute minimum level of crude protein necessary for winter maintenance can be set, since it will vary with the kinds and amounts of other nutritional factors in the forage, age of the animal, etc. Einarsen (1946) considered 5 percent as the critical level in wintering deer, and Bissell and Strong (1955) felt that 7 percent was adequate for maintenance. The National Research Council (1963, 1964) gave 7.6 as the minimal crude protein for overwintering pregnant domestic ewes and 7.5 for pregnant heifers. Around 7 percent would seem to be adequate for elk under most conditions. None of the grasses (or *Juncus*) or forbs of Owens Valley can supply this minimal level. However, most of the browse species retain adequate protein levels through the winter.

Nitrogen free extract (NFE).—This important energy component showed considerable variation within species during the season. Herbaceous plants showed a general trend from low in the early season to high in dried condition. Most browse

TABLE 8

Mineral Composition of Owens Valley Forage Plants Sampled Seasonally

Forage plant	Season	Ca %	P %	Ca/P	Mo ppm	Cu ppm	Mo/Cu	SO$_4$-S ppm
Sacaton	Spring	.40	.22	1.8	3.0	2.8	1.1	1335
	Summer	.28	.21	1.3	5.2	1.3	4.0	3450
	Fall	.50	.08	6.3	2.0	2.4	.83	5700
	Winter	.40	.07	5.7	2.4	14.6	.16	1580
Licorice	Spring	.20	.44	.45	1.0	14.0	.07	1600
	Summer	.50	.31	1.6	Tr.	9.3	0.0	1050
	Fall	3.6	.14	25.7	4.0	5.7	.70	1750
	Winter	1.54	.02	77.0	12.0	9.3	1.3	110
Juncus	Spring	.14	.16	.88	4.8	4.9	.98	1495
	Summer	.40	.10	4.0	1.0	2.7	.37	1250
	Fall	.45	.06	7.5	7.2	2.3	3.1	1650
	Winter	.42	.03	14.0	4.0	7.5	.53	850
Saltgrass	Spring	.70	.24	2.9	4.0	2.4	1.7	1440
	Summer	.28	.16	1.8	4.6	1.3	3.5	2300
	Fall	.30	.07	4.3	2.4	3.1	.77	1550
	Winter*	.12	.03	4.0	3.6	4.2	.86	560
Greasewood	Spring	.80	.36	2.5	24.8	7.7	3.2	935
	Fall	1.3	.12	10.8	44.0	6.3	7.0	7450
	Winter	1.29	.08	16.1	10.4	8.5	1.2	480
Quailbush	Fall	1.3	.11	1.2	4.0	4.4	.91	3700
	Winter	1.45	.09	16.1	5.6	4.6	1.2	2300

* This sample is repeated from the bimonthly samples. All other samples in this table are separate.

species started the season high in nitrogen free extract and fluctuated but little with time. In winter, NFE levels of all forage plants tested were similar.

The NFE fraction represents soluble carbodydrates in the forage. These are typically easily assimilated, so that plants with high levels of NFE are generally good sources of energy.

Crude fiber.—This fraction contains the main structural components of plants. Since these persist after drying, they tend to be quite high in winter. Crude fiber levels through the growing season were fairly stable. Grasses, and particularly *Juncus*, had comparatively high fiber content through the season. Once again, browse species were quite stable in this component, and were only slightly higher in the winter than during the growing season.

Crude fiber, an energy producing forage component, is made up of complex carbodydrates which are generally considered to be resistant to digestion. Negative correlations of crude fiber content and total digestibility of a forage have been reported by a number of authors, and Meyer and Jones (1962) have proposed a method of using crude fiber to evaluate quality of alfalfa hay. Yet the work of A. D. Smith (1952), Dietz et al. (1962), and others has shown that deer are able to

TABLE 9

NUTRIENT CONTENT OF OWENS VALLEY FORAGE PLANTS SAMPLED SUMMER AND WINTER

Foothill plants	Season	Dry matter	Protein	Ash	Fat	Fiber	NFE†
Winterfat*....................	Summer	58.4	11.4	11.3	2.0	24.8	50.5
	Winter	42.4	16.9	12.6	2.2	28.3	40.0
Bitterbrush...................	Summer	42.0	13.1	5.8	4.4	14.2	62.5
	Winter	55.1	9.1	4.5	7.0	24.1	55.3
Big sage.....................	Summer	42.6	10.7	6.7	10.8	15.2	56.6
	Winter	44.8	12.6	5.1	15.0	13.4	53.9
Desert needlegrass...........	Summer	73.4	5.1	7.2	3.1	29.9	54.7
	Winter	86.7	4.2	7.4	2.3	31.6	54.5
California buckwheat.........	Summer	48.8	7.1	7.7	1.6	11.5	72.1
	Winter	56.6	6.1	4.6	2.5	12.1	74.7
Globe mallow.................	Summer	28.9	22.8	11.4	2.4	18.4	45.0
Hopsage*.....................	Summer	44.1	10.7	18.2	1.5	21.3	48.3
	Winter	32.8	18.0	10.9	2.2	25.4	43.5
Goldenbush...................	Winter	50.7	6.6	7.0	17.0	13.8	55.6
Nevada ephedra..............	Winter	58.0	9.1	6.2	3.4	29.9	51.4
Green ephedra...............	Winter	55.8	8.8	9.7	4.4	22.2	54.9
Bottomland plants							
Willow (mature).............	Summer	....	12.7	8.7	2.9	11.6	64.1
Willow (immature)..........	Summer	34.0	14.7	5.9	1.6	15.9	61.8
	Winter	53.5	5.1	6.5	3.0	35.6	49.8
Sunflower...................	Summer	16.2	17.3	18.2	9.2	12.2	43.1
Wildrose....................	Summer	39.2	14.1	5.5	2.6	8.3	69.5
Cottonwood..................	Summer	27.6	13.4	13.4	4.6	12.8	55.8
Rabbitbrush.................	Summer	27.9	19.8	8.5	11.4	16.2	44.1
Slender wheatgrass..........	Summer	30.1	17.0	9.5	4.0	30.9	38.6
Giant wildrye...............	Summer	27.7	13.0	9.7	2.8	37.9	36.6
Wild barley.................	Summer	21.3	31.6	13.0	7.8	21.5	26.1
Alkali mallow...............	Winter	94.0	3.1	39.0	2.7	22.3	32.9
Shadscale...................	Winter	62.9	7.1	16.7	2.1	24.2	49.9

* Showed early green growth at time of winter collection.
† NFE = nitrogen free extract.

TABLE 10

MINERAL COMPOSITION OF OWENS VALLEY FORAGE PLANTS SAMPLED SUMMER AND WINTER

Foothill plants	Season	Ca %	P %	Ca/P	Mo ppm	Cu ppm	Mo/Cu	SO₄-S ppm
Winterfat*	Summer	1.6	.13	12.3	2.2	12.0	.18	829
	Winter	1.6	.24	6.7	1.4	10.2	.14	670
Bitterbrush	Summer	1.3	.19	6.8	2.8	6.9	.41	143
	Winter	1.14	.11	10.4	1.0	7.5	.13	110
Big sage	Summer	.94	.32	2.9	1.6	19.0	.08	1001
	Winter	.84	.23	3.7	3.6	12.3	.29	910
Desert needlegrass	Summer	.29	.08	3.6	5.4	2.7	2.0	944
	Winter	.28	.04	7.0	5.6	5.6	1.0	290
California buckwheat	Summer	1.6	.16	10.0	1.6	7.5	.21	458
	Winter	1.49	.14	10.6	1.4	6.5	.21	290
Globe mallow	Summer	1.2	.48	2.5	1.2	11.0	.11	3003
Hopsage*	Summer	.78	.10	7.8	1.0	5.6	.01	4290
	Winter	.65	.28	2.3	0.4	8.1	.05	1360
Goldenbush	Winter	1.42	.09	15.8	Tr.	3.5	.00	560
Nevada ephedra	Winter	1.93	.09	21.4	1.0	3.7	.27	400
Green ephedra	Winter	3.25	.09	36.1	1.0	1.7	.58	370
Bottomland plants								
Willow (mature)	Summer	1.3	.21	6.2	Tr.	4.7	0.0	2850
Willow (immature)	Summer	.72	.29	2.5	Tr.	5.1	0.0	1250
	Winter	1.89	.09	21.0	1.0	7.9	.13	450
Sunflower	Summer	2.1	.36	5.8	4.6	16.0	.29	7150
Wildrose	Summer	.52	.20	2.6	1.0	11.0	.09	600
Cottonwood	Summer	1.2	.21	5.7	1.0	7.6	.01	770
Rabbitbrush	Summer	.70	.30	2.3	1.0	16.9	.06	855
Slender wheatgrass	Summer	.08	.27	.3	6.6	2.7	2.4	620
Giant wildrye	Summer	.09	.15	.6	4.4	3.6	1.2	920
Wild barley	Summer	.35	.52	.7	3.4	9.3	−3.0	830
Alkali mallow	Winter	2.7	.11	24.5	9.8	27.3	.35	1040
Shadscale	Winter	1.32	.07	18.9	6.6	6.7	.99	2880

* Showed early green growth at time of winter collection.

digest fair amounts of crude fiber, and evidence to be presented later suggests that tule elk may be fairly efficient at digesting fiber.

Crude fat.—Crude fat was highest in the early growth and dropped through the season. The decline was greatest in forbs, with both grasses and browse retaining higher levels in the winter.

Although fats in all plants were relatively low, their energy values are higher than carbohydrates (about 2.25 times higher) because of the low amount of oxygen in relation to carbon and hydrogen in fat molecules. Some species such as big sagebrush and goldenbush were very high in fat content, but some of it is in the form of essential oils, which are not easily digested. Nagy et al. (1964) have reported that essential oils in big sage inhibit rumen fermentation. Yet, many workers (for example, Dietz et al., 1962) have found sagebrush to be a good deer food if fed along with other species. The relative importance of sagebrush in the winter diet of tule elk suggests that it is an important source of nutrients.

Total ash.—The ash fraction tended to decline with the season; however, in some species (*Juncus*, sacaton), the ash content increased. The differences between plant species were quite high, but in general bottomland species were higher in ash than foothill plants.

Sulfate.—This element is quite abundant in the plant tissues of Owens Valley. Most species showed the same trend of being high in sulfate in early growth, dropping off by midsummer, resurging in the fall, and dropping to a low level in the winter.

Molybdenum.—Owens Valley is an area of high soil molybdenum. Most plants tested were initially low in molybdenum, built up to a high point in midsummer, and trailed off in the winter. Jensen et al. (1958) have demonstrated that legumes are high in molybdenum, and this was found to be true of sweetclover in this study. However, the fact that greasewood also concentrates molybdenum has not, to my knowledge, been reported previously.

Copper.—This element was highest with the early growth, and dropped off by early summer. Thereafter changes within and between species were quite variable, with no clearly defined trend.

Molybdenum-copper ratio.—The relationship of molybdenum to copper is of interest in regard to molybdenosis (molybdenum poisoning), a disease suffered by domestic animals in Owens Valley. The symptoms appear when animals ingest excessive amounts of molybdenum. However, the disease is alleviated by injection of copper, or by furnishing adequate copper in the diet. Molybdenum poisoning in elk is discussed later.

The molybdenum-copper ratio was low in early season and rose to a high during midsummer. With the coming of fall and drying of plants, the ratio again fell.

Calcium.—Amounts of calcium were highest with first green growth, but by May had more or less leveled off. For most species there was little difference between summer and winter readings. According to the National Research Council (1963, 1964), wintering pregnant heifers have a minimum calcium requirement of 0.16 ppm and pregnant ewes 0.20 to 0.27 ppm. Most plants are well above these levels and it seems doubtful that deficiencies of this mineral occur.

Phosphorus.—This mineral was highest in the early spring, and dropped to its low point during the winter. The drop was most pronounced in the grasses and forbs, with browse showing in most cases a similar decline.

The National Research Council recommends a minimum level of 0.15 ppm phosphorus for pregnant heifers and 0.16 to 0.21 ppm for pregnant ewes. Growing stock requires even higher amounts. Of the species tested, only two (four-wing saltbrush and big sage) had levels of winter phosphorus above 0.15. Grasses and forbs dropped to very low levels. These readings suggest phosphorus may be a problem in winter in Owens Valley.

Calcium-phosphorus ratio.—Favorable ratios of calcium to phosphorus are around 2:1. When the ratios became too unbalanced, tricalciumphosphate an insoluble precipitate, is formed (Maynard and Loosli, 1962). Thus, these minerals are lost to the animal if the ratio between them is greatly out of balance.

In the forages tested Ca:P was most favorable in the spring growth and early summer. During fall, the ratios began to increase, and by winter, all plant species showed wide ratios. The lowest ratio, 3.7:1, occurred in big sagebrush, and the highest, 77:1, in licorice. Most species had ratios of about 10:1 or higher. These unfavorable Ca:P ratios almost certainly complicate the already limited winter phosphorus. The possible influences of phosphorus deficiencies will be discussed below.

Relationship of food habits of elk to nutrient levels.—The kinds of forage utilized seasonally by elk can be interpreted in light of the nutrient levels of various plants. Winter is the low time of year in available nutrients, and during this time, maintenance is the basic demand of the elk population. The browse species, which hold nutrients best, are most important during this season. With the coming of spring and the new green growth, there is an abundance of highly nutritious forage in the annual forbs which the elk turn to immediately. Active growth processes are initiated—body growth in young animals, fetal growth in cows, and antler renewal in bulls. As the annuals dry, the elk shift mainly to the summer annuals, perennial forbs, and some of the more palatable grasses. Heavy summer use of forbs by other elk has been reported by Pickford and Reid (1943) and Stevens (1966). This, too, is a time of nutrient abundance. As these herbaceous plants begin to dry in the fall, there is a gradual shift toward browse species which retain their nutrient levels better (particularly protein and minerals). This diet is supplemented with dried grasses, which are still good sources of energy.

The timing of life processes in elk has evolved in relation to the normally available kinds and amounts of forage. There is no single critical season; each seasonal "link" is as important as every other. Shortage of annual forbs in the spring due to drought can be every bit as critical during this season of high growth demands as insufficient browse in the winter.

COMPARATIVE NUTRITION OF TULE ELK POPULATIONS

Knowing the levels of nutrients in various forage species is highly valuable, yet many questions are left to be answered. Can the researcher pick forage as effectively as the grazing animal, so that the samples analyzed actually approximate the material ingested during grazing? Also, what proportion of the ingested material is actually digested and made metabolically available to the animal?

Digestibility is usually studied by feeding individually penned animals known amounts of food of known quality, and making complete fecal collections to establish how much of the nutrients has been excreted. This work has given some valuable information on digestibility of various foods by deer and domestic animals. But the artificial conditions which make these studies possible place in doubt their applicability to the natural range situations. Particularly unsettling is the fact that feeds give different results when fed singly than when fed in combinations (Dietz et al., 1962); wild animals normally take a mixed diet. The use of fecal collection bags with fistulated animals has somewhat extended nutritional work into the field with domestic animals, but these methods are clearly not suitable for wild unrestrained ungulates.

Two different approaches were used in this study in an attempt to circumvent these difficulties. With the great number of unmeasurable variables, it was unlikely that absolute values could be obtained; therefore the investigation was conducted as a comparative study of three tule elk populations: the Independence herd of Owens Valley, the Tupman Reserve herd, and the Cache Creek herd.

Digestibility by indicator techniques.—This technique relies upon an indigestible component of the forage. A comparison of the relationship of a digestible nutrient to the indigestible fraction in the feed and in the feces of the animal being fed allows a calculation of the percent of the nutrient which has been removed in passing through the digestive tract. In feedlot situations, indigestible chromic oxide can be added to the feed to serve as the indicator. Of naturally occurring plant components useful as indicators, the two most frequently used are lignin and plant chromogens (pigments). The merits of each as an indicator have been debated in the literature. However, because the forages taken by elk in this study most closely approximated the forages studied by Harris et al. (1959), the lignin technique was used. Geis (1954) used the lignin ratio technique to compare digestibility of three diets fed to penned Rocky Mountain elk. Also, the generally dry nature of the forages during the sampling period suggested that plant chromogens might occur in very low amounts.

Samples were obtained from five elk from the Independence herd killed in the legal hunt on October 10, 1964. The food habits of this herd, as determined from rumen analysis by Bruce Browning of the California Fish and Game Laboratory were 13.2 percent licorice, 7.2 percent willow, 15.5 percent forbs, and 64.1 percent grass by volume.

Samples of the Tupman herd were obtained from five cows removed during the reduction on October 13, 1964. The reduction was held at a time when the enclosure was without natural forage except for two irrigated pastures, which were closed off seven days before the collection. It was hoped that the herd could be restricted to the pelleted alfalfa diet. Unfortunately, the animals picked up coarse dry stems from the ground, apparently to serve as bulk.

Two adult cows from the Cache Creek herd were taken by me on November 23, 1964, under a collecting permit issued for the purpose by the California Fish and Game Commission. Their diet, as determined from rumen analysis by Bruce Browning was 10.0 percent forbs, 42.5 percent grass, 2.5 percent oak leaves, and 45.0 percent acorns by volume.

All samples were collected by the same technique. The rumen contents were stirred thoroughly with a long-handled spoon. Then the contents were dipped up as grab samples and placed in double-thickness cheesecloth bags, labeled, and allowed to drain and air-dry. The fecal samples were obtained by splitting the colon with a scissors, removing pelleted feces from the terminal portion, and placing the contents in labeled paper sacks, which were also allowed to air-dry.

The samples from the Tupman enclosure were analyzed individually to determine individual variation. The Owens Valley and Cache Creek samples were composited by taking equal weights of air-dried material from the individual samples.

Levels of protein, fat, fiber, ash, and nitrogen-free extract were determined by John P. Rible, Extension Technologist, Extension Service Laboratory, University of California, Riverside. Lignin determinations were done under contract by Edward P. Babcock and Sons, commercial agricultural chemists, Riverside, California, using methods specified by Association of Official Agricultural Chemists (1960).

Comparison of the alfalfa pellet sample (taken over a seven-day period before the animals were killed) with the material in the rumens of the Tupman elk shows a considerable difference in nutrient content, which can be accounted for by the ingestion of coarse dry stems by the elk (table 11). The fractions which markedly increased were the expected ones: crude fiber, NFE (and lignin which is contained partly in the fiber component, partly in NFE) and ash. Protein was greatly lowered, as would be expected. The individual variation in both rumen and fecal samples was quite low.

It appears that rumen samples do give a fair approximation of the nutrient levels of ingested forage. The habit elk have of feeding intermittently through the day minimizes the fluctuations in rumen nutrient levels caused by digestion and absorption. Although minerals and urea nitrogen may be added via saliva (Annison and Lewis, 1959) and urea through the rumen wall (Simonnet et al., 1957; Houpt, 1959) the data in table 11 suggest that these are of small enough quantities that they would not interfere with the use of the data on a comparative basis. Klein (1962) reached a similar conclusion about rumen samples from black-tailed deer.

Calculations of percent digestibility on the basis of lignin as an indicator resulted in totally erratic results (table 12). It is difficult to believe that discrepancies of this magnitude could be traced to differences in treatment of the samples or errors in lignin determinations, even though lignin determinations are subject to error (McCullough, 1959; A. D. Smith et al., 1956). The low standard deviations for lignin in both rumen and fecal samples (table 11) argues against errors of this sort. These data suggest that tule elk may indeed be able to digest significant quantities of lignin. Smith et al. (1956) gave evidence suggesting that mule deer might be able to digest lignin.

Examination of table 11 shows that ash was the fraction most consistently concentrated in the feces over that in the rumen in all three herds. Clearly, some ash could be exchanged along the digestive tract between the rumen and the colon, and bile is a possible source of additional salts. But ash was the most promising indicator for obtaining at least comparative results. Calculation of percent digesti-

TABLE 11

NUTRIENT LEVELS IN RUMEN AND FECAL SAMPLES FROM THREE TULE ELK POPULATIONS

Populations sampled	Protein (%)	Ash (%)	Fat (%)	Fiber (%)	Lignin (%)	NFE¶ (%)
Tupman pelleted alfalfa*......	16.9	12.0	1.6	20.5	5.97	49.0
Tupman rumen						
No. 4......................	13.9	15.3	1.4	27.3	13.74	42.1
No. 6......................	11.6	11.1	1.6	32.0	13.84	43.7
No. 7......................	11.6	12.1	1.8	30.7	13.82	43.8
No. 8......................	13.5	13.6	2.2	30.8	13.98	39.9
No. 9......................	13.9	14.5	1.9	31.4	14.09	38.3
Mean....................	12.9	13.3	1.8	30.4	13.89	41.6
SD.....................	1.198	1.718	.305	1.831	.109	2.412
Tupman feces						
No. 4......................	11.5	25.2	2.0	26.4	14.59	34.9
No. 6......................	9.7	26.5	1.8	24.4	14.58	37.6
No. 7......................	10.9	26.0	1.8	26.0	14.01	35.3
No. 8......................	11.6	25.5	1.7	26.3	14.02	34.9
No. 9......................	10.2	26.9	1.6	24.7	14.31	36.6
Mean....................	10.8	26.0	1.8	25.6	14.30	35.9
SD.....................	.823	.733	.148	.940	.283	1.197
Owens Valley rumen†.........	13.2	14.1	3.7	26.2	13.78	42.8
Owens Valley feces†..........	11.4	22.4	4.7	19.1	17.68	42.4
Cache Creek rumen‡..........	9.2	5.7	5.9	21.6	20.11	57.6
Cache Creek feces‡..........	17.1	14.6	3.3	16.8	12.59	48.2

* Sampled from pellets fed for 7 days prior to collection of elk.
† Samples composited from 5 individual adult females of the Independence herd.
‡ Samples composited from 2 individual adult females.
¶ NFE = nitrogen free extract.

TABLE 12

PERCENT DIGESTIBILITY OF FORAGE BASED UPON THE LIGNIN RATIO
TECHNIQUE FROM THREE TULE ELK POPULATIONS

Populations sampled	Protein	Ash	Fat	Fiber	NFE*
Tupman					
No. 4......................	22.0	neg.	neg.	9.0	22.0
No. 6......................	20.7	neg.	neg.	27.7	18.4
No. 7......................	7.3	neg.	1.5	16.2	20.5
No. 8......................	14.4	neg.	32.9	14.9	12.3
No. 9......................	27.8	neg.	17.0	22.6	5.9
Mean....................	18.4	neg.	5.1	18.1	15.8
SD.....................	7.840	....	14.536	7.230	6.663
Owens Valley.................	32.7	neg.	1.1	43.2	22.8
Cache Creek.................	neg.	neg.	10.6	neg.	neg.

* NFE = nitrogen free extract.

bilities based upon ash as an indicator is shown in table 13. The values obtained are much closer to what would be expected from digestion trials with domestic animals and deer. The only unusual result is the high digestibility of fiber; in view of possible digestibility of lignin this is not necessarily an error.

When the apparent digestibility of nutrients and total digestible nutrients (TDN) calculated from ash as an indicator are compared for the three herds (table 14), the results are in agreement with field observations. The Independence herd was living on a relatively low quality diet and was in only fair condition. The Tupman elk were fed primarily on pelleted alfalfa and were in good condition.

TABLE 13

PERCENTAGE OF DIGESTIBILITY OF FORAGE BASED UPON ASH-RATIO
TECHNIQUE FROM THREE TULE ELK POPULATIONS

Populations sampled	Protein	Fat	Fiber	NFE*
Tupman				
No. 4	49.8	14.1	41.3	49.7
No. 6	65.0	52.8	68.1	64.0
No. 7	56.3	53.7	60.6	62.5
No. 8	54.2	58.6	54.5	53.3
No. 9	60.5	55.0	57.6	48.5
Mean	57.2	46.8	56.4	55.6
SD	5.837	18.43	9.84	7.223
Owens Valley	45.6	19.8	54.1	37.6
Cache Creek	27.4	78.2	69.6	67.3

* NFE = nitrogen free extract.

The Cache Creek animals, with an acorn diet, were in excellent condition. Based on TDN's, the diet of Tupman elk was 1.31 times better than the Independence herd diet. The Cache Creek diet was 1.76 times better than the Independence herd diet and 1.35 times better than the Tupman diet.

Dietz et al. (1962) found TDN's of 53.1 to 55.3 using a high quality alfalfa and of 45.9 to 48.1 with poorer quality alfalfa fed to mule deer. These results would seem to be fairly comparable to the Tupman TDN of 49.55 when the levels of nutrients in the rumen samples are taken as a basis of comparison.

Nevertheless, the data derived by using ash as an indicator must be considered at best an inference. Enough variables are unknown that the results may be largely fortuitous. It is concluded, therefore, that (1) lignin is not a suitable indicator under the conditions studied: (2) failure of the method may have been due to ability of elk to digest lignin; and (3) using ash as an indicator gave results of expected kind, but of unproved validity.

Volatile fatty acids in the rumen liquor.—A second approach to evaluation of the nutrition status of tule elk herds was based upon the use of volatile fatty acid (VFA) determinations of samples of rumen liquor. In ruminants a large proportion of carbohydrate digestion occurs in the rumen through the activities of microorganisms. Carbohydrates are reduced to VFA's, principally acetic but also proprionic, butyric, and higher acids, which are absorbed directly through the rumen wall.

Numerous studies of rumen digestion in domestic animals are summarized in recent books by Barnett and Reid (1961), and Annison and Lewis (1959) and a symposium volume (Dougherty, 1965). Similar work on deer has been summarized in a paper by Short (1966). Artificial rumen assays have yielded much of the data

TABLE 14

CALCULATED TOTAL DIGESTIBLE NUTRIENTS (TDN) IN THE DIETS OF THREE TULE ELK
POPULATIONS, BASED ON DIGESTIBILITY DETERMINED BY ASH-RATIO TECHNIQUE

Nutrients and populations	Crude value in diet	Percent digestibility	Pounds digested per 100 lbs. feed
Protein			
Tupman............................	12.9	57.2	7.38
Owens Valley.......................	13.2	45.6	6.02
Cache Creek........................	9.2	27.4	2.52
Fat			
Tupman............................	1.8	46.8	1.89*
Owens Valley.......................	3.7	19.8	1.63*
Cache Creek........................	5.9	78.2	10.37*
Fiber			
Tupman............................	30.4	56.4	17.15
Owens Valley.......................	26.2	54.1	14.17
Cache Creek........................	21.6	69.6	15.03
NFE†			
Tupman............................	41.6	55.6	23.13
Owens Valley.......................	42.8	37.6	16.09
Cache Creek........................	57.6	67.3	38.76
TDN			
Tupman............................	....	....	49.55
Owens Valley.......................	....	....	37.91
Cache Creek........................	....	....	66.68

* Fat is multiplied by 2.25 to correct for its higher energy content.
†NFE = nitrogen free extract.

on rumen reactions. Yet as Shaw (1959) points out, there is some question of the applicability of these results to what actually occurs in the rumen.

The rationale of the studies reported here is based upon several conclusions reached by Shaw (1959). First, that the proportions of the individual VFA's in the rumen liquor do not change with time after feeding, and second, that the VFA's are absorbed by simple diffusion through the rumen wall. Therefore the rate of production of VFA's and the rate of absorption are in equilibrium (Annison, 1965). And, since tule elk feed throughout the day, a more or less stable food increment is maintained. Studies on domestic sheep by Moir and Somers (1957) showed that feeding every few hours greatly stabilized the rumen acid levels over feeding twice a day. If these assumptions are true, then the VFA concentration in the rumen is in dynamic balance, and determination of VFA's in the rumen liquor would reflect the energy being derived by the animal from this source. Shaw

(1959) felt that rumen liquor VFA determinations were useful for appraising various diets for milk production in domestic cows.

Again, the data are handled on a herd comparative basis. VFA samples were obtained from the same animals from which the lignin samples were taken. The rumen contents were strained through a double thickness of cheesecloth and the rumen liquor collected. Twenty-five ml of liquor were taken from each animal and acidified to kill the microorganisms and stop further fermentation. They were then taken into the laboratory in a coldbox where they were centifuged at intermediate speed to separate the solids. The individual samples were then composited by herd and kept frozen until analysis. Because there was no centrifuge available, the Cache Creek samples were frozen following acidification, and were centrifuged and composited at the time of analysis.

The analyses were performed under contract by Truesdail Laboratories, Inc., Los Angeles, California. The acids were analyzed by gas chromatography according to the method of Shelley et al. (1963). The results are given in table 15.

Acetic acid predominated as is typical of ruminants (Annison and Lewis, 1959). Diets rich in readily fermented carbohydrates favor proprionic acid production, so it is not surprising that the high acorn diet of the Cache Creek herd yielded very high levels of proprionic acid. In the Owens Valley animals, acetic acid predominated, as would be expected from a relatively poor diet. In total acids, Owens Valley animals were lowest, Tupman intermediate and Cache Creek highest.

In table 16 the levels of VFA's in the rumen liquor are converted to energy by multiplying the acids by their caloric values as given by Brody (1945). The total caloric value per volume of rumen liquor relative to the three herds' diets was as would be expected. Owens Valley diet was the lowest in caloric value. The Tupman diet was 1.1 times better than the Owens Valley, and the Cache Creek diet was 1.45 times better than Owens Valley and 1.31 times better than the Tupman diet. These results correlated with the results of digestibility based upon the ash ratio technique.

These data do not warrant attempting to calculate 24-hour energy budgets since too little is known about turnover rate of rumen contents. However, other things being equal, a larger animal is more efficient than a smaller one, and an animal with a high ratio of rumen to total body size is more efficient than one with a low ratio. Short (1963) has compared the white-tailed deer to domestic cattle and sheep on the basis of rumen capacity. The rumen volume is about one-tenth of the body weight in white-tailed deer, one-fourth in domestic cows, and one-third in domestic sheep. Based upon the work of Gill and Jaczewski (1958) on red deer, elk have a ratio of just over one-fifth, slightly less than that of the domestic cow. The relatively large rumen and large body size of elk help explain its comparative efficiency for a wild herbivore, and its strong competitive status.

Discussion of nutrition.—The following generalizations appear warranted by the results obtained from the ash indicator and VFA determinations. At the time tested (fall), the Tupman herd had a diet rich in proteins of high quality, as evidenced by high digestibility. Owens Valley animals also had a high protein diet, but of a much poorer quality than Tupman. Cache Creek, where the herbaceous forage was dry and only low quality browse species were available, had a relatively

poor protein regimen. In fats and NFE, the Cache Creek herd diet was far superior
to that of the other two herds, and Tupman was substantially better than Owens
Valley. Fiber is most useful in the Tupman diet, intermediate in Cache Creek and
poor in Owens Valley. All factors considered, the Owens Valley herd diet in the
fall of 1964 was neither good nor poor. The generally fair condition of the animals
taken in the hunt reflects the diet. Tupman elk were in good shape, with moderate
amounts of fat. The Cache Creek herd animals collected were very fat, due primarily to the extremely high carbohydrate diet, which more than compensated
for a relatively low protein intake.

On a seasonal basis, the Tupman herd has a reliable diet due to the feeding program. The wild herds suffer from the wide seasonal fluctuations in the quality of
diet. At times of abundance, e.g., the time of these studies of the Cache Creek herd,

TABLE 15

VOLATILE FATTY ACIDS IN RUMEN LIQUOR SAMPLES OF THREE TULE ELK POPULATIONS
(Expressed as milligrams of acid per 100 milliliters of liquor)

Populations sampled	Acetic	Proprionic	Butyric	Total
Owens Valley*	359	99	81	539
Tupman Reserve*	362	73	141	567
Cache Creek†	367	249	120	736

* Sample composited from 5 adult females.
† Sample composited from 2 adult females.

and the summer of 1963 in the Independence herd, quality of the diet of the wild
elk exceeds that of the Tupman elk. But the wild elk suffer during periods of low
quality, as for example the early summer of 1964 in the Independence herd.
Similarly, the Cache Creek herd is probably hard pressed to maintain an adequate
diet during falls when mast production is low.

MINERAL NUTRITION

Studies of mineral nutrition were prompted by the fragility of antlers of Owens
Valley elk. Molybdenosis (molybdenum poisoning) was suspected, but my studies
implicated poor phosphorus availability as the likely cause.

Cattle in the valley have suffered from molybdenum poisoning, and copper sulfate is routinely fed in supplements to prevent it. Some forage plants used by elk,
especially sweetclover and greasewood, are particularly high in molybdenum, and
many species in midsummer have unbalanced molybdenum-copper ratios. According to Jensen et al. (1958), when molybdenum exceeds 5 ppm on a dry basis, there
is danger of poisoning in domestic cattle.

One important symptom of molybdenum poisoning is poor bone structure resulting from interference with phosphorus metabolism (Comar et al., 1949). The
broken antlers suggested that this symptom was occurring in elk. Also, a number
of old skeletons had broken and mended bones, and the number of crippled animals
in relation to the population size seemed high.

Molybdenum is a problem mainly in the highly alkaline areas with a high water
table (Jensen et al., 1961; Dye and O'Harra, 1959) as typified in Owens Valley by

the bottomland areas occupied by grassland and greasewood-shadscale types (fig. 8). All of the bottomland herds live on excess molybdenum areas, while the Goodale herd on the Sierra foothills has no molybdenum problem. Goodale antlers show somewhat less breakage.

Samples of antlers were obtained from the Independence and Goodale herds, from the Tupman Reserve, and also, through the courtesy of H. Steven Logsden, from Roosevelt elk in Humboldt County, California. Roosevelt elk antlers show little or no breakage. To check for possible sex differences in mineral levels, samples of jawbone from males and females from the Independence herd taken in the legal hunt on October 17 and 18, 1964, were also analyzed. These analyses were performed by contract with Edward S. Babcock and Sons, Riverside, California. The results of the bone samples (table 17) suggest that if anything, cows are even less strong in skeletal structure than bulls.

TABLE 16

CALORIC VALUES IN KILOCALORIES PER 100 MILLILITERS OF RUMEN LIQUOR
FOR THREE TULE ELK POPULATIONS
(Based on caloric values of 3.49 kcal/g for acetic, 4.96 for proprionic
and 5.95 for butyric as given by Brody, 1945)

Populations sampled	Acetic	Proprionic	Butyric	Total
Owens Valley......................	1.253	.491	.482	2.226
Tupman Reserve...................	1.263	.362	.839	2.464
Cache Creek......................	1.281	1.235	.714	3.230

Lesperance and Bohman (1963) found that heifers incorporated molybdenum in significant amounts in bone. That structural weakness in elk antlers was not due to incorporation of molybdenum was demonstrated by analysis of the samples for molybdenum. In all cases molybdenum was less than one ppm, and probably as little as 0.1 ppm.

None of the antler samples from different herds showed statistically significant differences, but several consistent differences emerge (table 17). By weight, the Independence and Tupman herds show the greatest amount of calcium and phosphorus, yet these herds have the most pronounced breakage. But on a volume basis, the Goodale herd and particularly the Roosevelt elk are superior in the amount of both calcium and phosphorus. Similarly, these two herds have the highest proportion of phosphorus to calcium. It appears that the weakness of antlers in the Independence and Tupman herds is caused by structural deficiencies due to inadequate mineralization, particularly as regards phosphorus.

The vegetation chemical analyses indicated that calcium is more than adequate, but that phosphorus may be inadequate.

Still, there is the question of whether phosphorus is deficient in antlers because of inadequate levels and unbalanced calcium-phosphorus ratios in the forage, or because of interference with phosphorus metabolism by molybdenum. To indicate the levels of molybdenum in relation to copper levels in the bodies of elk, samples of liver were analyzed for these minerals (table 18). Samples of liver from Roosevelt elk were obtained for me from animals killed in Humboldt County by person-

TABLE 17

MINERAL COMPOSITION OF ANTLER AND BONE SAMPLES FROM TULE AND ROOSEVELT ELK POPULATIONS

(Volume expressed as gms/100 mls and weight as gms/100 gms. Sample size is 5 and standard deviations are given in the parentheses. Molybdenum was less than 1 ppm in all antler and bone samples.)

Samples and populations	Calcium		Phosphorus		Ca/P	
	Volume	Weight	Volume	Weight	Volume	Weight
Antler samples						
Tule elk						
Owens Valley						
Independence herd	15.7(1.40)	21.1(1.08)	8.1(.82)	10.8(.98)	1.94(.04)	1.96(.08)
Goodale herd	16.4(2.49)	20.6(1.32)	8.6(1.64)	10.7(.27)	1.92(.11)	1.93(.07)
Tupman Reserve	15.8(1.44)	21.7(.45)	8.0(.50)	11.1(.42)	1.97(.07)	1.96(.07)
Roosevelt elk	17.2(2.08)	20.7(1.10)	9.0(.94)	10.8(.57)	1.91(.10)	1.92(.07)
Bone samples						
Tule elk						
Owens Valley						
Independence herd						
females	14.1(.55)	23.5(.00)	7.6(.89)	12.6(1.02)	1.85(.16)	1.87(.15)
males	14.9(.82)	23.8(.45)	7.9(1.02)	12.6(.74)	1.90(.15)	1.90(.14)

nel of the Califorina Department of Fish and Game. The analyses of liver were also performed under contract by Babcock and Sons, Riverside, California.

The levels of molybdenum in the liver samples were very low in relation to copper (table 18). The copper-molybdenum ratios seem to be highly favorable. Livers of domestic heifers suffering from molybdenosis induced by high molybdenum feeds by Lesperance and Bohman (1963) showed Cu/Mo ratios of less than 4:1.

Therefore, it appears that molybdenosis does not occur in tule elk. It is well known that domestic stock can be selected to derive strains resistant to molyb-

TABLE 18

TULE AND ROOSEVELT ELK LIVER LEVELS OF COPPER AND MOLYBDENUM
EXPRESSED AS PPM ON A DRY WEIGHT BASIS
(Sample sizes were 5 except as indicated. Standard deviations are given in parentheses.)

Elk	Copper		Molybdenum		Cu/Mo	
Tule elk						
Owens Valley						
females......................	112	(38.99)	3.4	(.55)	34.3	(15.44)
males......................	142	(51.67)	4.4	(2.07)	39.3	(20.24)
Tupman Reserve						
females......................	84	(24.08)	4.0	(1.00)	21.0	(3.53)
males*......................	140	(22.70)	4.5	(1.29)	36.0	(30.67)
Cache Creek						
females†......................	135	(....)	3.5	(....)	39.2	(....)
Roosevelt elk						
females......................	116	(16.73)	2.0	(1.00)	74.7	(44.83)

* Sample size 4.
† Sample size 2.

denum poisoning. Since molybdenum levels were high in parts of the original tule elk range in the San Joaquin Valley, the high level of liver storage of copper and apparent excretion of molybdenum in these elk may have resulted from natural selection over a long period of time.

The poor antler structure is at least in part attributable to generally low phosphorus availability and the fact that there is little phosphorus storage in the body (Rerábek and Bubenik, 1956). This deficiency is no doubt intensified by the early maturation of the antlers in tule elk in which the breeding season is four to six weeks in advance of that of Rocky Mountain elk as reported by Murie (1951), and two to four weeks before Roosevelt elk as observed by Harper et al. (1967). Since casting and regrowth occur at about the same time as in other subspecies, maturation and mineralization in tule elk take place over a relatively short period of time. Perhaps the elk's system is unable to supply phosphorus fast enough to meet this demand.

COMPETITION WITH DOMESTIC STOCK

One of the most important aspects of the ecology of the tule elk is competition with domestic stock for native range forage. The term "competition" is used here in the strict sense of two species utilizing a resource in limited or potentially limited supply. Thus a simple overlap of food habits between two species does not necessarily indicate that competition is occurring. For example, both elk and cattle eat large amounts of greasewood in the spring, but there is such an abundance of greasewood available that the supply greatly exceeds the demands of both. Similarly, competition does not occur for bottomland annuals which are eaten by the elk during the summer when livestock are usually not present, and are dry and unpalatable when domestic stock is put on the range in the winter.

Season of use and numbers of domestic stock.—Domestic stock is usually kept in the bottomland in winter and moved to the higher country, mainly on public land grazing allotments, for the summer. Cattle are removed from the valley floor in the spring when the grazing season opens, and are generally returned to the valley in October and November.

The number of cattle wintering in the valley is difficult to determine. The Inyo County tax records show 10,955 beef cattle in 1963 and 11,588 in 1964, but the assessment is made on March 1, and some operators move their cattle out before this date to avoid paying tax on the animals. Also, about 15 percent of these animals are outside of Owens Valley proper. The 1959 United States Agricultural census showed 26,002 cattle in Inyo County, but this estimate appears high to me. Perhaps around 15,000 would be more nearly correct.

Pack stock, used to take recreationists and their supplies into the high Sierra during the summer, are also over-wintered in Owens Valley. In general, pack stock spends a greater amount of time in the valley than do cattle. Packing season runs mainly from June 15 to September 15, and on a very much smaller scale during the deer hunting season in October. The remainder of the time they are on the winter pastures. Horses and mules are most commonly used, and hereafter reference to horses includes both. Some burros are now coming into use but they represent a small portion of the pack stock at present.

An accurate census of horses is also difficult to obtain. The Inyo County Tax Assessor's Office reported 1,228 horses, mules, and burros in 1963 and 1,100 in 1964. About 12 percent of these were outside of Owens Valley in other parts of the county.

Thus, while keeping in mind the limitations of the estimates, there are about 15,000 cattle in Owens Valley for six months in the winter and 1,000 horses for about nine months.

Sheep raising is not an important endeavor in Owens Valley. The tax office shows 272 sheep, of which about 200 are in Owens Valley. However the Bureau of Land Management still maintains a sheep driveway on its land, which runs more or less parallel on the west side of Highway 395. Thousands of sheep are brought in by truck from the southern San Joaquin Valley, then trailed through Owens Valley to the high mountain summer areas to the north. The driveway is located well below most of the range of the Goodale elk herd and the winter range of the Tinemaha herd, so that little conflict occurs. However, the sheep take considerable forage which would otherwise be available to the cattle belonging to holders of permits along the driveway. The Bureau of Land Management has been intensifying regulations on trailing to keep the impact down, but the conflicts of the driveway with other interests are so great that the practice will probably be discontinued in a few years. Competition with local cattle interests and the fact that no taxes are paid in Inyo County on these sheep are continuing sources of irritation to the local people.

More important is the heavy camping and fishing use of the Sierra streams along the driveway. Herders move the sheep during the day from one stream to the next, camping by water. Grazing is very heavy along the stream courses where the best forage is available. The heavily cropped plants and the abundant quantities of droppings do little to enhance the natural beauty of the stream for recreational users. And public health authorities are concerned about contamination, since these streams are water sources for both recreationists and local towns.

Competition with cattle on foothill areas.—A number of cattle allotments are permitted on the Sierra alluvial fans by the Forest Service and the Bureau of Land Management. The leases of these agencies and of the City of Los Angeles have been coordinated in recent years, and this was a significant step toward regulating numbers of animals to benefit the range. Cattle allotments are closed in September, and all domestic stock is removed.

The food habits of cattle and elk overlap to a large degree in the foothill area. The elk tend to take more of the second class browse species under all conditions, but cattle will also take appreciable amounts when better forage is not available.

In good rainfall years, there is little competition between elk and cattle on the Sierra ranges. The tremendous herbaceous production is more than both species combined can utilize. Later, as the annual plants dry, use by both species of the grasses and browse increases. The total impact of livestock on the major winter browse species in such years is small.

Competition occurs during poor years when forage production is low. In 1964, when annuals were very sparse, cattle released on the lower part of the fan moved up to the head of the fan and began feeding heavily on bitterbrush. In areas where elk and deer occur, demand for bitterbrush is already heavy and in places excessive. Adjustment of numbers is required in such cases, and domestic stock have a lower priority on public lands since wild game is a public resource. Thus, continuing problems will occur in any foothill area where cattle, elk, and deer occupy the same ranges during poor years. This is as true of the White and Inyo ranges as of the Sierra.

Competition with livestock on the valley floor.—Competition of elk with domestic livestock in the bottomlands is a far more complicated problem. Besides variation in forage availability due to weather changes from year to year, there is the summer absence of most of the stock, the tendency of the two species to remain segregated geographically when both are present, and a great variation in the food habits of the different grazing animals. Both horses and mules depend overwhelmingly upon grasses and wireweeds (*Juncus, Eliocharis*) for their food. Forbs such as bassia and wild licorice are barely touched, even in the spring. Brush species are also little used by horses. The food habits of cattle overlap those of elk almost completely, but cows are able to utilize coarse dry grasses to a much greater extent than elk. Conversely, elk utilize browse species much more readily than do cows. Cattle do use browse if grass is not available, and also use browse (particularly greasewood) in the early spring when the new growth appears.

The food habits of both burros and sheep closely approximate those of elk, and potential competition with elk is absent at present only because of the very low numbers of these domestic animals and their distribution in areas not occupied by elk. Pickford and Reid (1943) reported strong competition between Rocky Mountain elk and domestic sheep.

Obviously, competition in the strict sense cannot be evaluated on a broad scale on the valley floor by direct observation. Precise measurements of lengths of time forages were used by various grazers, the numbers of grazers, the kinds and amounts of forage available, and their use are required to really understand the forage relationships. Therefore, the approach used in this study was a detailed examination of a particular area where competition was probable. Once the competition interactions for this area were understood, the degree and kind of competition in other areas could be evaluated on the basis of consistent direct observation.

The study area.—A large grassland area adjacent to (east of) the Los Angeles aqueduct near Fort Independence was chosen for study. The area was approximately four miles long and one mile wide, bordered on the north by a fence near Thibaut Creek, on the west by the aqueduct fence, and on the south and east by brush fields. It is divided by an east-west fence, so that approximately the northern two-thirds is used to winter pack horses and mules, and the southern one-third for wintering cattle (fig. 27). The area is used consistently during the summer by a major part of the Independence elk herd.

Methods of determining ground area of different types.—The study concentrated on those plant species which are of major importance to domestic stock in the winter. Any substantial use by elk in the summer, therefore, would reduce the number of domestic animals the area could overwinter. The important species are alkali sacaton, saltgrass, and *Juncus*. Other species occurring within the area are rabbitbrush, with almost no winter use, and some annual and perennial forbs which are dried before the stock are placed on the range. Most of the forbs occur in the horse pasture, and horses normally do not utilize these plants even when green.

The study area was mapped from aerial photographs and acreages determined from the map (fig. 27). The horse pasture study area contained 1,262 acres and the cow pasture 879 acres. Several types of vegetation (sacaton-rabbitbrush and sacaton-saltgrass) could be easily distinguished from photographs and were mapped accordingly. The remainder of the area contained mainly saltgrass and *Juncus;* also, it had a number of small dry ponds too numerous and irregular to map effectively. Area of these was estimated by another method.

To determine the area of saltgrass and *Juncus* toe-point samples were used (as modified from Wood et al., 1960). The first transect was located randomly in the one-half mile at the north end in each pasture, and the others located systematically at quarter-mile intervals. Transects were located along a line of sight to a point located by compass high on the Inyo Mountains in a due east direction. Seven transects were run in the horse pasture on June 11 and 12, and five in the cow pasture on June 13 and 15, 1964. The procedure was to take four paces along the transect, while keeping the eyes fixed on the location point high on the Inyos, and using the tip of the toe as the center of the sample plot.

Data were obtained on three sampling levels. The first level was the recording of the surrounding vegetation as to major type: *Juncus,* saltgrass, sacaton-saltgrass,

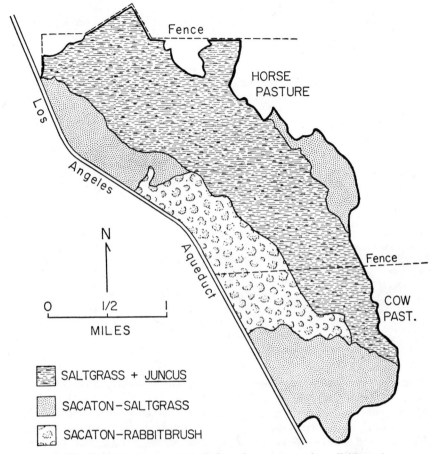

Fig. 27. Vegetation map of the Independence pasture where elk-livestock competition was studied.

sacaton-rabbitbrush, or pondbottom. The second level was to record the dominant plant species within a circular plot of 1.75 feet radius (area = 9.6 sq. ft.) from the tip of the right toe. From these data, the acreage of saltgrass, *Juncus,* and sacaton as they occurred on the ground in greater than 5 percent cover was determined ("Actual forage acres" of tables 20 and 22). Any plot with less than an estimated 5 percent plant cover was recorded as bare ground.

The third level of data involved the precise "hit" of a pinpoint extending from the point of the toe. The exact "hit" or "point" was quite easily determined in this vegetation where cover was quite low by keeping the eyes on the line of sight until the foot was firmly planted. From these data the cover by species, interplant bare ground, and litter was obtained for each forage type (table 19).

Estimation of grazing pressure.—Estimations of numbers of cows, horses, and elk and of the length of time each spent in the study area were necessary, since the

TABLE 19

Percentage of Cover in Forage Types Sampled for Production
and Utilization in the Independence Pasture

Pasture	Forage type			
	Saltgrass	*Juncus*	Sacaton-saltgrass	Sacaton-rabbitbrush
Horse pasture				
bare ground...................	41.7	24.8	40.8	48.8
litter.........................	27.2	29.0	28.0	30.4
saltgrass......................	29.7	14.3	16.3	4.4
sacaton.......................	0.0	0.0	12.0	15.8
Juncus......................	0.4	26.5	0.8	0.1
other.........................	1.0	5.5	2.1	0.5
Total "hits"................	1498	238	485	866
Cow pasture				
bare ground...................	48.1	31.6	37.9	42.5
litter.........................	33.0	31.6	27.3	34.9
saltgrass......................	18.9	5.3	14.6	2.4
sacaton	0.0	0.0	17.0	16.9
Juncus......................	0.0	31.6	2.7	2.4
other.........................	0.0	0.0	0.5	0.9
Total "hits"................	185	19	1099	332

eastern edge of the grassland was not fenced, and the animals could move freely back and forth. A sampling technique was used which involved counting all of the animals within the study area with the aid of binoculars and spotting scope on Monday mornings at approximately 10 o'clock. The area forms a shallow basin which is clearly visible from the raised aqueduct road, and the eastern border was quite distinctly marked by the beginning of brush fields. Animals bedded in the ponds or tightly bunched in groups undoubtedly led to minor error in counting, but difficulty in counting was the exception rather than the rule. Newborn calves of cattle in the spring were not included in the count, while elk calves running with the herd were.

Numbers of animals and season of use are shown in figure 28. The relatively good separation of periods of use by elk and domestic livestock is apparent. Also apparent is the amount of "trespass" domestic stock (i.e., horses in the cow pasture and vice versa). Part of this is due to breaking of fences by elk, which move about from pasture to pasture. At times the domestic stock also breaks fences. Most trespass is accidental but some local operators, if not actually aiding trespass, at least do little to stop it. The elk are often blamed by the lessees for forage taken during the summer by trespass stock.

Forage production.—Production was determined with the aid of wire cones which protect sample plots of 9.6 sq. ft. from grazing (pl. 8). The cones have been described in detail in the food habits section.

Paired plot sites as nearly alike as possible were selected subjectively but the one to be coned was picked by the flip of a coin. In the horse pasture, where there would be considerable use by horses in the spring, the plots were selected to approximate the average production of the pasture. Five cones were placed in saltgrass, two in *Juncus,* and three in sacaton-saltgrass and sacaton-rabbitbrush, which were considered as one unit in the horse pasture. Times of establishment of plots are shown in figure 28. The cones were replaced to measure production continuing after clipping following spring use by horses, and four additional cones were placed in *Juncus* type (fourteen total cones).

In the cow pasture, nine cones were installed: two in saltgrass, one in *Juncus,* two in sacaton-rabbitbrush and four in sacaton-saltgrass. The latter two types were considered separately in the cow pasture, since the area without rabbitbrush differed mainly in having been burned, and I wanted to evaluate the influence of burning on production. Only elk used the cow pasture during spring and summer, and since my previous observations of food taken by elk suggested that the use of the grass species would be light, I did not attempt to approximate the production over the whole pasture. Rather, I selected the very best sites for cones, since any utilization of forage by elk would be most readily detected on the most palatable forage sites.

Utilization.—Utilization was determined by two methods. The first was based on the production cones through the use of paired plots. Before installation, two plots, separated by ten feet or more, were selected to be as identical as possible. A coin was then flipped to decide which plot should be protected by the cone as a control, and which left open to grazing. When a grazing season ended, the forage from both plots was clipped (times of clipping are given in fig. 28), air-dried, and weighed. The difference between the two plots allowed calculation of percent utilization during the period.

The second method involved extensive plot clipping over the full extent of the pasture. Plots used were smaller than the 9.6 sq. ft. cone plots, since it was found by prior trials that using a large sample of small plots gave a lower variance than using a small sample of large plots. A compromise plot size of 2.4 sq. ft. (onequarter of the frame) was finally settled on for clipping.

Plots were located by subdividing the various types into squares and sampling each square randomly. On the ground this was accomplished by pacing. Final plot selection was made by rolling the circular plot frame and clipping the forage in a previously marked quarter of the frame where it fell, unless it fell upon bare ground (less than 5 percent estimated cover) in which case the frame was rolled a second time. In many parts of the pastures the distribution of *Juncus* was so spotty and irregular that subjective judgment was required, but all plots were determined by a roll of the plot frame.

In the horse pasture, sample sizes of 100 plots were used for each of the three types for each sampling period. In the cow pasture 100 samples were taken of sacaton-saltgrass, 50 of saltgrass, 25 of *Juncus,* and 50 of sacaton-rabbitbrush at each sampling period. Clipping times are shown in figure 28.

All clipped material was placed in labeled paper sacks which were stapled shut. The sacks were air-dried at least a month in a dry room, then for two more weeks in an open but roofed area in relative humidities of less than 20 percent during

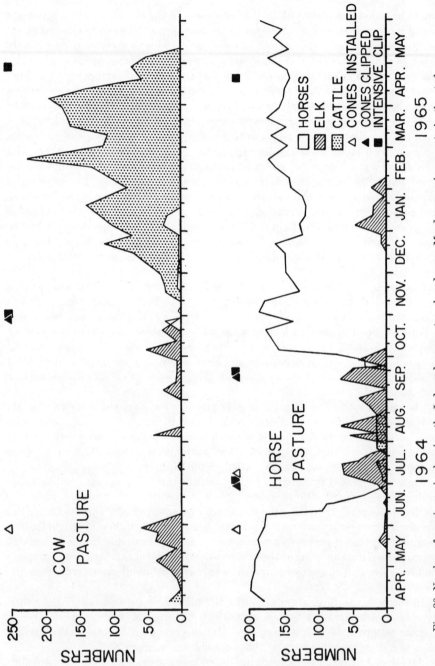

Fig. 28. Number of grazing animals using the Independence pasture based upon Monday morning counts in the study area.

the day. After the sacks had stabilized in weight, they were weighed in grams on a triple beam balance, and final weights were obtained by subtracting tare weight.

Horse pasture results.—Production in the horse pasture is shown in table 20. Based upon the ten cones, utilization by horses in the spring amounted to 45.3 percent of the pasture forage. This compares closely with the 46.4 percent estimate derived from the extensive pasture samples (table 21). Based on fourteen cones, the summer utilization by elk was 0.2 percent as compared to 3.1 percent for the

TABLE 20

HORSE PASTURE PRODUCTION DURING THE 1964 GROWING SEASON

Forage type	Total acres	Actual forage acres	Production (air-dried lbs/acre)	Total pasture production (tons air-dried forage)
Saltgrass.......................	1242.0	597.1	2724	813.3
Juncus........................	94.9	94.9	4448	211.0
Sacaton-rabbitbrush...........	683.5	570.0	1589	452.9
Total........................		1262.0		1477.2

TABLE 21

HORSE PASTURE UTILIZATION BY HORSES AND TULE ELK IN TONS OF AIR-DRIED FORAGE
(Percents are given in parentheses.)

Forage type	Total production	Spring horse utilization		Summer elk utilization		Winter horse utilization		Total utilization	
Saltgrass...........	813.1	431.0	(53.0)	21.1	(2.6)	260.3	(32.0)	712.4	(87.6)
Juncus..............	211.0	123.9	(58.7)	7.2	(3.4)	56.5	(26.8)	187.6	(88.9)
Sacaton............	452.9	130.4	(28.8)	16.8	(3.7)	271.7	(60.0)	418.9	(92.5)
Total..............	1,477.2	685.3	(46.4)	45.1	(3.1)	588.5	(39.8)	1,318.9	(89.3)

extensive method. This difference could easily be due to sampling error. Cones were not used for the winter period, but the extensive sampling showed 39.8 percent utilization by horses (table 21).

Cow pasture results.—Cow pasture production is given in table 22. Utilization of the cow pasture by elk based upon cones (the only method applicable) gave a negative value for the mean of the nine cones. That is, the protected plots showed less production than unprotected plots (see pl. 8). Based upon positive values only, elk use was 0.1 percent (table 23). The use of the cones to estimate production for the pasture is not valid. Since they were purposely placed in the most favorable sites. But since elk utilization was virtually zero, the extensive sampling method gives a fair estimate of the forage production (table 22). Winter utilization by domestic cattle (table 23) amounted to 74.2 percent of production based upon the extensive samples.

Discussion of competition between elk and domestic stock.—Table 21 shows clearly that during the spring, green saltgrass and *Juncus* were heavily utilized by horses. However, in the fall and winter, sacaton use was proportionately higher, so that at the end of the grazing season the utilization of each species was about the same. Similarly, cattle placed on the range in the fall took mainly sacaton (table 23). A summer preference by elk for both sacaton and *Juncus* over saltgrass is also suggested by these data (table 21) but the differences are small.

The relatively heavy grazing by horses during the growing season was expected to reduce forage production, but if anything it stimulated growth (compare production for each pasture, tables 20 and 22). While the cow pasture is not directly comparable, since it is higher and drier than the horse pasture, I had expected that

TABLE 22

Cow Pasture Production During the 1964 Growing Season

Forage type	Total acres	Actual forage acres	Production (air-dried lbs/acre)	Total pasture production (tons air-dried forage)
Saltgrass	190.5	62.9	1307	41.1
Juncus	10.5	10.5	2109	11.0
Sacaton	435.2	394.9	1796	354.6
Sacaton-rabbitbrush	242.7	165.8	1096	90.9
Total	878.9	634.1	....	497.6

TABLE 23

Cow Pasture Utilization in Tons of Air-Dried Forage
(Percents are given in parentheses.)

Forage type	Total production	Summer elk utilization*	Winter cow utilization	Total utilization
Saltgrass	41.1	0.4(1.0)	15.8(38.4)	16.2(39.4)
Juncus	11.0	0.0(neg.)	5.6(50.7)	5.6(50.7)
Sacaton-saltgrass	354.6	0.0(neg.)	272.0(76.7)	272.0(76.7)
Sacaton-rabbitbrush	90.9	0.0(neg.)	76.0(83.6)	76.0(83.6)
Total	497.6	0.4(0.1)	369.4(74.2)	369.8(74.3)

*Based upon paired plot cone method.

the moderate grazing program in the cow pasture would have resulted in a more nearly equal forage production. In fact, production in the horse pasture was substantially higher, even in the sacaton-rabbitbrush, in which type the two pastures were most nearly alike.

On the basis of these studies, it seems that the amount of moisture available is by far the most important factor in forage production. If there is good rainfall, or if the pastures are irrigated, production will be high; in a drought year the production will be low. The overwhelming importance of rainfall and its great fluctuation from year to year on these ranges overshadow the influence of the kind of grazing program for the most part. Also, there is no strongly competitive invader in the saltgrass and *Juncus* areas. Heavy grazing leads to a reduction in existing cover, but not invasion by undesirable plants. In the drier sacaton areas, rabbitbrush slowly increases in importance, even in moderately grazed pastures.

The comparison of production of sacaton-saltgrass (burned) with sacaton-rabbit-brush (unburned) in the cow pasture clearly shows the increase in forage production that can be realized by the removal of rabbitbrush (table 22).

The area studied is probably the grassland most persistently used by elk in the valley. These results clearly demonstrate that the impact of elk upon the native grasslands is light and explain why elk are rarely seen in many good grassland areas even when the domestic stock is out of the valley in the summer.

Indeed, during the summer the tule elk relies mainly upon subclimax vegetation. All of the important summer foods are subclimax species: bassia and sunflower in disturbed flatlands, licorice in burned areas, and willows and other streamside vegetation along ditches and canals.

To summarize, competition between elk and domestic stock is minor in most bottomland areas. Where domestic cattle are summered in the valley there may be some competition for bassia in poor growth years. Elk also take some streamside vegetation which would otherwise be available for winter use by stock. The ditches represent a very small proportion of the total area, but the forage is some of the best nutritionally.

AGRICULTURAL DAMAGE

Alfalfa.—Alfalfa damage is the most important form of conflict between the elk and agriculture. Owens Valley ranchers, like ranchers everywhere, tend to exaggerate their losses, but there is no question that in poor years elk do cause damages which reduce the livestockmen's profits. Besides the alfalfa eaten, much is knocked down by bedding so that it is difficult to harvest. And since much use of alfalfa occurs during the rut, the thrash-urinate act of the bulls causes further damage.

Damage by elk does not discourage raising alfalfa. In fact, during this study alfalfa acreage expanded in the most persistently damaged area. The amount of damage at present is limited and measures taken to control it are minimal. Some ranchers patrol their fields at night, but these efforts are usually sporadic. No one has seriously considered constructing elk-proof fences, nor has any experimentation been made with electric fences. The degree of damage does not warrant such measures at present. The low lease and irrigation water costs paid to the City of Los Angeles for alfalfa land allow a rather wide margin of profit so that there is not great pressure for efficiency.

Fences.—Damage to fences is the second most important agricultural problem with elk. Most of the fences in the valley are old, with rotting posts and rusted barbed wire, and are rather easily broken by elk. Given the opportunity, elk usually crawl under fences. Even large bulls will carefully place their antlers under the fence one at a time, and then push under. Elk will continue to use certain places to cross fences where the wire is loose (e.g., under a wire gate) or where the fence is already down. Leaving the lower strand loose at crossing points would reduce the damage done by elk.

Most fence breakage is caused by alarmed herds running into the fence. Posts are broken off and barbed wire strands broken or knocked loose from the posts. Solitary alarmed bulls usually jump over a fence, frequently knocking the top strand loose. During the rut, bulls use wooden fence posts to polish antlers, systematically pulling out the staples which hold the barbed wire. On one occasion I observed a pugnacious bull knock a fence down before walking through, and on another occasion an alarmed bull hit a fence three times full force with his antlers before going partly over and partly through the fence.

Damage to fences is more a frustration than an economic burden. The time necessary to keep fences in repair is not great, as I learned in attempting to keep the fences up in the Independence pasture to stop trespass stock during my competition studies. Yet the job does not stay done, and the added burden of separating mixed stock must be considered. There is little possibility for alleviating this sort of damage.

Supplemental feed.—It is believed by some livestockmen that elk eat much of the winter supplement put out for livestock to correct deficiencies in the native winter forage. This supplement usually contains protein, copper sulfate, and about 30 percent common salt to hold down consumption. I made special efforts to observe the Bishop elk cow herd which spent several months in the winter of 1963–1964 in an area where supplement was being fed. Feeder areas were searched periodically and systematically for the presence of elk droppings. No depredations on the supplement nor elk droppings in the vicinity of feeders were observed. A similar check in early spring of 1964 of thirty-six feeders throughout the valley in known areas of wintering elk showed only one with possible depredations. Three cattlemen in the valley told me that they had never had any trouble with elk taking their supplement.

I can see no reason why elk would not eat the supplement; but these results suggest that the problem, if it does exist, is a local one, and not of great significance for the valley as a whole.

COMPETITION BETWEEN ELK AND DEER

The area at the foot of the steep Sierra scarp which is occupied by the Goodale elk herd is also used during the winter by deer (*Odocoileus hemionus inyoensis*). According to Jones (1954), these deer summer along the crest or just over on the west slope. At present, there are two major deer ranges within the range of the Goodale elk. The most important competition is on the Goodale deer range, roughly from Division Creek north to Goodale Creek. The other deer range, Oak Creek, is located west of Independence in the region of Gray's Meadow. At present, the elk are just penetrating the latter area. Deer are sparsely scattered through the bitterbrush type as far south as Whitney Portal, but are nowhere abundant. To the north of Goodale, the large deer population once present around McMurray Meadows has dropped to a very low level.

The main overlap of deer and elk range is in the bitterbrush area by the mouth of Goodale Canyon at the foot of the scarp between Goodale Creek and the lava flow to the south. Within this area is a stand of bitterbrush which covers approximately 670 acres.

Bitterbrush can be considered a key browse species; that is, by virtue of its common occurrence and high palatability, it shows excessive grazing before other plants. Thus, if bitterbrush is not overused, neither are the other species. Studies were concentrated on bitterbrush as the species most likely to demonstrate the existence of elk-deer competition.

Within the bitterbrush stand, the United States Forest Service had already established two permanently marked belt transects of 1/13 acre (660 feet by 5 feet) (Wood et al., 1960). I carried on my intensive studies on these two transects during 1963–1964 and installed four more transects for 1964–1965. The Forest Service, particularly Edward R. Schneegas, gave considerable assistance with this phase of the study.

Bitterbrush production.—Production was measured in late October on five marked plants on each transect. Terminal leaders were measured and recorded to the nearest one-half inch on a minimum of fifty leaders on all parts of the bush within grazing reach. The mean length of leader was calculated from all of the bushes. This method gives an index to production, rather than the actual figure, since the total number of leaders produced was not determined. Yet, there is a reasonably close correlation between length of individual leaders and the total number produced.

As with other kinds of forage, the production of bitterbrush varies considerably with the amount of effective precipitation (fig. 29). Thus the amount of forage available to elk and deer from season to season fluctuates widely, with about twice as many years below the mean as above (fig. 29).

Grazing pressure from deer and elk.—The use of the area by grazing animals was determined from pellet counts made quarterly (on approximately the 20th of October, January, April, and July) on the belt transects. All deer and elk pellet groups were counted and cleared from the transects. There was little difficulty in distinguishing the droppings of elk from those of deer with the exception of some elk calf droppings. But most of these occur during the summer when deer are out of the area, and most calf droppings tend to be distinctive in form.

The mean number of pellets per transect is also the mean number of deer days per acre because the transect is 1/13 acre in area, and deer defecate approximately 13 times a day (McCain, 1948; A. D. Smith, 1964, and many others). The same direct conversion factor was used to derive elk days per acre, since the defecation rate is quite close to that of deer (12.52 pellet groups per day reported by Neff et al., 1964). The animal days per acre for the study area are shown in figure 30. Deer used the area in both winters, but not during the summer. Elk used the area both summers. During the first winter studied, the area was used by elk but not as heavily as during the summer; the second winter, elk use was low.

Since the number of acres in the study area and the length of time between pellet counts are both known, an estimate of animal numbers can be derived by the formula

$$\frac{\text{animal days per acre} \times \text{total acres}}{\text{days on range}} = \text{number of animals.}$$

Numbers derived from this calculation are shown in table 24. The calculation of the peak population is, of course, the best estimate of the total populations of deer and elk, while the seasonal population is most meaningful in the amount of range browsing pressure.

The total estimates derived from pellet counts compare favorably with those of other methods. Counting deer sighted during walks of a systematic route through

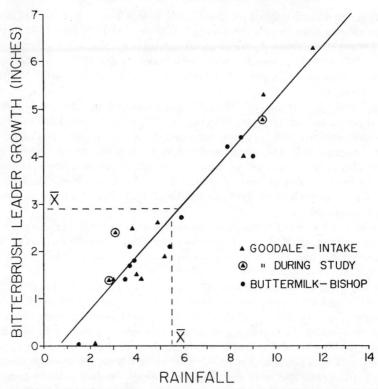

Fig. 29. Bitterbrush leader growth in relation to rainfall from 1951–1952 through 1964–1965.
(Buttermilk-Bishop is a winter range for deer 8 miles west of Bishop.)

the Goodale bitterbrush area (fig. 31) gave a maximum count of 129 deer in 1964–
1965. This is near the peak population estimate from pellet groups of 132 (table
24). Since many deer move onto the foot of the scarp and to other protected areas
during the day, the foot counts would be expected to give a lower number, so that
132 deer is probably on the conservative side.

The elk estimates are compared with the maximum accountable numbers based
upon direct observations. In 1963 a minimum of 27 cows, 11 calves, 1 spike, and
9 older bulls were accounted for, a total of 48 elk. On the basis of adding the
minimum number of calves in 1964 there were 63 head. Since these estimates are
both on the conservative side, and 1965 was a good calf year, the pellet group
estimate of 80 head is about the expected number.

Utilization of bitterbrush.—Utilization of bitterbrush was determined from
readings on 20 permanently marked plants on each transect, taken quarterly at
the same time as pellet counts. The technique was to tally the number of grazed
and ungrazed leaders, striving for a minimum of 50 leaders from all parts of the
plant within grazing reach. The percent of cropped leaders was calculated for each
plant, and the percent utilization for the transect was the mean of the percents for
the 20 marked plants. This measure is an index of utilization, since the browsing

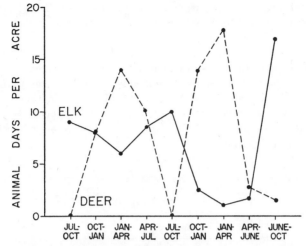

Fig. 30. Use of the Goodale bitterbrush area by elk and deer based upon quarterly pellet group counts.

animal does not always remove all of the leader, but may leave the basal portion. Therefore, the method slightly overestimates the percent of total production which is utilized. Leaders which had the bark and leaves stripped off leaving the woody portion of the twig were tallied as grazed.

Determining what proportion of the bitterbrush utilization was attributable to elk and what to deer depended upon the absence of deer use during the summer. In figure 32 the number of elk pellet groups is plotted against the amount of bitterbrush utilization for each transect after summer elk use, but before deer use (October 20 sample), and a regression line drawn through the points. The following transect reading in January showed both elk and deer use of the area. The number of cumulative elk pellets was determined by adding the new groups to those counted in the previous period, and the expected total elk utilization was read from the regression curve in figure 32. This amount is subtracted from the actually measured utilization, and the remainder was plotted against the number of deer pellet groups per plot.

The elk and deer regression lines were then used to predict the utilization thereafter on the basis of the cumulative pellet groups of each. The predicted value was compared to the actual value as it was measured at the time the pellet counts were taken (figs. 33 and 34). The mean of all six transects for 1964–1965 is shown in figure 35. The fact that the predicted values and the measured values were quite close suggests that this method of determining the relative forage removal by each species was essentially reliable.

The deviation of predicted from actual values after January of 1965 (figs. 33, 34, and 35) was caused by the extremely early green growth, which resulted in the deer's shifting to the new forage to a very large extent. This points out that the regression lines in figure 32 imply that bitterbrush makes up the same proportion of the total forage grazed irrespective of grazing intensity. Thus, the sudden appearance of green growth highly palatable to both deer and elk results in a decline of the proportion of bitterbrush taken in relation to alternate forage. In order to correct for the new forage availability, a new regression line would have to be established under these conditions. But since the concern here is with competition for the permanent range, and specifically for bitterbrush, we can consider the appearance of the new growth as the effective termination of the winter season. In the previous year, the new growth failed to appear until late in the summer because of drought, and the total growth was very small. Most seasons would fall between these extremes.

TABLE 24

ESTIMATES OF DEER AND ELK NUMBERS BASED ON PELLET GROUP COUNTS
ON THE GOODALE RANGE BITTERBRUSH AREA
(670 acres)

Season	Deer				Elk			
	Seasonal		Peak		Seasonal		Peak	
	Days	No.	Days	No.	Days	No.	Days	No.
1963–1964............	270	79	90	104	270	58	90	63
1964–1965............	270	85	90	132	338	30	90	74
Summer 1965.........	...	..	..	...	140	80	..	..

Discussion of competition between deer and elk.—From figure 32 it is apparent that the slope of the regression lines for deer is much steeper than for elk. This emphasizes the fact that elk have relatively broad food habits and are able to utilize a wide range of other forage species of secondary importance, while deer are much more dependent upon bitterbrush as a winter food. This conclusion is further supported by the fact that the poor production in 1964–1965 resulted in a great drop in the rate of use of bitterbrush by elk (figure 32) while there was a demonstrable increase in use by deer.

Estimates of animal numbers based on both pellet groups (peak populations, table 24) and direct observations showed substantial deer and elk increases in the second year. Yet there was a marked decline of occupation of the area by elk during the drought year (table 24), and they left the area entirely during the winter. In the good production year, the deer moved onto the area much earlier than in the poor year (figure 31). In the poor year the deer must have remained higher up on the scarp for a longer time, since deep snows on the crest assured that they were no longer on the summer ranges. Deer left the area at about the same time both years. These results indicate that good forage conditions attract and hold these grazing animals, while poor conditions lead to use of alternative areas.

The interaction of numbers of animals, length of time on the range and relative importance of bitterbrush in the diet determine the ultimate bitterbrush utilization by each species. In 1963–1964, based upon the mean of the two transects, total bitterbrush utilization was 82.2 percent, of which elk took 38.8 percent and deer 43.4 percent. In 1964–1965, six transects gave a total utilization of 39.8 percent, of which elk took 6.0 percent and deer 33.8 percent. In short, the utilization of bitterbrush by elk depends upon the production; it is used heavily in years when it is abundant and lightly when it is scarce. Deer, by contrast, tend to use bitterbrush consistently regardless of other factors.

Hormay (1943) considered that 60 percent utilization of bitterbrush was about the maximum the plants could stand without loss of vigor. By July of 1964, the

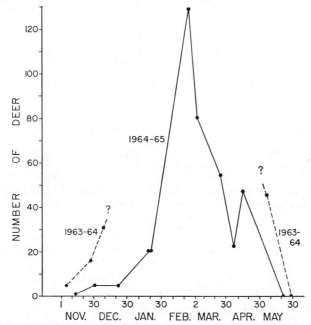

Fig. 31. Counts of deer on the Goodale bitterbrush area made along a hiking transect.

six bitterbrush transects averaged 84.3 percent utilization. Even taking into account the overestimate of the utilization determination method, this degree of browsing is detrimental to the vigor of the stand. Utilization in 1964–1965 was also increasing at a rapid rate, and without the fortunate early green growth, would probably have exceeded 60 percent.

The bitterbrush in this area is quite drought resistant, and this ability to persist through unfavorable rainfall periods is also apparent under the stress of heavy grazing. Few of the plants are actually being killed, but the amount of production and the general vigor of the stand are being reduced.

Competition between Elk and Bighorn Sheep

The Sierra Nevada bighorn (*Ovis canadensis californiana*), like the tule elk, is a rare form; Jones (1950) estimated the population at about 400. Bighorns occupy the high peaks of the Sierra in the summer, but move down on the east slope in the winter. The largest herd of sheep, the Mount Baxter herd, winters in the canyons from Sawmill to Thibaut Creeks near where many of the Goodale elk winter.

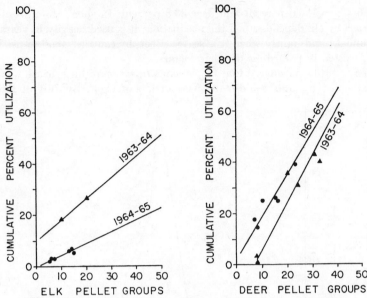

Fig. 32. Correlation of elk and deer pellet groups and bitterbrush utilization
on Goodale transects.

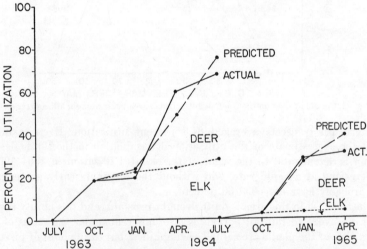

Fig. 33. Relationship of actual bitterbrush utilization measured on Transect G-3 and
utilization predicted from the regression lines in figure 32.

The possibility of competition between two rare forms prompted examination
of their relationship, which has been reported in detail elsewhere (McCullough
and Schneegas, 1966). To summarize, it was found that bighorn sheep tended to
use the steep rocky canyons where elk could not penetrate, and that only the
fringes of their respective ranges overlapped. Therefore, there is little likelihood
of competition between them.

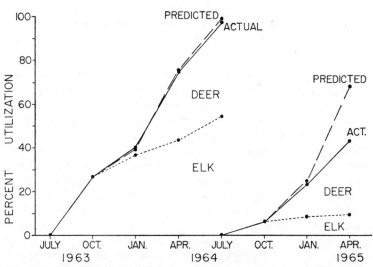

Fig. 34. Relationship of actual bitterbrush utilization measured on Transect G-5 and utilization predicted from the regression lines in figure 32.

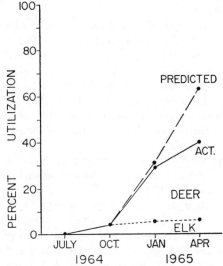

Fig. 35. Comparison of mean measured bitterbrush utilization and predicted utilization based on regression lines in figure 32 for all six transects in 1964–1965.

If the Goodale elk herd expands into the large bitterbrush stands between Independence Creek and Whitney Portal they will be adjacent to the winter range of the bighorn sheep of the Mount Williamson herd. Again, the possibility of competition seems slight. The tule elk is physically and behaviorally not equipped to invade the steep, rough, and rocky terrain which is the heart of the bighorn range.

TULE ELK POPULATION DYNAMICS
Census Method

Since 1943, elk population data in Owens Valley have been obtained by the Department of Fish and Game by aerial census (fig. 36). The early counts were made in a large airplane which necessarily had to remain high and travel fast, and the system of coverage was not carefully regulated. Thus counts up to about 1950 were subject to a fair amount of error. The high 1949 count, for example, may well be based upon a repeat count of some animals.

Since about 1950, a smaller single-engine plane has been used. In recent years it has been a Cessna 182 carrying three observers. The bottomlands are covered by flying a grid with one-half mile spacing between lines in an east-west direction, then repeating the grid in a north-south direction to crosscheck. Special problem areas, for example the willow covered "island" in the Lone Pine herd area, are covered not only by the grid, but are carefully searched by flying directly over on one side, then the other. Because the bottomlands are virtually flat, it is possible to fly very low, literally having to gain altitude to clear power transmission lines. The foothill areas on either side of the valley are flown on the contour at about one-half mile intervals, and crosschecks are not feasible. The rough terrain and uncertain air currents require that a much greater altitude be maintained for safety.

The amount of error in the elk count varies with the location of the animals. Counts of elk in the bottomlands are quite accurate, but in the foothills elk are much more difficult to spot. Also when elk are in the foothill areas they normally maintain smaller groups which are harder to find. Therefore counts are generally highest when most animals are concentrated in the bottomlands from about July through December. Census counts decline from January through May. The Goodale herd, which remains in the Sierra fans all year long, is always difficult to census. At present the calf-cow ratio count is conducted in early July and the total count in early December.

Counting the same animals twice is unlikely with the present census method. The area is covered so quickly, and elk can be seen at such great distances that no real problem is encountered. The only risk of repeated counting would be in a long movement of elk from one area to another overnight. This is circumvented by breaking off the day's work at natural boundaries between herds.

Failing to see elk under trees is a minor problem, even when the leaves are on, if the wooded areas are searched carefully. Even in the "island," tree cover is sparse enough so that the animals can be seen. A few may be missed, but this number is insignificant compared to those missed in the foothill areas.

Observer proficiency varied from excellent to very poor, and this factor is extremely important since it influences the count results from all areas. A good observer can counteract many of the inherent difficulties of censusing, while the best designed technique cannot overcome the incapability of an inept observer.

Errors in tallying the number of individuals within elk bands vary with the size of the group; the higher the number, the greater the difficulty in counting. Small groups can be counted with no trouble. Elk do not run when being buzzed

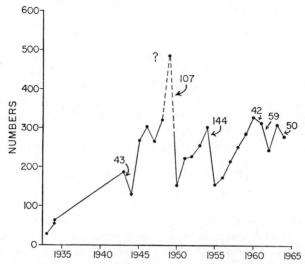

Fig. 36. Owens Valley elk population based upon aerial counts made by the California Department of Fish and Game. Numbers indicate legal harvests.

by an airplane (in fact, they hardly move) and this behavior greatly reduces the problem of counting the herd. Repeating the count until all observers agree on the number reduces the error to a very low level. In a group of fifty, for example, there might be an error of one, or occasionally two. This error is very small compared to that arising from locating small scattered groups, so that it is advantageous to conduct the counts during times when the elk are in large groups.

Several errors in classification can occur. Very small calves are difficult to count in large groups, since they are literally tucked under their mothers, or they may drop down and hide. This problem can be avoided by holding the count after the calves are somewhat larger. Another problem, that of confusing nubbin yearling males with cows, is difficult to solve. Nubbins are invariably tallied as cows, and the magnitude of the error depends upon the number of nubbins in the herd.

The overall accuracy of the aerial counts can be estimated by comparison with known counts from the ground. The December 1963 aerial count of the Independence herd was 20 bulls and 63 antlerless for a total of 83, as compared to a known 29 bulls and 56 antlerless for a total of 85. It is apparent that the difference in the totals is small considering the many variables involved. But the large difference in classification according to sex is primarily due to the larger number of nubbins in the herd that year, which from the air could not be distinguished from cows.

The Goodale herd in 1963 was censused at 5 bulls and 35 antlerless (total 40) as compared to a known minimum of 10 bulls and 38 antlerless (total 48). Even the latter count was not complete. Thus in this herd the error with the best aerial count is probably 10 to 20 percent, and in some years it may be much greater.

But as wildlife population censuses go, the tule elk aerial censuses are quite good. The Department of Fish and Game correctly interprets the counts as *minimum* numbers, and judiciously has avoided using a correction factor. It is best to continue this approach, but to strive for improvement of the census by including several modifications. The timing of the cow-calf ratio counts could be set later in the season, to better distinguish calves and to avoid missing late-born calves not yet with the herd, or those which drop down and hide. Also, the total count should be set ahead if possible, before bulls and cows begin to move into the foothills, with the consequent breakup of the larger groups. In fact, both statistics might be obtainable with a single count. In terms of the life cycle, the best time would probably be at the height of the rut for these reasons: (1) the calves are large enough to be seen easily, and they are all with the herd; (2) nearly all of the elk are in the valley for the rut (the Goodale herd being an obvious exception); (3) bulls tend to be grouped in close proximity to the cow groups which are bunched by the master bulls; (4) the cow groups are broken into two or three sub-herds by the secondary bulls, and are thus easier to count; and (5) nearly all of the nubbins are driven out of the herd and are with the bachelor bull cohorts; any cowlike animals in the bull groups could be given special attention. The best timing, to coincide with the peak of the rut, would be approximately August 25 to September 5. Obviously, the shift to a single count should not be made before adequate testing.

Improving the Goodale count will require a more intensive coverage of the ground. The high speed of the Cessna (about 120 mph) is a disadvantage in spotting elk in the relatively high brush cover and rough terrain. Perhaps using an aircraft of slower flight speed and also reducing the contour flight interval would give better results in the Sierra alluvial fans, and perhaps also in the White and Inyo foothills.

POPULATION GROWTH

The buildup of elk following the original introduction into Owens Valley is shown in fig. 36. It can be seen that during times of maximum increase (for example, 1955 to 1960) the herd grew at about 14 to 15 percent per year. Furthermore, the early growth rate from introduction (1934) to the first count (1943) was between 14 and 15 percent. This seems to be the basic rate of growth for the population within the density the population has thus far reached, indicating that they are not being limited by density dependent factors. The number of elk has increased continually, being controlled only by the periodic legal hunts.

NATALITY AND MORTALITY

Table 25 shows the proportion of cows conceiving, based upon examination of reproductive tracts from legal kills (examination performed by Oscar Brunetti of the Department of Fish and Game Laboratory in Sacramento). Including a few yearlings (which in tule elk breed commonly, as previously discussed), 90 percent of the cows examined carried a fetus. As pointed out by Halazon and Buechner (1956) and Morrison (1960b), corpora lutea counts do not necessarily indicate ova unfertilized at the time of conception; secondary ovulation following conception may occur.

By July, when the newborn calves had joined the herds with their mothers, the cow-calf ratio was about 100:33 (table 26). Thus, sometimes between early

TABLE 25

RESULTS OF EXAMINATIONS BY CALIFORNIA FISH AND GAME LABORATORY OF
FEMALE REPRODUCTIVE TRACTS FROM LEGALLY KILLED TULE ELK

Year	Number examined	Corpora lutea	Embryos	Percent pregnant
1961..........................	17	29	15	88.2
1962..........................	31	53	27	87.1
1964..........................	15	20	15	100.0
Total.........................	63	102	57	90.5

TABLE 26

SEX AND AGE RATIOS OF THE OWENS VALLEY TULE ELK POPULATION BASED
UPON A COMBINATION OF AERIAL AND GROUND COUNTS
(Sample size on which ratio is based is given in parentheses.)

Season	Per 100 cows		Percent of population
	Bulls	Calves	
1963 season			
July............................	40 (199)	34* (190)	19.4 (247)
December.......................	55† (308)	33‡ (218)	18.0† (308)
1964 season			
July............................	56 (245)	24¶ (194)	13.0 (282)
December.......................	55† (279)	25‡ (166)	20.0† (279)
1964 season			
June (aerial)....................	66 (149)	34 (121)	17.0 (180)

* Ground classification of Tinemaha and Goodale herds added to the aerial counts of the other herds.
† Corrected on the basis of ground counts of cow:calf ratio since calves are not separated in the December aerial count.
‡ Ground count.
¶ Ratio abnormally low because of the failure of the Independence herd calf crop. Based on only the other herds, a ratio of 100:33 was obtained.

pregnancy and the time the calves join the herd after birth, there is a very high mortality. When this mortality occurs is an unanswered question. Abortion or resorption of the fetus may contribute to the mortality or it may occur at or following birth, or both. At least one of the reproductive tracts examined contained a resorbing fetus. Attempts to determine pregnancy by external appearance of cows before the calving season were unsuccessful. The earlier discussion of the life of newborn calves illustrated that considerable mortality can occur at this time. Also, ground counts during early June of 1965 gave a ratio of 100 cows to 56 calves based on a sample of 89 as compared to 100:34 by the aerial census on June 15 to 17. This difference may reflect continuing calf mortality, or merely the fact that the aerial count was held too early for the most reliable results. In all but one case where the same herds were classified by both methods, a higher absolute number of calves was obtained on the ground with a smaller sample size.

Therefore, the question of when the mortality occurs cannot be resolved at present. Suffice to say that some time between early pregnancy and about one month of age, about 64 percent of the potential calf crop is lost.

The mortality by age and sex is shown in the provisional life tables (table 27) and survivorship curve (fig. 37). These data must be considered provisional because of the generally small sample sizes, and the necessity of integrating several different sources of data to obtain the full table. The number of animals born has been based upon a 90 percent conception rate, so that the 0–1 year class actually includes a good part of the prenatal period. Data on the males through four years and females through two years are based upon actual survival as observed in the

TABLE 27

PROVISIONAL LIFE TABLE FOR OWENS VALLEY TULE ELK

x = age in years
d_x = number dying during age interval per 1,000 born
l_x = number surviving at beginning of age interval out of 1,000 born
q_x = percent mortality during age interval
e_x = life expectancy of those attaining age interval

Males					Females				
x	d_x	l_x	q_x	e_x	x	d_x	l_x	q_x	e_x
0–1	624	1000	62.4	2.1	0–1	624	1000	62.4	2.7
1–2	22	376	5.9	3.7	1–2	13	376	3.5	5.4
2–3	44	354	12.4	2.9	2–3	22	363	2.5	4.6
3–4	45	310	14.5	2.3	3–4	27	341	7.9	3.8
4–5	88	265	33.2	1.6	4–5	35	314	11.1	3.1
5–6	89	177	50.3	1.1	5–6	49	279	17.6	2.4
6–7	65	88	73.9	0.8	6–7	53	230	23.0	1.8
7–8	20	23	87.0	0.7	7–8	62	177	35.0	1.2
8–9	2	3	66.0	0.8	8–9	97	115	84.3	0.7
9–10	1	1	100.0	0.5	9–10	18	18	100.0	0.5

field. Calculation of life table data based upon aging of legally killed animals (aged by Oscar Brunetti of the Fish and Game Laboratory) is not valid for the younger age classes, since older animals are purposely selected during the hunts. However, the kill data for four years and older were used for deriving this portion of the male curves, since after this age there is probably little distortion by selection and this information cannot be obtained by direct observation. The older female curve is based upon the distribution of age classes in the legal kill with some extrapolation on the basis of a 55:100 bull-cow ratio.

It is obvious that most of the mortality occurs in the very young calves. Comparison of July cow:calf ratios with those of December (table 26) shows that calves which live to join the herd have a good survival rate through the first winter. The higher ratio in December than in July of 1964 is a reflection of the legal harvest of cows during that fall. The greatest increase in cow:calf ratios occurred in the herds from which the highest numbers of cows were removed.

Spring cow:calf ratios to measure over-winter mortality are difficult to obtain because of the general scattering of the herds to the high country. In 1964 a March cow:calf ratio of 100:57 was obtained in a sample of 110. This left approximately 100 cows untallied, and the number of calves with them obviously must have been much lower. But in terms of absolute numbers, most of the calves were accounted for, including all but one in the Independence and Tinemaha herds. Hence, the over-winter mortality on calves was also low. The number of calves which join the herd a month or two after birth is virtually the recruitment rate. The increment of calves amounts to about 18 to 20 percent of the herd per year (table 26).

The longevity of Owens Valley elk is about 10 years. The oldest animal taken in the hunts, in which the older animals are purposely selected, was aged at 12, and this was the only animal out of 84 examined which was aged over 10.

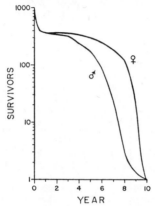

Fig. 37. Provisional survivorship curve for Owens Valley tule elk.

The mortality rates of male and female calves are similar. However, from the yearling year onward the mortality of bulls is considerably higher than that of cows (fig. 37). The most reliable bull:cow ratios are about 55:100 (table 26). The mortality rate of bulls (about twice that of cows) was also reflected in animals found dead. Of 41 carcasses or skeletons of yearling or older animals found in a random fashion, 28 were bulls and 13 were cows. This difference is probably due to sexual behavior. The aggressiveness of the male, and his stronger tendency to wander widely as an individual, results in greater vulnerability; a good proportion of older bulls engage in serious fights and occasionally are struck hard blows by the opponents' antlers; and many bulls go into the winter in poor condition as a result of the rutting activities. All of these factors, and probably others, result in increased mortality of males as is common among mammals.

Legal hunt mortality.—There is little question that the legal hunts have been the single most important cause of mortality over the years. Some 453 head have been removed in six hunts in Owens Valley. In the period 1960 to 1964, 10 percent of the herd was removed in each of three open seasons. To the kill must be added the crippling losses. In the early years, when permit holders were allowed to hunt without restriction, crippling losses were very high. "Flock shooting" of running herds was common. For 304 legals kills in the first three hunts, there were 37 known cripple losses (12 percent of the take-home kill). No doubt many other cripples died undiscovered. The warden guide system used in recent hunts has reduced the crippling loss to a low level. In the 1964 hunt that I observed, there were two cases out of 50 animals taken where mortally wounded animals that ran some distance before dropping were overlooked by the warden-guide. The total crippling loss in recent years has probably been less than 5 percent, and this could be further reduced if the wardens were instructed to watch the fleeing herd carefully with binoculars to detect wounded animals which veer from the herd and collapse. Some of these animals at first show no sign of being hit, and run off with the herd even though fatally wounded.

Illegal shooting.—Estimates of mortality by causes other than legal shooting are based upon reliable reports, animals found dead, and old skeletons. A total of 55 deaths were known in Owens Valley (table 28), 41 of which were from unknown causes.

TABLE 28

SUMMARY OF TULE ELK MORTALITY BY CAUSE, AGE, AND SEX, DERIVED FROM
ALL SOURCES OF DATA OTHER THAN LEGAL HARVESTS

Cause	Males			Females				Uniden- tified	Total	Percent
	Year- ling	Mature	De- crepit	Year- ling	Mature	De- crepit	Calves			
Unknown ..	5	17	1	1	9	0	2	6	41	74.5
Shot.......		5			1		1		7	12.7
Accident...		3						1	4	7.3
Coyote.....							2		2	3.6
Cougar.....					1				1	1.8
Total......	5	25	1	1	11	0	5	7	55	
Percent....	9.1	45.5	1.8	1.8	20	0	9.1	12.7		

Among adults, shooting was the most frequently identified cause of mortality. In some cases part of the meat was taken, but more often the carcass was left. A few local ranchers are the most frequent offenders, but other people, both local residents and outsiders, occasionally shoot elk. There is some local poaching for meat, but this has declined to a low level in recent years.

During the study a tame young bull, which was being kept by a local resident with his cattle near Fort Independence, was killed by a shotgun blast in the head. Only the hindquarters were taken. Forks, a bull which played an important role in the 1963 Independence herd rut, was shot and killed in June, 1964, and only the canine teeth taken.

Killing of elk by ranchers to stop damage was once common, but has declined greatly in recent years. Harassment, primarily chasing with horses to move the elk onto the neighboring lease, is a far more common practice today. Still some elk are being shot, and I observed .22 caliber rifles being used; blood was drawn, but no mortalities were known to occur. There is a widespread belief among the ranchers that dragging elk entrails along a fence will act as a repellent to the elk. Killing of elk for this purpose occurred during the study.

The number killed each year by livestockmen is difficult to determine, but based upon my own impressions and conversations with ranchers and other in formed persons, I would guess that between five and ten animals are killed per year. Nearly everyone agrees that the bragging far outweighs the actual killing, that the number killed is gradually declining, and that most of the shooting is being done by a few individuals. To the credit of Owens Valley ranchers, it should be clearly stated that most of them take a tolerant view of the elk and are willing to work within the existing management program of the Department of Fish and Game.

Accidental mortality.—Accidental death is a fairly common occurrence. When the Goodale herd used to cross Highway 395 near Aberdeen Resort to the Independence herd area, elk were regularly struck by cars. There has been no problem since the elk stopped crossing there in recent years. The Tinemaha herd is the only one to cross the highway at present. During the study two elk were struck and killed by cars near Poverty Hills. This will continue to be a problem area.

Fences cause some mortality among elk. Two deaths were known to be caused by entanglement of antlers in barbed wire. One bull could not escape the entanglement and died on the spot. The other bull dragged trailing wire until he eventually become exhausted and died. The skull of this animal is now in the possession of Mr. Charles Connor of Big Pine. Mr. Connor also reported a young bull found dead with its foot twisted in the upper wires of a new fence.

An unusual accidental death occurred in the case of a large bull found dead in Big Pine Canal, which is only two to three feet deep, but with abrupt sides. The elk cross it regularly. When the skelton was cleaned at the Museum of Vertebrate Zoology, an antler point was found imbedded in the spine, having been driven entirely through the spinal cord between the last two lumbar vertebrae. The point was a surroyal, probably the back one. If it had come from another bull, it seems unlikely that he would have struck in the middle of the back, particularly with a surroyal, and with such force. Most serious fighting occurs between master bulls and challengers, and the only bull with cows in the vicinity had all of his points intact. If the point were from the same animal, the angle of entry showed that it would have to have been from the left antler. Lifting and turning of the head to the left brings the antler into contact with the lumbar area. The bull's left surroyal was broken, but too badly to allow a match. The most likely explanation seems to be that the bull fell or summersaulted on his own antler, perhaps in a running group crossing the canal. With the abrupt bank, a misstep or bump from another animal could easily have put him off balance. With the hindquarters paralyzed he would have been unable to get out of the canal.

Predation.—The three predators capable of preying on elk in Owens Valley are the coyote, bobcat (*Lynx rufus*), and the mountain lion or cougar (*Felis concolor*). Of these, the coyote is by far the most important because of its great abundance. It is totally ineffective against the adults and also calves once they join the herd. However, as pointed out in the section on reproduction, coyotes can prey successfully on the newborn calves.

Bobcats are of little concern because of their rarity, and because, like the coyote, they can be effective only against the small calves. Only six observations of bobcats were made during the study, most of these in the higher country or around lava flows in the valley. However, one bobcat was seen in the Independence herd calving area during the decline of the calf crop in 1964, and possibly it was attracted by the availability of vulnerable calves. Nevertheless, little weight can be assigned to a single observation.

Mountain lions occur in both the Sierra and the White-Inyo range, but are never common. Sign of lions was found on several occasions in the upper parts of the Goodale herd area, including two deer kills which were probably due to lions. Lions would be able to kill adult elk, and it was presumed that an occasional animal was taken. This supposition was substantiated in the winter of 1965–1966 when Vernon Burandt, Game Warden of Lone Pine, identified as a lion kill a prime adult elk cow found near Black Canyon on the Goodale range. On another occasion, the skull of a large bull was spotted in the steep rocks of Black Canyon where no elk would have ventured. This either had fallen from the top of the cliff or had been dragged there by a predator. In any event, predation by mountain lions must be considered a curiosity.

Eagles, ravens, and other avian predators would hardly be effective against even the calves, and elk of all ages pay them no heed.

DISEASE

Disease appears to be a minor problem in tule elk. Samples of blood sera were obtained from various herds, and through the cooperation of Bishop veterinarian Joseph Hird and the San Gabriel Animal Pathology Laboratory, they were tested for common diseases of large ungulates. All of the animals tested were negative for leptospirosis and brucellosis. Tested animals were:

```
Owens Valley population.....................16
    Bishop herd .....................3
    Tinemaha herd ...................1
    Independence herd ...............8
    Lone Pine herd ..................4
Tupman Reserve population ....................9
Cache Creek population .......................2
```

However, of 2 Tinemaha, 8 Independence, and 2 Cache Creek elk sera tested, 1 Tinemaha and 5 Independence animals were suspect for infectious bovine rhinotracheitis (IBR). This is a viral disease with symptoms in the upper respiratory tract much like those of a common cold. In feedlot domestic cattle this disease occasionally causes severe loss; in range cattle the clinical symptoms are rarely observed and the disease is extremely difficult to diagnose. Dr. Joseph Hird has found the disease among cattle in Owens Valley where abortion was occurring in cows otherwise normal in appearance. Certainly direct mortality from this disease is not occurring among elk. The symptoms were never observed. However, abortion due to IBR as a possible cause of the large mortality between conception and one month of age should not be discounted. Further sera collections would seem to be warranted to study this possibility. With the limited evidence at hand the only thing that can be said is that the elk have probably come into contact with the virus at some time in the past.

One adult cow with a lumpy jaw suggestive of necrotic stomatitis was observed.

Spherophorus necrophorus, the organism causing this disease, was found in the liver of one sample examined by Dr. M. L. Murdock of the San Gabriel Laboratory. However, none of the jaws of old skeletons or animals found dead showed abcesses. Murie (1951) found this disease to be prevalent in Jackson Hole elk, and it was something of a problem in the Tupman herd when baled hay was fed. With the present pelleted diet the disease has not been a problem at Tupman, and the Owens Valley occurrences, if indeed necrotic stomatitis, seem to be isolated cases.

Histopathological examinations of liver samples were performed by Dr. M. L. Murdock of the San Gabriel Laboratory on 5 males and 5 females from Owens Valley and Humboldt County, 4 males and 5 females from Tupman Reserve, and 2 females from Cache Creek. Cirrhosis and other abnormal conditions occurred in approximately 40 percent of the samples, involving all of the tule elk herds and the Humboldt County Roosevelt elk herd as well. Cause of this liver damage and its impact upon the well being of the various herds is not known. Visually, the livers appeared to be healthy. Perhaps such abnormalities are more common among wild ungulates than is presently suspected because careful histological examinations are seldom made.

In 1963 there was an outbreak of anthrax among cattle west of Highway 395 just north of Big Pine. This is an area where elk have never occurred and they did not come into contact with the disease. But this outbreak clearly illustrates the ever-present danger of introduction of a virulent contagious disease into the elk herd. Since the study, a second outbreak of anthrax has occurred (see below).

(see below)

PARASITES

Although time was not available for careful parasitological studies during hunts, the general impression was that parasite loads were exceptionally low. Only a moderate number of ticks were found on the Owens Valley and Tupman elk. However, the Cache Creek animals carried large numbers of ticks.

In the winter, many Owens Valley animals showed bare patches on the back of the neck just forward of the shoulder, and at first this was thought to be due to scabies. However, examination of large patches of shed hair showed nothing but dried blood and the dried bodies of ticks. The bare patches did not enlarge or occur on other parts of the body even though a third of the Independence herd and also some animals of other herds developed them. It soon became apparent that the hair was being rubbed loose when the elk crawled under fences and that there were no pathological implications. These same bare patches occurred in the winter of 1964–1965.

A number of flies and other biting insects bother the elk in the summer, particularly when the wind is low. Insect harassment was much greater in 1963 than in 1964, the drought year.

Internal parasites are also not common. Liver was handled regularly, but no flukes were found. Examination of 50 fresh fecal samples, 10 from each herd, for parasite eggs and larvae resulted in finding one unidentified strongylid egg and one ascarid egg. Four blood smears were sent to Dr. Murdock, and he did not find any of the common blood parasites.

Without doubt a careful parasitological examination would reveal a wide variety of parasites, but all evidence at present indicates low parasite populations. The last elk shot outside of the Tupman enclosure in the San Joaquin Valley were examined by a parasitologist; they also were found to be almost without parasites (E. Raymond Hall, 1933, Field Notes in Museum of Vertebrate Zoology). The low elk population levels may account for the low levels of both diseases and parasites.

DISCUSSION OF POPULATION DYNAMICS

The Owens Valley animals are obviously not increasing at a rate anywhere near the potential for the species. Murphy (1963) reported 28.2 percent as the increase rate of a captive Rocky Mountain elk herd with a preponderance of females. However, maximum rate of increase with a balanced sex ratio and no mortality is about 27 percent per year (fig. 38). Actual increase is between 14 and 15 percent per year. Since the recruitment of calves is about 18 to 20 percent per year, this means that 4 to 5 percent of the yearling and older elk succumb to mortality caused by factors other than the legal hunts. The other 12 to 13 percent (the difference from the theoretical potential of 27 percent) results from failure to breed (3 to 4 percent) and fetal or early calf mortality. Thus, losses due to poaching, adult predation, etc. account for a small part of the total mortality.

These data also show that a legal kill of about 14 to 15 percent of the herd is necessary just to remove the increase. If hunts were to be held at greater intervals, a larger percent of the herd would have to be removed in each hunt. This topic is discussed more fully in the management section.

In contrast to the Owens Valley population, the Tupman population is growing at nearly the 27 percent per year theoretical maximum. Nearly all of the cows bear calves and the calf survival rate is almost 100 percent. Thus the population increases each year from 32 to more than 40, and it is necessary to remove 10 to 12 animals in most years to keep the limit to 32 head.

At the opposite extreme is the Cache Creek population, which is virtually static. Obviously the recruitment rate and the mortality rate are approximately equal, but how this adjustment is brought about is not known at present. Low recruitment is the likely situation. Based upon my sightings during September, 1963, the cow-calf ratio was 100:11 and in November, 1964, it was the same (table 29). Although these ratios were based on small samples, they suggest that calf recruitment is poor.

TUPMAN RESERVE AND CACHE CREEK TULE ELK POPULATIONS

Certain aspects of the other tule elk populations have been mentioned in comparison with results obtained from Owens Valley. This section will summarize the status of these herds.

TUPMAN RESERVE

The refuge contains 953 fenced acres of flatland just north of Tupman in the San Joaquin Valley. However, the refuge is transected by a water canal, and the elk do not cross the bridge to the southern part; hence the area used by elk is about 350 acres.

The southern part of the refuge formerly contained a watercourse which was lined by willow trees, and other perennial plants were found over the area. The

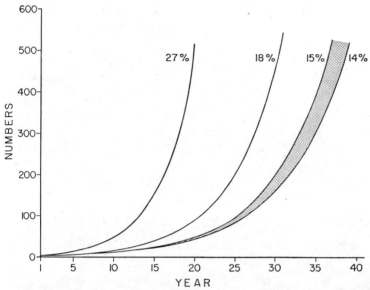

Fig. 38. Curves representing rates of population growth in percent per year based upon a balanced sex ratio at birth and a single calf per cow. The 27 percent curve is the maximum theoretical rate with no adult mortality. The 18 percent curve is the increase with the present Owens Valley recruitment rate assuming no adult mortality. The 14 to 15 percent curve is the actual Owens Valley increase rate without legal hunting.

willows were a favorite haunt of elk in early years. But heavy overgrazing resulted in elimination of the better forage species and the condition of the elk became very poor. Disease and calf failure took a heavy toll. Construction of the Miller Canal dried up the natural streamcourse and the willows and other water plants died.

The area presently supports a carpet of green annual grasses and forbs during the winter and spring, but these dry by early summer. In late summer and fall, the ground is virtually bare. Two fenced five-acre irrigated pastures remain green throughout the summer. These contain perennial grasses and clovers and are moderately used by the elk. The elk are fed alfalfa pellets and phosphorus and copper supplement.

The present herd of 32 is quite healthy. Nearly all of the cows breed and the calf crop is about 10 to 14 per year. Calf survival is nearly 100 percent. In November of each year, the surplus animals are removed and the meat given to a state prison.

Thus the Tupman herd is kept in a healthy state by artificial means in unnatural surroundings. Besides the barren appearance of the enclosure in summer, the 350-acre area is transected by a large water pipe and a telephone line.

CACHE CREEK

The Cache Creek herd is poorly known and has generally received little attention. The best information on it is an unpublished report prepared in 1956 by James Bower of the California Fish and Game Department. The discussion pre-

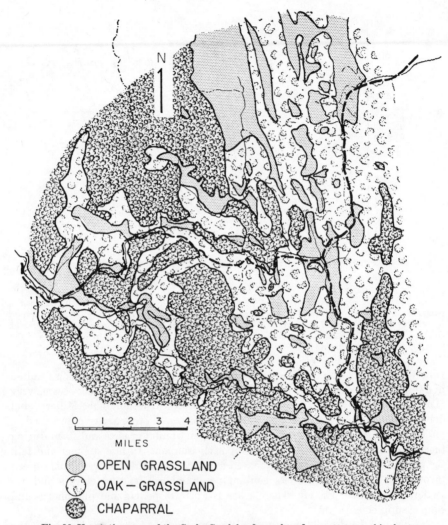

Fig. 39. Vegetation map of the Cache Creek herd area based upon topographic sheets
and ground surveys.

sented here is based partly upon his work, and partly upon my own brief studies
in the area.

The Cache Creek area represents the opposite extreme in tule elk range from
that of Owens Valley and lower San Joaquin Valley. The terrain is quite broken,
with ridges descending into narrow valleys. Most of the area is privately owned,
but there is a large block of Bureau of Land Management land southwest of the
Lake-Colusa county line.

Three main vegetation types occur in the area (fig. 39). Open annual grasslands

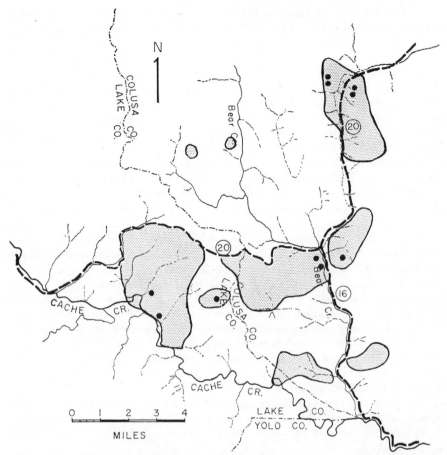

Fig. 40. Elk concentration areas in the Cache Creek herd based upon the report of James Bower and my own observations of sign and of animals (dots).

occur in the larger valleys, and on favorable upper slopes. These grade into mixed annual grasslands with good stands of blue oak (*Quercus Douglasii*). The third type is chaparrel, which occupies the drier steeper slopes. Chamise (*Adenostema fasciculatum*) is most abundant and occupies the large south and southwest facing slopes in the southwestern part of the region. Other major species include digger pine (*Pinus Sabiniana*), wedgeleaf ceanothus (*Ceanothus cuneatus*), manzanita (*Arctostaphylos glandulosa*), and many others.

The population changes over the years are virtually unknown, but Bower concluded from accounts of local residents that the herd rose to a peak, then declined to the present level of an estimated 60 to 80 animals. Aerial counts have not been very successful because of the heavy cover and rough terrain. The highest counts were 52 on January 24, 1955, and 53 on March 6, 1956. Aerial counts were taken only between 1954 and 1956.

Distribution of elk based upon the aerial counts, Bower's ground surveys, and my observations is shown in figure 40. In general, during the green growth stage the elk scatter widely in small groups to graze the new forage and to give birth, similar to the Owens Valley animals. As the grasses begin to dry, the elk are forced to the vicinity of water supplies. There are many stock dams in the area, but most of these also dry up late in the season. The elk then tend to concentrate on the Payne Ranch (south of Highway 20, west of Highway 16 to the Lake-Colusa county border) where large stock dams retain water; in the large canyons between Cache Creek (where they water) and Highway 20 on Bureau of Land Management lands; and in other pockets where water is available.

In November of 1964 I accounted for a minimum of 35 animals on lands other than the Payne Ranch (access to the latter was denied). Since most of the elk are known to concentrate on this ranch during this time of year, an estimate of 80 animals seems reasonable. On September 13, 1955, 54 animals were located on the Payne Ranch proper by the Department of Fish and Game.

The population structure of the Cache Creek herd is not well known. The sex ratio of about 22 bulls:100 cows (table 29) obtained from various classifications is probably too low because the bulls would tend to be more scattered than the cows. Bower's 1956 count of new calves gave a relatively low 33:100 ratio, but the previous year's calf crop, which had survived the dry season, appeared to be quite good (table 29). My counts indicate a low calf survival in 1963 and 1964. Of the two cows I collected, one was nursing a calf but did not carry a fetus, and the other was dry but carried a fetus. The rut appears to occur at about the same time as for the Owens Valley and Tupman populations. On September 11, 1963, my observations showed that the rut was on and this would agree with Bower's belief that the peak of calving occurred around May 1.

Little is known about adult mortality. I found a recently dead old cow and two weathered skeletons. Some poaching occurs. This herd has never been open to a legal hunt, but some elk have been mistaken for deer and killed during the deer season.

Acorns made up 45 percent of the rumen contents of the two elk collected, and mast was undoubtedly responsible for their good condition. Perhaps calf success depends, in part, upon the mast crop of the previous year. Other important foods were grass, 42.5 percent; filaree, 10 percent; and oak leaves, 2.5 percent. Traces of forbs and clovers were present, and during the growth stage these probably are quite important. In a burned area on the Bureau of Land Management lands I found the new chamise sprouts were being taken by elk. Bower found that redberry (*Rhamnus crocea*), birchleaf mahogany (*Cercocarpus betuloides*), wedgeleaf ceanothus, and scrub oak (*Quercus dumosa*) were browsed by elk. Utilization of brush was light to moderate in his study, and my observations are in agreement.

The amount of damage being caused by the Cache Creek herd is questionable. Some owners complain of heavy range use and damaged fences. Others feel that the elk do little damage, and actually encourage elk on their lands. Croplands are not common in the area so there is little crop damage. The land of the most persistently complaining owner has been severely overgrazed by cattle, and the accusation that elk take too much forage is not very convincing. Fences are sometimes broken. One owner complained to me that a herd of running elk had broken down his fence. He then volunteered that he had been chasing them with a horse to get them off his property. What seemed to annoy him most was that they were physically able to jump over the fence, but instead ran through it. In general, the amount of damage caused by this herd appears to be relatively light, and quite local in nature.

MANAGEMENT AND PRESERVATION OF TULE ELK
PRESENT POLICY

The present policy of the California Fish and Game Commission recognizes that the value of California's elk herds is primarily esthetic. Even managed to the ultimate for sport hunting, the harvest of elk would be minor in relation to the demand. The commission policy calls for management of elk herds consistent with land uses by other big game species and by agriculture and forestry.

According to the commission, these policy goals will be accomplished by:

1. Protection of elk herds through enforcement of laws and regulations.
2. Protection of elk habitat in cooperation with public and private agencies.
3. Managing elk herds on the basis of natural forage without recourse to artificial feeding.
4. Selective removal of animals when necessary to control elk numbers for the benefit of the herd or to alleviate agricultural or forest damage.
5. Plans will be formulated for the management of each of the elk herds in the state based on biological, economic and other factors determined from research and investigations.

The management plan for the Owens Valley tule elk herd is given in full below:

It is the objective to preserve the Owens Valley elk herd in a safe and thrifty condition. The herd will be counted and its condition ascertained regularly and at least once a year.

Regulations will be proposed by the Fish and Game Commission to accomplish the following:

1. The herd will be maintained at between 250 and 300 animals. Whenever the herd needs reduction, annual removal of selected animals on a cull basis will be authorized.
2. Each reduction of the herd will be controlled by the Department of Fish and Game under regulations established by the Fish and Game Commission. Each hunter or group of hunters (not to exceed four in number in each group) will be accompanied by a regular employee of the department who will designate which animals are to be taken, the objective being a selective removal of the poorer animals.
3. Successful applicants will be required to demonstrate good markmanship and safe handling of firearms.
4. Department employees will be authorized to carry guns and to insure that any animals that are wounded are dispatched humanely if the occasion demands.

At present, wardens serve as guides for the hunters. The warden determines which hunter shoots first, selects the animal, and tells the hunter when to shoot. Since the department is responsible for transporting the hunter back to his car at the check-station, four-wheel drive pickups are used to transport the dressed elk carcass as well.

This policy evolved over a period of years as the controversy over the elk herd grew. The early hunts were declared in response to pressure from livestockmen to reduce agricultural damages. The first three hunts resulted in relatively large reductions. The 1943 hunt effected a 23 percent reduction and the 1949 hunt 22 percent, not counting the significant crippling losses. These hunts caused considerable concern among sportsmen and conservationists about the ultimate survival of the elk. The livestockmen continued to demand the complete removal of the herd. In 1952, meetings between the opposing interests and the Department of Fish and Game led to the adoption of a policy of holding the number of elk between 125 and 275.

The next hunt was held in 1955 when 144 elk were killed out of an estimated 301

TABLE 29

COMPOSITION COUNTS OF THE CACHE CREEK TULE ELK POPULATION

Date	Bulls	Cows	Calves	(bulls:cows:calves)
Jan.–May 1956* (1955 calves).......	16	67	32	24:100:48
July 1956*.........................	6	27	9	22:100:33
Sept. 1963.........................	2	19	2	11:100:11
Nov. 1964..........................	6	27	3	22:100:11

* Based on counts made by James Bower.

(48 percent). Shooting from vehicles into running herds, and other unsportsmanlike behavior, was rampant, and the crippling loss was thought to be excessive. The need for closer control over the behavior of hunters and reduction of the number of elk killed in a hunt was clearly felt by conservationists. Thus when the Department of Fish and Game proposed that another hunt be held in 1960 with 150 permits to be filled from an estimated 285 elk, a storm of opposition broke. A citizens committee, the Committee for the Preservation of the Tule Elk, was organized, and served as a main rallying point for opposition to the hunt. Public pressure was so strong that the hunt was called off and the policy reviewed. After hearings in the winter of 1960–1961 the present management policy of holding the herd between 250 and 300 by highly controlled hunts was adopted by the Fish and Game Commission.

The hunts in recent years have removed a moderate proportion of the population, and the control of hunters has reduced crippling loss to an insignificant level. The 300 maximum has been interpreted strictly; if 300 or more elk are counted in the aerial census, a hunt will be proposed, while if less than 300 are counted, no hunt is held.

The Owens Valley cattlemen realize that there is no hope that the elk will be removed, or that the number will be reduced below that set by the present policy. The more progressive ones also realize that the conservation movement and the demand for recreation are steadily increasing, and that pressure in favor of the elk will increase. They fully recognize that it is in their own interest to support the present policy, and they do so. By and large, organized sportsmen's groups also support the commission's policy.

The land management agencies, the Los Angeles Department of Water and Power, the United States Forest Service, and the Bureau of Land Management support the present policy. Each of these agencies has broad responsibilities for managing a spectrum of natural resources to various ends, and they view tule elk as only one element, albeit an important one, in the total program. There has been a substantial increase in cooperation between these agencies in recent years, and many programs have been coordinated to the benefit of all. This trend speaks well for the continued improvement of management of all natural resources, including the tule elk.

A NATURE RESERVE PROPOSAL

The Committee for the Preservation of the Tule Elk, based in Los Angeles, is dedicated to the same basic objective as the Department of Fish and Game, and the land management agencies—saving the tule elk from extinction. However, they strongly disagree about the means by which this objective should be attained. The committee has opposed all Owens Valley elk hunts, and has advocated creation of a reserve for the elk which would encompass the southern half of the valley. They would have all competing activities removed from the reserve. It is believed by the committee that the elk would be able to increase their number, and that they would in time become tame enough to allow close approach by tourists and photographers.

The policy of the committee does not call for a containing fence. However, the suggestion that a drift fence be constructed running east-west across the valley at Tinemaha Reservoir dam and extending up the steep face of the mountains on either side to contain the elk has been commonly associated with the reserve proposal. Such a fence would have the serious consequences of splitting the Tinemaha herd range in half, and on that basis should be strongly opposed. The use of an area by a herd is not merely fortuitous. Movements are directed to utilize the available resources in the most efficient manner. The economy of the Tinemaha herd could not help but be hindered by the construction of such a fence; this herd's persistent alfalfa damage attests to already limited summer forage.

The establishment of a nature reserve for elk in the southern part of the valley may give the ranchers in the northern part a political lever to obtain the removal of elk from the remainder of the valley. The ranchers could logically argue that if the reserve is specifically for elk, then why should not all of the elk be in it? And that if the reserve is truly a solution to the elk survival problem, why allow elk in the remainder of the valley where they conflict with agricultural interests? The end result could well be the elimination of the Bishop herd.

But a more basic consideration is whether or not the establishment of a reserve would indeed secure the survival of the elk. Implicit in the demand for a reserve is the assumption that the elk are in danger of extinction under the present management plan. In fact, however, the biological data suggest that the likelihood of extinction under the present plan is remote. An increase rate of 14 to 15 percent per year is respectable for a wild elk herd. Clearly, the herd is in the accelerating phase of the growth curve (fig. 38), so that the rate of increase is nearly maximum for existing conditions in Owens Valley. The animals are in good health, and the loss of about 4 percent of the adults to natural causes and poaching is not excessive.

Legal hunting is the major cause of mortality, and this is within control. The relatively large reductions practiced in early years certainly were cause for concern, particularly in view of the undetermined total crippling loss. Yet throughout its known history, the tule elk has displayed a remarkable ability to build up from reduced numbers. This is in marked contrast to typical cases of endangered species, in which the populations are dwindling due to failures of reproduction or survival, the causes of which are poorly or not at all understood. The recent tule elk hunts have barely removed the annual population increment. The practice of scheduling the hunts on a minimum actual count of 300 assures that a known population is present, and there are no errors in estimation. This is not an argument against maintaining more animals if capacity to support them is present; but the assumption that the present population is inadequate to preserve the form is not borne out by biological data.

Another tenet of protectionist philosophy is that there is safety in numbers. This approach in managing large ungulates has led to some of the worst mistakes of the conservation movement. The rise and crash of the Kaibab deer herd is a classical example. A given range will support only a limited number of big game animals on a sustained basis, and failure to recognize this has occurred again and again. Fortunately, the National Parks have recognized the need for animal control, and Yellowstone Park has begun necessary reductions of their famous elk herd. Many other control programs for big game animals are now underway, including reduction of elephants, hippos, and other excess game populations in African parks. These programs rest on the recognition that most of the natural controls (predation, aboriginal hunting, etc.) of large animals are no longer present, and that the role of regulation must be assumed by man; furthermore, that safety lies not in the accumulation of large stocks, but rather in maintaining a population well within the capacity of the land. The fundamental error has been in giving too much attention to the animal itself, and not enough to the health of the natural ecosystem in which it lives.

Most protectionists are motivated to a great extent by a desire to prevent killing of wild animals. It is not surprising, therefore, that reduction programs are vigorously opposed and thus are rarely implemented before serious habitat damage has been done. One alternative that is tried, artificial feeding, leads to a sorry end. The miserable state of the Jackson Hole elk herd is an object lesson. These animals are virtually welfare cases. Continued winter feeding has resulted in the complete destruction of natural forage on the winter range, so that the elk are largely dependent upon artificial winter feed. Stopping the feeding program would all but eliminate the elk herd (Anderson, 1958).

The very people who avidly seek inviolate sanctuaries also abhor the inevitable habitat destruction which follows. The protectionists are appalled by the Tupman Reserve, which has gone through the entire sequence of protection, overpopulation, range destruction, artificial feeding, disease, and eventual (with no other choice) herd reduction—after virtually none of the natural values were left to save. How much wiser it would have been to have instituted a herd control program in the first place.

A similar course of events might well occur if a nature reserve for the tule elk were established. Sooner or later (and, in fact, sooner) it would be necessary to control the herd, and this would be resisted by protectionists; the possible need for herd control is never mentioned in the literature advocating creation of a reserve. Needless to say, the likelihood of ultimate survival of the elk would be greatly reduced by deterioration of the natural habitat.

It is assumed that removal of domestic stock will allow a proportionate number of elk to occupy the range vacated. My range studies clearly show that the kinds of food taken in the bottomlands by domestic cattle and horses in the winter are of little importance to the elk. In fact, they take very little of this forage during the summer when stock is out of the valley. The poorest condition observed in elk during the two years of the study occurred in the Independence herd in June, 1964, when grasses shown in plate 8 were widely available and no stock was present. The critical factor was the absence of adequate forbs because of drought. The fact of the matter is that complete removal of domestic stock would be of minor benefit to the total carrying capacity of the *valley floor* for tule elk.

This is not to say that higher numbers of elk could not be reached, but rather that such higher numbers would be obtained at the expense of the general health of the herd, since the present resources would necessarily be divided among more animals. At present, summer resources in dry years are in low supply, as evidenced by the observation given above on the Independence herd, and by the sharp increase in alfalfa depredations during drought years. Since drought years are so frequent, it seems wise to base carrying capacity of elk on natural forage available in poor years. Any substantial increase in the bottomland herds will mean inadequate resources during drought years in areas where alfalfa is not available, and where it is available, an increase of damage to alfalfa.

Increasing the number of bottomland elk would have a second, and usually unrecognized, danger. Population pressure would tend to cause the closing of the gaps now present between most of the Owens Valley herds. In the event of an outbreak of a virulent disease, there would be nothing to prevent it from passing throughout the entire population from one end of the valley to the other. The significant danger of a disease catastrophe was abundantly emphasized by the outbreak of anthrax in Owens Valley cattle in 1963. Fortunately for the elk, it occurred in an area they had never occupied. Subsequently to the study in the summer of 1968 a second outbreak of anthrax occurred in cattle in an area where elk do frequent. A search by the Department of Fish and Game resulted in the finding of 13 elk carcasses. They were in too advanced a state of decomposition to be certain that negative results obtained from anthrax tests were reliable. Even though all cattle and elk carcasses were burned and the disease arrested, the possibility of further outbreaks of infectious disease is an everpresent hazard to the ultimate survival of the elk. If the population were allowed to become distributed continuously, an infectious disease contracted at any point in the population would be liable to sweep from one end of the valley to the other. While the gaps between herds exist, there is a fair chance of a disease outbreak running its course within one herd area, or being checked by sacrificing only one herd by shooting.

In summary, on the basis of the biology of the tule elk, there is little justification for creating an inviolate sanctuary in Owens Valley. However, I wish to make very clear that this should not be interpreted as an argument against managing Owens Valley as a natural area for esthetic reasons. Certainly, the valley is an area of exceptional beauty and of unusual interest. At the present time, recreation is far and away the most important factor in the local economy, and the demand is rapidly growing; the Los Angeles metropolitan area is only a short day's drive away. The Forest Service, Bureau of Land Management, and the Department of Water and Power in cooperation with Inyo County are rapidly expanding recreational use by development of campsites, etc. Virtually all of the land is already owned by these large agencies, and at present is open to use by the general public.

Owens Valley is not a prime area for agriculture, and livestock raising accounts for a small part of the total economy. Its relative importance will continue to decline as recreational use increases. It is almost inevitable that eventually the valley will be managed for recreational purposes.

The tule elk is an important esthetic resource in the area, and will continue to grow in value. Owens Valley cannot support a vast elk population; yet, managed according to their biological needs, elk can be an important and interesting element of a healthy, natural ecosystem.

DIVERSITY FOR PRESERVATION

The well-known principle of "diversity" as a hedge against instability is applicable to preserving remnant populations of elk. The objective is to spread the resource, so that a catastrophic loss removes only a part of the total. A breeding stock remains to reestablish populations which may be lost. Given the limitations of enhancing the existing tule elk populations, the most logical positive strategy to assure preservation is to establish additional herds.

In a statistical sense, independent probabilities are accumulated by multiplication rather than addition. Assume, for purposes of illustration, that the probability of extinction in each tule elk population is equal only to the number of animals in it. The Owens Valley elk would have an extinction probability of 1 in 300, the Tupman elk 1 in 32, and the Cache Creek elk 1 in 80. The combined probabilities of the latter two herds would be 1 in 2,560 ($\frac{1}{32} \times \frac{1}{80}$). In other words, the 112 elk in these two herds would have a survival probability more than eight times as great as that of the Owens Valley elk. The combined probabilities of all three population would be 1 in 768,000. Thus it is apparent that the addition of even one new herd would yield a greater probable survival of the race than any conceivable increase in the existing herds.

OWENS VALLEY BOTTOMLAND HERDS

It is desirable to maintain as many elk as the limited Owens Valley habitat will support. From figure 38 it can be seen that the Owens Valley herds should not be reduced to below about 200 head. This is the point on the population growth curve where the curve approaches maximum steepness. The recent practice of removing 50 from a herd of 300 or more (16 percent) is a sound one, since it removes only slightly more than the usual annual increase (14 to 15 percent). Thus, hunts would usually be conducted every other year, which will result in less disturbance than holding annual hunts.

At present the hunts are not culling operations simply because culls are so uncommon. Instead, effort has been directed towards taking the oldest animals. Perhaps in future hunts greater efforts could be made to remove bulls with deformed antlers, particularly those with cocked-over pedicels, regardless of the age of the bull. The reason for taking these animals is not to attempt to eliminate this trait from the population; such attempts would probably be unsuccessful. Since these bulls are not able to compete for cows during the rut, and the trait persists, it must be either due to a recessive genetic character or environmentally induced. But these bulls should be taken because they are, in fact, culls, in the sense that they do not contribute to the continuance of the population.

The recent increase in the unhunted Goodale herd means that while many more animals are being counted there in aerial censuses, all of the harvesting is being conducted in the bottomlands. Thus the bottomland herds are being disproportionately harvested. The bottomlands should support at least 250 head distributed approximately 65 in the Bishop herd, 40 in the Tinemaha herd, 80 in the Independence and 65 in the Lone Pine herd. Thus the further increase in Sierra alluvial fan herds should be in addition to the 250 in the bottomlands.

Whether the removal of excess animals should be done by state employees or by the present sport hunting arrangement is a question more political than biological. There is little doubt that the hunt could be conducted more efficiently by state employees. Nevertheless, the hunters, by and large, do enjoy the experience despite the fact that an airplane is used to spot elk (not to drive them, which is largely ineffectual) and that the stalk is coordinated by two-way radios.

I talked to many of the 1964 hunters and found the response generally quite favorable, as had been indicated by questionnaire surveys made by the Department of Fish and Game following previous hunts. Several complaints were made about one of the warden guides, but most of the wardens were praised for their conduct. The warden I observed most closely during the 1964 hunt developed an exceptional rapport with his hunters and did a fine job of conducting the hunt safely and diplomatically.

My talks with participants in the unruly hunts of earlier years convinced me that the guiding system should be retained for safety reasons and to control crippling loss. At present, the $25 elk fee income does not begin to cover the expense of conducting the hunt. A substantial increase in the fee would seem reasonable to help defray costs.

Goodale Herd

This herd has boomed since 1960, and is contining to grow at present. The Goodale and Division Creek bitterbrush stands are being excessively grazed under the combined use of elk and deer. It is apparent that to relieve the pressure upon the bitterbrush will require a reduction in animal numbers, and this, in turn, will require a marked departure from the hunting regulations as now set.

At present, there is virtually no harvest of either deer or elk in the Goodale area. The deer season usually ends about November 1, and the deer do not start to move onto the area until about that time (fig. 31). A few hardy hunters climb the higher country to hunt, but the total kill is insignificant. In 1962 only three bucks were killed in the Goodale Unit and in the last few years 5 to 10 bucks have been taken per year. Antlerless hunts have never been held in the Goodale area.

An adequate harvest of deer will require a much later season and the taking of deer of either sex. The obstacles to obtaining a special late season are great, for many of the local people are opposed to antlerless hunts. There has been a marked decline of deer in much of Inyo County, and this decline has occurred over a period of time when antlerless hunts have been urged by the Department of Fish and Game, and a few hunts actually held. The number of antlerless deer killed was small, and deer declined in areas where antlerless hunts had never been held, as well. Yet, a great many of the local sportsmen are convinced that antlerless hunts caused the decline. The Inyo County Board of Supervisors has the power to veto antlerless hunts, a prerogative that they have exercised.

Neither have elk been harvested from the Goodale range. The absence of roads over much of the area means that most of the stalking would have to be done on foot. Elk in this area are more difficult to spot from the plane, and there is little hope of getting a four-wheel drive vehicle to the kills.

A harvest of Goodale elk will require a warden guide of unusual ability and willingness. I believe that a guide will be desirable, both to control crippling loss and to assure that the hunters are successful. Also, the hunter would have to arrange for transporting the carcass out of the area by pack stock or other means.

A first approximation of the numbers of animals that can be supported in balance with the Goodale bitterbrush can be obtained from a simple model. Since the regression lines in figure 32 predicted with fair accuracy the amount of bitterbrush actually utilized, they can further be used to predict the carrying capacity of the area. The first problem is the great variation in the amount of use, particularly by elk, depending upon the bitterbrush production. Thus it is necessary to select the production level which is the most meaningful on a long-term basis. In figure 29, it is apparent that the mean bitterbrush production (2.9 inches) lies above the majority of past measurements of production. The mode (approximately two inches) is probably a better reflection of the long term production, and this value is used in the model. The regression lines for utilization on animal days per acre for two inches of bitterbrush protection as extrapolated from figure 32 are shown in figure 41.

It is next necessary to establish the amount of bitterbrush utilization that the plants can withstand on a sustained basis. The 60 percent given by Hormay (1943) is the best-substantiated figure available. The number of deer- and elk-days that can be supported is predicted by reading over from 60 percent utilization to the regression lines and down. Animal days per acre can be converted to number of deer for the 670 acres on a 270-day winter season, and to number of elk on a year-long (365 days) basis.

Table 30 shows various carrying capacities calculated under different management programs. Clearly the Goodale area will carry far more elk, due to their broad use of the range, than deer. While the validity of the calculated capacity of 235 elk alone is questionable due to the great extrapolation, in fact 80 elk were on the range for 140 days in the summer and early fall of 1965 and consumed less bitterbrush than the model would predict. The combined deer and elk use as measured by pellet groups gave a prediction of 14 percent utilization while the actual measured utilization was 12.9 percent. Nevertheless, it would be foolhardy to accept the 235 figure at face value without a great deal more testing.

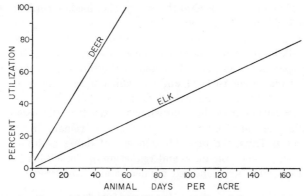

Fig. 41. Regression lines of bitterbrush utilization on elk and deer grazing pressure based upon an extrapolation from the lines in figure 32 to two inches of leader growth. See text for a full discussion.

The significant point is that greater animal numbers (not to consider biomass) can be supported by favoring elk over deer on this area. Similarly, more pressure can be removed from the critical plant, bitterbrush, by reduction of the deer population. It is therefore recommended that on the Goodale area, elk should receive priority in management plans, and that efforts be made toward an effective reduction of deer. At the same time, to assure the continued health and vigor of the herd, the elk population should be stabilized. It is suggested that a conservative figure of between 50 and 80 head be planned for the area, the former figure if reductions of deer cannot be obtained, and the latter if deer reduction can be accomplished. Clearly studies of the Goodale bitterbrush should be continued to assess the effects of management and to point out further adjustments should they become necessary.

The probable results of failure to obtain control of elk and deer populations are several. First, the Goodale elk herd will continue to expand into new areas where grazing pressure is not so heavy. Concurrently, the elk in the present Goodale range will decline in general health, with consequent decline in reproductive and

TABLE 30

CARRYING CAPACITIES OF RANGE AND SIZES OF DEER AND TULE ELK HARVESTS BASED ON VARIOUS MANAGEMENT PLANS FOR THE GOODALE RANGE AS DERIVED FROM A MODEL

(See text.)

Management goal	Carrying capacity		Estimated present population		Harvest indicated	
	Elk	Deer	Elk	Deer	Elk	Deer
Manage for elk only...................	235*	0	80	132	0	132
Manage for deer only..................	0	87	80	132	80	45
Manage for present elk population......	80	50	80	132	0	82
Manage for elk population of 50........	50	67	80	132	30	65

* This number involves such a large extrapolation that the regression line at this point, or the assumption that bitterbrush is the first species to show grazing damage, may not be valid.

survival rates. During the period of this study, the Goodale herd was the healthiest herd in Owens Valley. To a large extent the margin of difference was the high quality forage provided by bitterbrush. Elimination of the bitterbrush would not result in the elk herd being eliminated, since they are able to utilize a number of other forage species successfully. But loss of the bitterbrush would probably be the margin between a robust herd, and one which merely survives.

However, the strong dependence of deer upon bitterbrush as a winter food means that elimination of the bitterbrush would result in the essential elimination of the Goodale deer herd. A few deer would always remain, but at nowhere near the present level. Thus, the probable outcome of doing nothing in the Goodale range is a virtual loss of the deer, and reduction of the elk herd to a subsistence level. Such a situation was reported for deer and elk in Oregon by Cliff (1939).

The "Whitney Herd"

The natural spread southward of the expanding Goodale herd will probably soon colonize the large bitterbrush stands on the alluvial fans between Independence Creek and Lone Pine Creek, adjacent to Mount Whitney. There are few deer on these National Forest lands at present, and livestock allotments are conservative. This area should support 80 to 100 elk, and these animals should definitely be in addition to the 300 allowed in other areas. But in the meantime, effective methods of harvesting Sierra elk herds should be worked out on the Goodale herd. Eventually it will be necessary to control all of the Sierra herds to prevent range deterioration, particularly as regards bitterbrush.

Thus a total population of about 400 head is suggested for Owens Valley when the Whitney herd develops.

Predator Control

The fact that coyotes kill some of the newborn calves may prompt demands for predator control. These demands should be resisted. The goal of the elk management program is to maintain the herd basically for esthetic reasons, and increasing recruitment of calves above the present level will not enhance the esthetic value of the herd. The possible slight increase in elk harvests does not warrant coyote control, since increased hunting should not be the goal of the management plan, but rather a by-product. Further, whether or not the ultimate recruitment rate of calves would increase is unknown; the very fact that calf mortality is heavy at birth may be partially responsible for the low calf mortality thereafter.

A second reason for not controlling coyotes is that coyotes also have high esthetic value. Recreationists enjoy seeing them and hearing their choruses at night. Many sportsmen enjoy coyote hunting in the off season. These recreational uses are increasing the value of having coyotes as part of the natural fauna.

Habitat Manipulation

Because it is desirable to maintain the herd in a natural condition, little in the way of manipulation of the habitat is possible. Growing of feed specifically for the elk should not become part of the management program. However, some manipulations may be feasible within the natural system. For example, a brief flooding of the ponds in the Independence herd area in the early summer of drought years would substantially increase the growth of bassia for summer elk food, if the Department of Water and Power would agree to such a program. The waterways to accomplish flooding are already present. Similarly, in the flats just below Tinemaha Reservoir there is potential for encouraging bassia growth in order to furnish summer forage and reduce the alfalfa damage caused by this herd.

During this study, the Forest Service cleared several plots in the Goodale area in an attempt to establish a new stand of bitterbrush. The attempt was unsuccessful. In this region of low rainfall, establishment of browse is an extremely difficult task. Such clearings do create areas of good forb growth, but the benefits derived probably do not justify the disruption of the naturalness of the area. And the basic problem of too many animals for the amount of forage still remains to be solved.

Tupman Reserve

The present system of herd regulation at the reserve has proven quite satisfactory, and there seems to be little reason for changing it. However, vast improvements in the appearance of the enclosure could, and should, be made. Obviously the area cannot be restored to anything approaching the primitive state; but neither is it necessary to retain the present eyesore. The techniques of park planning to enhance the natural appearance of small areas have advanced rapidly in recent years. Imaginative planning and adequate funding could bring vast improvements.

Cache Creek Herd

There is no reason to believe that the Cache Creek herd is anything but a pure stock of tule elk, and as such, it is an important factor in the preservation of the form. My studies of this herd were too brief to allow me to make any management suggestions. Therefore, the first requirement is a more complete investigation of its status and year-round life cycle. Development of a practical technique for determining year to year population changes, at least on a trend basis, should be one goal of such a study.

San Luis Island

The desirability of establishing tule elk herds in new areas has already been discussed. One prospective area for the development of a herd within the original range is San Luis Island, about eight miles north of Los Banos in Merced County. The island comprises about 14,000 acres and lies between the San Joaquin River on the east and Salt Slough on the west. Both of these streams are slow-flowing creeks today. This is the last large parcel of unfarmed grassland in the San Joaquin Valley bottomland. The essentially natural characteristics of the island give it unique esthetic and scientific values. It is highly desirable that this remnant of the original landscape be preserved in its natural state.

The United States Fish and Wildlife Service has an option on the southern part of the island (7,630 acres) for acquisition as a waterfowl refuge. This property has rights to 91.9 acre feet of water, and at present has the canals and pumps necessary to put the water on the land.

With the concept of a natural area, it is desirable that the tule elk, once native here, be reintroduced. The ultimate value of the elk on San Luis Island will depend upon how well it is integrated into the total environment.

Since the streamcourses on either side of the island do not present a barrier to the tule elk, a suitable fence will have to be erected to prevent the elk from moving onto the adjacent agricultural lands. The area enclosed should be very large to retain the impression of a small free-roaming herd in a natural area.

Animals for the introduction can be the surplus animals from the Tupman Elk Reserve. This stock has the advantage of being easily obtained and is relatively tame, which will aid in handling and transporting, and ease the adjustment to the new environment.

There is little question that the elk will build up to destructive levels if allowed to increase without check. It is extremely important that the elk be held to a level which will not endanger the habitat of the other native species, or cause alterations in the natural vegetation.

SUMMARY

A study of the tule elk (*Cervus elaphus nannodes*) was conducted to determine its history and present status and to establish its ecological relationships. Between January, 1962, and June, 1963, a taxonomic study and an intensive historical literature review were carried out on the Berkeley campus. A two-year field study of the living populations was conducted from July, 1963, to July, 1965, under a grant from Resources For the Future, Inc.

The tule elk is a small, light-colored form which was probably derived from the Rocky Mountain race (*C. e. nelsoni*). It is adapted to living primarily on open valley bottomlands, although foothill areas were used at certain seasons originally, and are yet today. It is specialized for living in semi-arid conditions. It originally occupied the Sacramento and San Joaquin valleys of California and favorable larger valleys of the coast ranges from approximatley Santa Barbara north to near the Russian River in Sonoma County.

In pristine times, the tule elk was abundant through much of its range. Settlement by European man began in 1769, and although elk were reduced locally in the following years, they maintained good populations over most of the range until the gold rush in 1849. In the following decade market hunting caused the population to crash. By 1870 only a single small band remained in the tule swamps of Buena Vista Lake in Kern County. All of the present populations were derived from this remnant.

The Tupman Reserve herd near Tupman, California, is kept in an enclosure near the remnant range. This herd is maintained largely on artificial feed and is held to a winter population of 32 head. A second population, the Cache Creek herd, is free-roaming over the grass-oak and chaparral hillsides in the inner coast range about the Lake-Colusa county line. The herd was derived from a transplant, and the present population is estimated to be about 80. A third wild population, also established by transplanting, lives in Owens Valley on the east side of the Sierra Nevada in Inyo County. This area was outside the original range of tule elk, but they have prospered here, and are now held to a maximum of 300 head by periodic controlled hunts. Field work was concentrated on this population, with the other two visited infrequently to obtain comparative data.

In Owens Valley, the elk range from Bishop on the north to Lone Pine, some 80 miles to the south, and into the foothills on either side of the valley. The elk occur in five fairly distinct herds having little interchange between them, with the exception of bulls wandering during the rut. Four, the Bishop, Tinemaha, Independence, and Lone Pine herds, use favorable locales in the bottomlands through most of the year, but make some use of foothill areas during the winter and spring. The fifth, the Goodale herd, lives on the Sierra alluvial fans throughout the year. Intensive field observations were made on the Independence herd.

Social hierarchies are well developed in both sexes and are basically linear. The herding habit is strongly developed and herds are highly integrated and coordinated. Leadership is usually by adult females, but no single individual is the fixed leader. Rather, the animal taking the initiative serves as the leader. Bulls and cows tend to remain separated during much of the year. Bulls join the cow groups during the rut. Cow groups break up during the calving season.

The timing of the rut, and indeed, of the entire life cycle, varies from year to year depending upon forage conditions. Under good conditions the rut is early, while in poor years it is late. The largest bulls come out of velvet earliest. The bull which comes out of velvet first (primary bull) controls the cows during the early part of the rut.

During the rut, a cohort of bulls remains near every cow herd and is kept out of the herd by the master bull. These bulls, plus the rebellious cows, keep pressure on the master bull. Serious challenges do not occur until the master bull is nearly exhausted. Only the dominant bull of the cohort is a potential challenger. Usually challenges occur following a copulation, when the bachelor bull cohort rushes into the herd and mills about. When the primary bull is defeated, the herd is split up among two or three secondary bulls, which are the next in the hierarchy. These, in turn, are replaced by the next rank of bulls (tertiary). Outside bulls take their appropriate places in the hierarchy and their contribution to the rut depends upon their rank.

In a herd of about 50 cows and calves, about 12 bulls out of 29 play an important role. The largest bulls perform nearly all of the copulations.

Most tule elk cows breed as yearlings. Examination of reproductive tracts of females taken in the fall hunts showed that about 90 percent of the females carried a fetus at that time. Calves are born in April and May after a gestation of about 250 days. They weigh about 20 pounds at birth and grow at about a pound per day during early life. Calves tend to remain in the same general area when the cow is absent. The cow normally remains nearby to defend the calf.

By the time the new calves join the herd, only about 33 percent of the cows are with calves. Whether most of this mortality occurs *in utero* or after birth is not known. However, coyotes do kill some of the newborn calves. Calves which live to join the herd usually survive to the yearling stage. Mortality of yearling and older elk was about twice as high among males as among females.

Recruitment of calves is about 18 to 20 percent of the herd per year. The typical rate of increase of the herd when not hunted is about 14 to 15 percent. Thus 4 to 5 percent mortality of adult animals due to causes other than legal hunts must occur. Most adult mortality is caused by illegal shooting and accidents. Parasites and diseases appear to be minor problems. Over the years legal hunting has accounted for a large proportion of the total mortality.

Foods during the spring and summer consist largely of forbs and ditch bank vegetation, including willow leaves and twigs. In winter, browse supplemented with dry grasses is more important. Chemical analysis of forage species showed spring to be the time of highest nutritional content. Most growth processes, such as antler regrowth, molt, and calving, occur during this season. Most nutrients declined through the summer. Browse species remain more stable through the year than herbaceous species.

Comparative studies of nutrition suggested that the Tupman Reserve elk, which are artificially fed, are on a good diet, while that of the wild Owens Valley and Cache Creek elk fluctuates greatly depending upon forage conditions. Studies of mineral nutrition suggest that the brittle antlers of the Owens Valley elk are not due to molybdenum poisoning, but rather to a combination of insufficient phosphorus and early maturation of antlers.

Damage to alfalfa fields by elk is the most important conflict with agriculture in Owens Valley. The amount of alfalfa damage is inversely related to the availability of native forage, which in turn is dependent upon the amount of rainfall. Damage to fences is another important conflict, while depredation of supplemental feed put out for livestock seems to be a minor problem.

Competition between elk and cattle in the foothill areas may occur whenever the two species occupy the same range. Competition between cattle, horses, and elk in the bottomlands is minor, since the elk take mainly forage which is unavailable in winter for domestic stock. On the other hand, elk make relatively light use of coarse, dry grasses, the major winter forage for stock. Competition between deer and elk occurs in the Goodale area where both species make heavy use of bitterbrush. Competition between Sierra bighorn sheep and elk is slight due to the marginal overlapping of their respective ranges.

The potential for increasing the elk population in Owens Valley even if domestic stock were reduced is quite limited. Most of the potential for increased numbers lies in expansion to presently unoccupied range. Diversification by establishing many separate herds is discussed as a strategy for preservation as an alternative to accumulation of numbers. With this rationale, it is highly desirable that additional herds be established in new areas.

Maintenance of esthetic value should continue to be the primary objective of management programs, with hunting as an incidental benefit stemming from the need for herd control. Management programs should preserve the natural environment, and maintain the elk as a self-sustaining component of the ecosystem.

ACKNOWLEDGMENTS

I want to thank Resources For the Future, Inc., for the two-year grant which supported the field study. Also, I want to express my appreciation to Mr. Horace Albright for his long-time interest in the tule elk, and his special efforts in making this study possible.

Mineral determinations on tissue samples were supported by a grant from the Union Foundation Wildlife Fund of the Museum of Vertebrate Zoology.

Dr. A. Starker Leopold supervised the entire project. Advice in special areas was given by Drs. Seth B. Benson, Harold F. Heady, Arnold Schultz, H. H. Biswell, and J. J. Hird, and by Messrs. P. Dean Smith, Jack Beer, William Dasmann, Everett Doman, Edward Schneegas, and Paul Lane.

Dr. Robert T. Orr allowed me to examine specimens in the California Academy of Sciences. Dr. Raymond F. Dasmann facilitated my study of the skulls in the Humboldt State College collection. Messrs. Charles Repenning, Shirley Weise, Carlo DeFerrari, and William Edmands allowed me to study specimens in their possession.

The cooperation received in my field work was outstanding, and I am pleased to give credit for this assistance. Without it, many of the studies reported here could not have been carried out.

The California Department of Fish and Game gave assistance at all levels. At the local offices, Jack Beer, Mark Halderman, Chuck Monroe, Vern Koontz, Morris Anderson, Charles Kanig, Vern Burandt, and Jake Meyers helped me in many ways. Dick Davidson, Game Supervisor for Region V, cleared much red tape, and Pat Symons, pilot, besides being extremely competent at his profession, gave me much information on previous censuses. Special thanks are due to the wardens and biologists who helped to collect biological samples during the 1964 hunt.

In Sacramento, Director Walter Shannon, Chief of Game Ben Glading and Game Supervisor Wallace MacGregor cleared the way for several important facets of the study. Oscar Brunetti and Bruce Browning of the Fish and Game Laboratory performed analyses which are beyond my competence. Howard Leach arranged for my survey of San Luis Island. In Region II Harvey Russo and Roy Erwin assisted with my work on the Cache Creek herd. In Region I Kenneth Conrad and Fred Ross obtained comparative samples from the Roosevelt elk.

In the Forest Service, special thanks go to Edward Schneegas, Wildlife Biologist of Inyo National Forest, for the considerable field assistance he gave me in the Goodale elk studies, and for collecting biological samples during the first day of the 1964 hunt. Also deserving thanks are Joseph Radel, Hatch Graham, Harold Hunter, Nick Zufelt, Hal McElroy, Tyson Harold, Ben Casad, and Marion Borrell.

Derrel Fulwider of the Bureau of Land Management assisted me in many of the range studies. Other bureau people who gave field assistance include Ed Smith, Bob Springer, Ray Brubaker, and Jim Garner.

My work at the Tupman Elk Reserve was advanced by former State Park Ranger William Walker, and present Ranger John P. Anderson and Assistant Ranger Dick Carr. John Michael, Lewis Wakefield, Leonard Penhale and Lloyd Lively all assisted me in obtaining samples of these animals when they were needed.

Paul Lane, Northern District Engineer for the Los Angeles Department of Water and Power, gave me full access to their files and maps, and aided in many other ways. Bob Phillips, Chief Aqueduct Engineer, also encouraged the study, and many department employees passed on important observations, particularly those whose normal work brought them into frequent contact with elk. Harold (Skinny) Gates, Archie Woodward, and Lewis Prange deserve special mention.

The nutritional studies were conducted in cooperation with P. Dean Smith, Inyo-Mono County Farm Advisor, who aided me in numerous ways. John Rible, Extension Technologist at Riverside, performed the chemical analyses of vegetation. Mrs. Alice McClosky, Extension Botanist at Davis, identified many plant specimens.

Joseph J. Hird, Bishop veterinarian, cooperated with the molybdenum poisoning studies; he furnished collection equipment, technical advice, and use of analytical equipment. M. L. Murdock, Robert V. Lewis, and John S. Orsborn of the San Gabriel Laboratory performed tests for brucellosis, leptospirosis, and infectious bovine rhinotracheitis.

Local ranchers John Lacey, Charles and Mike Connor, and packer Herb London allowed special studies to be carried out on their leases. The local cattlemen and packers, almost without exception, were very cooperative and passed on their observations made over the years. Although many of them questioned my motives at first, mutual confidence developed with time, and many frank discussions ensued.

In the Cache Creek area, ranchers Terhel Sartain and Edgar Mitchell were cooperative in allowing access and furnishing information. Steven Logsden of Humboldt State College furnished antler samples from the Roosevelt elk which he obtained during his studies of this race. Alvero D. Sousa of Los Banos arranged and guided my tour of San Luis Island.

Numerous other individuals gave me the benefit of their observations, and continuously reported sightings of elk. For this information and numerous kindnesses I am grateful, and regret that it is not possible to mention the individuals. Such a list would read very much like the Owens Valley telephone book.

The greatest assistance came from my wife Karen. At various times she served as laboratory assistant, calculator operator, receptionist, secretary-typist, editor, and dispenser of advice, part of which was solicited.

APPENDIX A

DESCRIPTION OF SKULL MEASUREMENTS AND MEASUREMENT DATA OF WESTERN NORTH AMERICAN RACES OF CERVUS ELAPHUS

DESCRIPTION OF SKULL MEASUREMENTS

Condylobasal length—greatest length from the rear of the condyles to the tip of the premaxilla.

Zygomatic arch width—greatest width across the skull on the outsides of the zygomatic arches.

Orbital width—greatest width taken across the skull from orbit to orbit.

Mastoid width—greatest width across on the outsides of the mastoids.

Brain case width—greatest width of the brain case in the periotal-occipital region.

Condyle width—greatest width across from the outside of one occipital condyle to the outside of the other.

Foramen magnum width—greatest inside width across the foramen magnum.

Upper toothrow—greatest length from the anterior of premolar 2 to the posterior of molar 3, always measured on the left side unless that side was clearly abnormally deformed.

Upper diastema—shortest length from the anterior alveolus of PM^2 to the tip of the premaxillary.

Canine width—greatest width across the maxillaries just above the canines.

Palatal length—least length from the anterior tip of the premaxillaries to the posterior edge of the palatines above the sphenoid canals.

Maxillary ridge width—least width across the ridge on the maxillaries approximately one-half way between the canines and PM^2.

Width across PM^2—greatest width taken across on the outsides of the PM^2.

Width of PM^2—greatest width of the left first premolar.

Width across M^2—greatest width across taken outside of the second molars.

Width of M^2—greatest width across the second molar.

Nasal length—greatest length of the left nasal bone from the anterior tip to the posterior suture with the frontal bone.

Nasal width—greatest width across both nasals at their widest points just anterior to the lacrimal bones.

Lower toothrow—greatest length from the anterior of PM^2 to the posterior of M^3 on the left ramus.

Lower diastema—least length of the left ramus from the posterior of the canine alveolus to the anterior of PH^2 alveolus.

Infraorbital width—greatest width across at the openings of the infraorbital canals.

DESCRIPTION OF SKULL QUALITATIVE CHARACTERS

Condyle projection—the degree to which the occipital condyles project downward as opposed to rearward.

Foramen magnum groove—the conformation of the foramen magnum groove as viewed from the ventral surface.

Bullae conformation—fullness as opposed to flatness of the anterio-ventral portion of the bullae.

Alisphenoid canal—development as opposed to reduction of the alisphenoid canal.

Ovale-alisphenoid groove—development or lack of a groove connecting the foramen ovale and alisphenoid canal.

MEASUREMENT DATA

	Males				Females			
	N	x̄	SD	Range	N	x̄	SD	Range
Condylobasal length								
nannodes								
Buttonwillow ..	19	416.3	13.83	392–434	6	397.5	5.20	393–405
Owens Valley ..	5	423.4	6.76	414–432	1	384	....	.....
South coast*...	1	429(442)	....	.....	..	....	....	.....
Cache Creek...	..	....	....	.....	3	399.3	....	395–402
nelsoni..........	6	470.3	15.05	460–500	4	419	....	409–434
roosevelti........	11	451.9	9.31	434–463	6	434.5	14.05	420–448
Zygomatic arch								
nannodes								
Buttonwillow ..	19	167.4	7.27	154–183	6	160.2	4.49	154–166
Owens Valley...	9	175.6	4.36	170–181	1	160	....	.....
South coast....	2	175.5(175)	....	174–177	..	....	....	.....
Cache Creek...	..	....	....	.....	3	161.3	....	158–164
nelsoni..........	7	187.3	3.76	183–193	4	169.8	....	161–175
roosevelti........	11	183.9	5.99	172–189	6	171.8	6.97	163–180
Orbital width								
nannodes								
Buttonwillow ..	19	189.5	7.66	178–204	6	174.7	2.15	171–177
Owens Valley ..	8	195.9	4.19	190–202	1	171.0	....	.....
South coast....	3	191.3(210)	....	182–197	..	....	....	.....
Cache Creek...	..	....	....	.....	3	178.0	....	173–183
nelsoni..........	8	208.4	3.82	204–215	4	181	....	171–187
roosevelti........	11	203.7	5.35	193–213	6	184.5	2.42	173–192
Mastoid width								
nannodes								
Buttonwillow ..	19	143.9	6.38	134–158	6	127.0	3.58	122–130
Owens Valley ..	11	146.5	5.82	130–152	1	122.0	....	.....
South coast....	4	150.5(160)	....	143–160	..	....	....	.....
Cache Creek...	..	....	....	.....	4	127.3	....	122–130
nelsoni..........	8	161.4	4.60	154–168	4	135.3	....	131–142
roosevelti........	13	159.8	7.29	148–173	7	140.9	2.12	131–149

* The first value given is for subfossil specimens. The second value given in parenthesis is from the recent specimen transplanted from Buttonwillow to Monterey.

MEASUREMENT DATA—*Continued*

	Males				Females			
	N	$\bar{x}$	SD	Range	N	$\bar{x}$	SD	Range
Brain case								
nannodes								
Buttonwillow ..	19	103.7	2.75	101–112	6	97.7	2.53	94–100
Owens Valley ..	11	104.6	3.33	96–108	1	96.0	....	.....
South coast....	3	107.7(111)	....	103–113	..	....	....	.....
Cache Creek...	..	....	....	.....	4	93.8	....	92–98
nelsoni..........	8	113.2	2.90	109–118	4	103.3	....	97–111
roosevelti.........	13	111.5	4.86	102–115	7	102.0	3.51	97–107
Condyle width								
nannodes								
Buttonwillow ..	19	80.2	2.94	74–85	6	76.2	1.88	74–79
Owens Valley ..	11	79.2	2.14	76–82	1	72.5	....	.....
South coast....	4	84.9(81.7)	....	79–87	..	....	....	.....
Cache Creek...	..	....	....	.....	4	74.1	....	69–76
nelsoni..........	8	91.0	3.31	86–96	4	85.6	....	81–91
roosevelti.........	13	91.9	3.18	88–99	7	86.3	4.03	82–92
Foramen magnum								
nannodes								
Buttonwillow ..	19	31.5	2.72	25.4–37.7	6	33.6	5.33	23.5–39.1
Owens Valley ..	11	30.4	2.06	27.0–33.0	1	34.7	....	.....
South coast....	4	33.1(32.0)	....	30.2–34.5	..	....	....	.....
Cache Creek...	..	....	....	.....	4	34.4	....	32.2–35.6
nelsoni..........	8	36.15	2.83	31.2–38.9	4	41.0	....	36.7–44.8
roosevelti.........	13	41.9	2.56	38.0–46.0	7	42.5	1.62	40.0–44.5
Upper toothrow								
nannodes								
Buttonwillow ..	19	143.0	2.92	136–147	6	139.5	2.41	137–144
Owens Valley ..	7	138.5	6.02	127–146	1	128.9	....	.....
South coast....	1	135(135)	....	.....	..	....	....	.....
Cache Creek...	..	....	....	.....	3	132.3	....	130–137
nelsoni..........	8	135.4	6.57	121–144	4	130.3	....	125–137
roosevelti.........	9	134.8	7.18	125–145	7	134.1	4.10	130–139

MEASUREMENT DATA—*Continued*

	Males				Females			
	N	$\bar{X}$	SD	Range	N	$\bar{X}$	SD	Range
Upper diastema								
nannodes								
Buttonwillow ..	19	131.0	5.45	123–138	6	128.9	2.89	126–134
Owens Valley ..	5	131.4	2.34	130–135	1	122.8	....	.....
South coast....	1	139(141)	....	.....	..	....	....	.....
Cache Creek...	..	.....	....	.....	3	132.3	....	129–135
nelsoni..........	6	150.2	4.27	147–157	4	138.3	....	135–142
roosevelti........	9	144.8	4.42	140–154	6	141.5	6.62	133–150
Canine width								
nannodes								
Buttonwillow ..	19	83.8	4.74	76–92	6	77.2	2.78	73–80
Owens Valley ..	6	87.8	3.14	84–91	1	77	....	.....
South coast....	1	87(95)	....	.....	..	....	....	.....
Cache Creek...	..	....	....	.....	3	80.2	....	78–82
nelsoni..........	8	89.9	3.03	86–94	4	76.3	....	73–79
roosevelti........	9	90.5	3.31	86–94	6	80.8	3.11	76–84
Palatal length								
nannodes								
Buttonwillow ..	19	251.8	9.48	240–268	6	248.2	3.55	244–253
Owens Valley ..	5	261.2	5.32	255–269	1	244	....	.....
South coast....	1	265(271)	....	.....	..	....	....	.....
Cache Creek...	..	....	....	.....	3	254	....	252–257
nelsoni..........	6	287.2	7.89	281–300	4	260.3	....	250–269
roosevelti........	4	272.0	....	270–273	4	269.5	....	264–277
Maxillary ridge width								
nannodes								
Buttonwillow ..	19	40.3	3.46	34.8–48.0	6	36.4	3.23	31.4–39.9
Owens Valley ..	7	43.6	4.50	41.3–46.0	1	42.2	....	.....
South coast....	1	36.5(41.9)	....	.....	..	....	....	.....
Cache Creek...	..	....	....	.....	3	39.7	....	38.0–41.1
nelsoni..........	8	40.63	2.90	37.7–45.4	4	35.4	....	32.6–37.2
roosevelti........	9	41.22	4.23	32.7–45.0	6	38.1	3.43	34.0–42.6

MEASUREMENT DATA—*Continued*

	Males				Females			
	N	$\bar{\text{x}}$	SD	Range	N	$\bar{\text{x}}$	SD	Range
Width across PM²								
nannodes								
Buttonwillow ..	19	84.2	4.34	78.3–92.6	6	83.3	4.04	77.4–89.2
Owens Valley ..	6	98.2	4.18	92.3–104.5	1	92.1	....	.....
South coast....	1	88.7(95.7)	....	.....	..	....	....	.....
Cache Creek...	..	....	....	.....	3	93.2	....	91.1–95.3
nelsoni..........	8	93.3	2.31	88.3–96.0	4	86.6	....	80.4–89.7
roosevelti........	7	92.1	6.99	83.8–105	6	91.3	3.26	87.7–96.0
Width of PM²								
nannodes								
Buttonwillow ..	19	17.6	.76	16.3–19.3	6	16.8	.45	16.1–17.3
Owens Valley ..	7	17.9	.85	16.6–18.9	1	16.1	....	.....
South coast....	1	17.2(18.7)	....	.....	..	....	....	.....
Cache Creek...	..	....	....	.....	3	17.2	....	16.4–18.0
nelsoni..........	8	18.7	.67	17.7–19.8	4	17.8	....	17.3–18.2
roosevelti........	7	16.7	.68	16.0–18.0	7	17.5	1.50	15.0–19.7
Width across M²								
nannodes								
Buttonwillow ..	19	121.9	5.25	107–130	6	121.6	4.03	116–128
Owens Valley ..	7	127.5	5.96	117–133	1	124.0	....	.....
South coast....	1	121(137)	....	.....	..	....	....	.....
Cache Creek...	..	....	....	.....	3	129.0	....	125–133
nelsoni..........	8	131.3	3.37	129–139	4	124.7	....	122–131
roosevelti........	7	125.9	3.25	121–128	6	127.9	5.80	119–134
Width of M²								
nannodes								
Buttonwillow ..	17	27.3	1.27	24.8–29.8	6	26.7	.88	25.5–27.8
Owens Valley ..	7	26.9	1.76	24.2–28.5	1	25.0	....	.....
South coast....	1	28.6(30.9)	....	.....	..	....	....	.....
Cache Creek...	..	....	....	.....	3	26.7	....	25.9–27.3
nelsoni..........	8	28.7	.74	27.5–29.8	4	27.7	....	26.7–28.6
roosevelti........	7	29.2	.67	28.0–30.0	7	28.7	1.10	27.3–30.5

MEASUREMENT DATA—*Continued*

	Males				Females			
	N	X̄	SD	Range	N	X̄	SD	Range
Nasal length								
nannodes								
Buttonwillow ..	19	149.5	8.50	149–162	6	136.6	6.25	130–145
Owens Valley ..	7	159.1	3.85	152–165	..	....	....	.....
South coast....	1	162(162)	....	.....	..	....	....	.....
Cache Creek...	..	....	....	.....	3	141.0	....	134–147
nelsoni..........	8	166.3	8.63	158–183	4	150.0	....	144–159
roosevelti........	7	169.4	9.42	151–182	6	156.6	8.61	146–170
Nasal width								
nannodes								
Buttonwillow ..	19	61.4	3.15	56–68	6	56.4	1.25	53–60
Owens Valley ..	7	61.8	3.50	58–67	..	....	....	.....
South coast....	..	....	....	.....	..	....	....	.....
Cache Creek...	..	....	....	.....	3	52.2	....	51–54
nelsoni..........	7	67.0	5.52	61–77	4	59.9	....	53–65
roosevelti........	7	65.0	3.97	60–69	6	62.5	5.86	53–70
Lower toothrow								
nannodes								
Buttonwillow ..	17	150.5	4.09	141–156	6	146.8	1.84	144–149
Owens Valley ..	7	146.9	4.31	139–152	1	139.3	....	.....
South coast....	1	149(149)	....	.....	..	....	....	.....
Cache Creek...	..	....	....	.....	3	142.7	....	139–149
nelsoni..........	6	145.7	6.74	135–156	3	139.0	....	138–140
roosevelti........	4	146.8	....	136–156	6	143.7	0.42	139–149
Lower diastema								
nannodes								
Buttonwillow ..	17	99.4	5.97	92–113	6	95.8	3.65	92–100
Owens Valley ..	7	101.5	4.31	97–108	1	91.1	....	.....
South coast....	1	104(113)	....	.....	..	....	....	.....
Cache Creek...	..	....	....	.....	3	98.7	....	94–103
nelsoni..........	6	115.1	4.40	109–122	3	100.1	....	98–103
roosevelti........	4	103.8	....	99–111	6	104.5	8.06	94–115

MEASUREMENT DATA—*Continued*

	Males				Females			
	N	X̄	SD	Range	N	X̄	SD	Range
Infraorbital foramen width								
nannodes								
Buttonwillow ..	19	75.0	4.02	68–85	6	71.1	2.61	67–73
Owens Valley ..	8	79.8	4.61	74–88	1	73.9	....	.....
South coast....	1	77(80)	....	.....	..	....	....	.....
Cache Creek...	..	....	....	.....	3	70.9	....	69–73
nelsoni..........	8	83.2	4.88	74–89	4	68.9	....	65–73
roosevelti........	7	83.6	4.57	78–88	6	74.5	4.84	68–81

APPENDIX B

RECORDS OF OCCURRENCE OF ELK
USED TO PLOT THE ORIGINAL DISTRIBUTION

RECORDS OF CERVUS ELAPHUS NANNODES

ALAMEDA COUNTY: Altamont Pass (Manly, 1894); Berkeley (Font: Bolton, 1931); near Livermore (J. Clyman: Camp, 1928); Oakland near Mill College (J. Crespi: Bolton, 1927).

BUTTE COUNTY: Feather River, 15 mi. N of confluence with Yuba River (J. Work: Maloney, 1945); Feather River at Honcut Cr. (J. Smith: Sullivan, 1934); near Oroville (J. Work: Maloney, 1945); Sacramento River, 7 mi. N Chico Cr. (J. Smith: Sullivan, 1934); Sacramento River at Chico Cr. (J. Work: Maloney, 1945); Sacramento River, 19 mi. N Butte Cr. near Jacinto (ibid).

COLUSA COUNTY: Sacramento River, 7 mi. NW Butte Cr. (J. Smith: Sullivan, 1934); Sacramento River at Butte Cr. (J. Work: Maloney, 1945); at edge of plains W of Williams (ibid).

CONTRA COSTA COUNTY: near (east of) Antioch (Font: Bolton, 1931); Los Madanos (Lyman, 1931); Martinez (H. C. Banta: Evermann, 1915); Moraga Valley (Bosqui, 1904); San Ramon Valley (W. Brewer: Farquhar, 1949).

FRESNO COUNTY: Fresno (H. C. Banta: Evermann, 1915); left bank of San Joaquin River, 37°N, 119° 40′ W (Edgar, 1893).

GLENN COUNTY: 10 mi SW Jacinto (J. Work: Maloney, 1945); Sacramento River (ibid).

KERN COUNTY: Buena Vista Lake (H. C. Banta: Evermann, 1915); Buttonwillow (4 specimens in MVZ); 6 mi. SW Buttonwillow (2 specimens in MVZ); 4 mi. S Buttonwillow (specimen in MVZ); 4½ mi. S Buttonwillow (specimen in MVZ); Township 30 N, R 25E (3 specimens in MVZ); China Grade Bluffs, 4 mi. NE Bakersfield (5 specimens in MVZ); Kern River (Grayson, 1920); 10 mi. E. McKettrick (specimen in MVZ); 2½ mi. SW Tupman (specimen in MVZ).

KINGS COUNTY: Lake Fork of the Tulare River near the lake (Frémont, ed. Nevins, 1956); Tulare Lake (Grayson, 1920); Whisky Slough, Tulare Lake (H. C. Banta: Evermann, 1915); Tule Lake Island, Tulare Lake (J. C. Adams: Hittell, 1911).

LAKE COUNTY: Clear Lake region (Gibbs, 1860); S side of Clear Lake (J. Work: Maloney, 1945).

MADERA COUNTY: a small stream just N of San Joaquin River, lat. 37° 08′, long. 120° 45′ 22″ (Frémont, ed. Nevins, 1956).

MARIN COUNTY: Bolinas (C. A. Allen: Evermann, 1915); Limantour Bay, Point Reyes (P. S. Shafter: Evermann, 1915); Point Reyes Peninsula (Revere, 1922); San Francisco Bay from Angel Island N to San Rafael (Duhaut-Cilly, 1934); San Geronimo (Joseph Mailliard, letter in MVZ, June 23, 1912) ; Tomales Bay (P. S. Shafter: Evermann, 1915) ; mouth of Tomales Bay (C. A. Allen: Evermann, 1915).

MERCED COUNTY: Merced River at the foothills (Frémont, ed. Nevins, 1956) ; opposite side of river from above (ibid) ; Merced River E of San Joaquin River (Manley, 1894) ; San Joaquin River opposite Merced (ibid) ; Sulphur River (?), 40 mi. E of Mission San Juan Bautista (Z. Leonard: Quaife, 1934) ; base of hills at the mouth of Yosemite Valley (ibid).

MONTEREY COUNTY: Monterey Bay (Vizcaino, 1891; Chinard, 1937; Humboldt, 1811; Fisher, 1934) ; Salinas Valley (F. Mauk: Evermann, 1915) ; between Salinas River and Watsonville (ibid) ; Watsonville Junction (J. Pillesier: Evermann, 1915).

NAPA COUNTY: near Monticello (J. Work: Maloney, 1945) ; Napa Valley one-half way between San Francisco Bay and Clear Lake (J. Clyman: Camp, 1926)

SACRAMENTO COUNTY: Grand Island (H. C. Banta: Evermann, 1915) ; Sacramento City (J. Work: Maloney, 1945) ; Sacramento River, 12 mi. N American River (J. Smith: Sullivan, 1934) ; Sacramento River, 1 day N American River (Wilkes, 1845) ; Sacramento River, 19 mi. S Woodland (J. Work: Maloney, 1945) ; Sacramento River near Cordelia (ibid) ; 20 mi. E of Sacramento River around a lake (ibid) ; Sacramento River, 8 mi. N Cosumnes River (ibid) ; Sacramento River, 10 mi. N Mokelumne River (ibid) ; mouth of Sacramento River, S shore (J. Rockwell: Evermann, 1915) ; mouth of San Joaquin River (J. Smith: Sullivan, 1934).

SAN BENITO COUNTY: near Hernandez (Grinnell, 1933).

SAN FRANCISCO COUNTY: Fort Point (Font: Bolton, 1931) ; mouth of San Francisco Bay (Dana, 1840).

SAN JOAQUIN COUNTY: near (S) Bethany (Font: Bolton, 1931) ; French Camp (J. Work: Maloney, 1945) ; 12 mi. S French Camp (ibid) ; Middle River (San Joaquin) (California Fish and Game, 1918) ; Mokelumne River (J. Work: Maloney, 1945) ; San Joaquin City (H. C. Banta: Evermann, 1915) ; N Fork San Joaquin River near Mokelumne River (ibid) ; Stanislaus River (J. Smith; Sullivan, 1934) ; Stockton (J. Work: Maloney, 1945).

SAN LUIS OBISPO COUNTY: Cuyama Valley (Grinnell, 1933).

SAN MATEO COUNTY: Pacifica (fossil specimen in MVZ) ; Purisima Cr. (specimen in Calif. Acad. Sciences).

SANTA BARBARA COUNTY: Cuyama Valley (Grinnell, 1933) ; Rincon Point (Fisher, 1930) ; Santa Barbara coast (Rodgers, 1929; Gifford, 1940).

SANTA CLARA COUNTY: S end of San Francisco Bay (Grinnell, 1933).

SANTA CRUZ COUNTY: College Lake or Pinto Lake near Watsonville (J. Crespi: Bolton, 1927) ; Pajaro Valley (F. Mauk: Evermann, 1915).

SHASTA COUNTY: Cow Cr. 10 mi. N confluence with Sacramento River (J. Work: Maloney, 1945) ; Cow Cr. 8 mi. N confluence with Sacramento River (ibid) ; Cow Cr. at Sacramento River (ibid).

SOLANO COUNTY: Sacramento River, 27 mi. S Woodland (J. Work: Maloney, 1945) ; Sacramento River ± 40 mi. below Sacramento (N. Kingsley: Teggart, 1914) ; Suisun Marsh (Ellsworth, 1931; J. Paine: Evermann, 1915; N. Kingsley: Teggart, 1914) ; one day N Suisun Marsh at headwaters of Suisun Cr. (J. Work: Maloney, 1945) ; edge of the hills near Vacaville (ibid).

SONOMA COUNTY: Buena Vista Canyon near Buena Vista (Ellsworth, 1930) ; Green Valley (Gregson and Gregson, 1940) ; between Healdsburg and Geyserville (Finley, 1937) ; Petaluma (Gregson and Gregson, 1940) ; Petaluma Cr. (MacKenzie: Evermann, 1915) ; Sonoma Cr. (J. Altimira: Finley, 1937) ; 8 mi. W Sonoma Cr. (J. Work: Maloney, 1945).

STANISLAUS COUNTY: Dry Cr. near (E) Turlock (Bosqui, 1904) ; Newman (H. C. Banta: Evermann, 1915) ; San Joaquin Ferry, 1 day S of Tuolumne River (Hill's Ferry?) (Clarke, 1852) ; San Joaquin River at mouth of Tuolumne River (Frémont, ed. Nevins, 1956) ; Stanislaus River (J. Work: Maloney, 1945) ; Stanislaus River, 25 mi. E of confluence (Frémont, ed. Nevins, 1956) ; between Stockton and Merced (Bosqui, 1904) ; a tributary S of Tuolumne River, 5 mi. E of San Joaquin River (Frémont, ed. Nevins, 1956).

SUTTER COUNTY: Feather River, 10 mi. N confluence with Sacramento River (J. Smith: Sullivan, 1934) ; Feather River near Nicolaus (J. Work: Maloney, 1945) ; Feather River confluence (J. Smith: Sullivan, 1934) ; NE side Marysville (Sutters) Buttes (J. Work: Maloney, 1945) ; Sacramento River, 11 mi. S Butte Cr. (ibid) ; Sacramento River, 23 mi. N American River (J. Smith: Sullivan, 1934).

T<small>EHAMA</small> C<small>OUNTY</small>: French Crossing on Sacramento River, one day S Pine Cr. (J. Work: Maloney, 1945); Sacramento River, one day N Chico Cr. (ibid); Sacramento River, 6 mi. N Deer Cr. (ibid); 2 mi SE South Yolla Bolla Mt. (specimen in MVZ).

T<small>ULARE</small> C<small>OUNTY</small>: Tule Swamp S of Kaweah River (Grayson, 1920).

Y<small>OLO</small> C<small>OUNTY</small>: at edge of plains W of Dunnigan (J. Work: Maloney, 1945); Knight's Landing Ridge near Guinda (ibid); Putah Cr. near the hills (ibid); Sacramento River near Woodland (ibid).

Y<small>UBA</small> C<small>OUNTY</small>: Bear River, 10 mi. above confluence with Feather River (J. Work: Maloney, 1945); Feather River at Yuba River (ibid); Feather River, 9 mi. S Marysville Buttes (ibid); Yuba River, 8 mi. above Feather River (ibid); Yuba River, 10 mi. above Feather River (ibid); 14 mi. SE Yuba River (ibid).

R<small>ECORDS OF</small> C<small>ERVUS ELAPHUS ROOSEVELTI</small>

D<small>EL</small> N<small>ORTE</small> C<small>OUNTY</small>: Crescent City (Prescott, 1925); Island Lake (ibid); Klamath River on Del Norte Co. line (J. Smith: Sullivan, 1934); ± 5 mi. S Lake Earl (ibid); Smith River, 6 mi. NE Lake Earl (ibid); 5 mi. SE Wilson Cr. (ibid); Wilson Creek at the coast (ibid); 7 mi. N Wilson Cr. (ibid).

H<small>UMBOLT</small> C<small>OUNTY</small>: Arcata (Coy, 1929); Bear Buttes (Gibbs, 1860); Cape Mendocino Ridge (specimen in MVZ); Eel River, 8 mi. from coast (Gibbs, 1860); Gold Bluff (specimen in MVZ); Iaqua on Yager Cr. (Barnes, 1925); Klamath River, within sight of the coast (J. Smith: Sullivan, 1934); Little River (Davison: California Fish and Game, 1928c); Orick (specimen in MVZ); one mi. N Orick (ibid); 2 mi. N Orick (ibid); 7 mi. N Orick (ibid); Sec 22 R 12 N, T 1 E (ibid); 2 mi. from Redwood Cr. (Greenleaf Curtis: E. R. Smith, 1953); Trinity River, 20 mi. NW of Klamath River (J. Smith: Sullivan, 1934).

M<small>ENDOCINO</small> C<small>OUNTY</small>: Albion River (J. Work: Maloney, 1945); Big River (ibid; Ryder, 1948); Upper Eel River (J. Work: Maloney, 1945); Garcia River (ibid); 10 mi. N Gualala River (ibid); Mount Sanhedrin (Stone, 1904); Navarro River (J. Work: Maloney, 1945); Noyo River (ibid); 1 mi. upstream, Noyo River (specimen of William Edmands, Reno, Nev.); Ten Mile River (J. Work: Maloney, 1945).

S<small>ISKIYOU</small> C<small>OUNTY</small>: Elk Lake, Marble Mts. (Doney, et al., 1916).

S<small>ONOMA</small> C<small>OUNTY</small>: Gualala River, along coast (J. Work: Maloney, 1945); near Plantation (specimens in Fort Ross Museum).

T<small>RINITY</small> C<small>OUNTY</small>: Trinity River (de Massey, 1931).

R<small>ECORDS OF</small> C<small>ERVUS ELAPHUS NELSONI</small>

CALIFORNIA

S<small>HASTA</small> C<small>OUNTY</small>: Brock Mt. (McAllister, 1919); on Pit River, 7 mi. N, 3 mi. W Fall River Mills (specimen in MVZ); north bank of Pit River S of Brock Mt. (McAllister, 1919).

S<small>ISKIYOU</small> C<small>OUNTY</small>: near Mt. Dome (specimen in MVZ); headwaters of the McCloud River (J. Work: Maloney, 1945); Mt. Shasta (Merriam, 1899); E base of Mt. Shasta (Townsend, 1887); Sisson (Merriam, 1899).

T<small>RINITY</small> C<small>OUNTY</small>: Scott Mts. (Merriam, 1899).

OREGON: tule swamp on Blitzen River between Malheur Lake and Steens Mts. (Bailey, 1936); Blue Mts. (ibid); Burns (ibid); headwaters of Deschutes River (ibid); Malheur Lake (ibid).

NEVADA: vicinity of Mountain City (Hall, 1946); Stevenson's Canyon, Snake Range (ibid). Records from other states are from Hall and Kelson (1959), except for Charleston Mts., Nevada (Merriam: Murie, 1951).

LITERATURE CITED

AINSWORTH, A. R.
  1932. The tule elk. Calif. Fish and Game 18(1) :81–83.
ALTMANN, MARGARET
  1960. The role of juvenile elk and moose in the social dynamics of their species. Zoologica 45(pt. 1, no. 4) :35–39.
ANDERSON, C. C.
  1958. The elk of Jackson Hole. Wyo. Game and Fish Comm. Bull. No. 10. 184 pp.
ANNISON, E. F.
  1965. Absorption from the ruminant stomach. Pp. 185–197 in Physiology of digestion in the ruminant, ed. by R. W. Dougherty. Washington, D.C.: Butterworth, 480 pp.
ANNISON, E. F., and D. LEWIS
  1959. Metabolism in the rumen. London: Methuen and New York: John Wiley. 184 pp.
ASSOCIATION OF OFFICIAL AGRICULTURAL CHEMISTS
  1960. Official methods of analysis. 9th ed. Washington, D.C. 832 pp.
AUDUBON, J. W.
  1906. Audubon's western journal: 1849–1850. Cleveland: Arthur H. Clark. 249 pp.
BAILEY, V.
  1936. The mammals and life zones of Oregon. N. Am. Fauna No. 55. 416 pp.
BANCROFT, H. H.
  1888. California pastoral. San Francisco: The History Co. Vol. 34 of the works of Bancroft. 808 pp.
BARLOW, H. B., R. M. HILL, and W. R. LEVICK
  1964. Retinal ganglion cells responding selectively to direction and speed of image motion in the rabbit. J. Physiol. 173(3) :377–407.
BARLOW, H. B., and W. R. LEVICK
  1965. The mechanism of directionally selective units in rabbit's retina. J. Physiol. 178(3): 477–504.
BARNES, E. P.
  1925. A few Roosevelt elk still exist in Del Norte County. Calif. Fish and Game 11(3) :142.
BARNETT, A. J. G., and R. L. REID
  1961. Reactions in the rumen. London: Edward Arnold. 252 pp.
BARRETT, R. H.
  1966. History and status of introduced ungulates on Rancho Piedra Blanca, California. Unpubl. master's thesis. Univ. Michigan, Ann Arbor, Michigan. 141 pp.
BATEMAN, P. C.
  1962. Geology. Pp. 100–122 in Deepest valley, ed. by Genny Schumacher. San Francisco: Sierra Club. 206 pp.
BISSELL, H. D., and HELEN STRONG
  1955. The crude protein variations in the browse diet of California deer. Calif. Fish and Game 41(2) :145–155.
BISSONNETTE, T. H.
  1941. Experimental modification of breeding cycles in goats. Physiol. Zoöl. 14(3) :379–383.
BOLTON, H. E.
  1927. Fray Juan Crespi. Berkeley: Univ. Calif. Press. 402 pp.
  1931. Font's complete diary. Berkeley: Univ. Calif. Press. 552 pp.
BOSQUI, E.
  1904. Memoirs. San Francisco: privately printed. 281 pp.
BOURNE, N.
  1653. Sir Francis Drake revived. London. 60 pp.
BRODY, S.
  1945. Bioenergetics and growth. New York: Reinhold. 1023 pp.
BRYANT, E.
  1848. What I saw in California. New York: Appleton. 455 pp.

BUBENIK, A., R. PAVLONSKY, and J. RERÁBEK
    1956. Trophik der Geweihbildung. Zeitschrift für Jagdwissenschaft 2(3):136–141.
BUECHNER, H. K.
    1961. Territorial behavior in Uganda kob. Science 133(3454):698–699.
BUECHNER, H. K., and C. V. SWANSON
    1955. Increased natality resulting from lowered population density among elk in southeastern
        Washington. Trans. N. Am. Wildl. Conf. 20:560–567.
BURCHAM, L. T.
    1957. California range land. An historico-ecological study of the range resources of California.
        Sacramento: Calif. Dept. Nat. Resources. 261 pp.
BURCKHARDT, D.
    1958. Observations sur la vie sociale du cerf (*Cervus elaphus*) au Parc National Suisse.
        Mammalia 22(2):226–244.
BURTCH, L. A.
    1934. The Kern County elk refuge. Calif. Fish and Game 20(2):140–147.
CALIFORNIA FISH AND GAME
    1918. Few elk in 1859. 4(3):144.
    1922. Elk moved. 8(4):229–230.
    1928*a*. An elk refuge needed. 14(1):58.
    1928*b*. Looking backward. 14(3):217.
    1928*c*. Humboldt County elk. 14(3):251.
    1930*a*. Wanted—a home for elk. 16(3):253.
    1930*b*. Division activities. 16(3):262–264.
CAMP, C. L.
    1928. James Clyman, American frontiersman 1792–1881. San Francisco: Calif. Hist. Soc. 247
        pp. + index.
CHINARD, G.
    1937. Le voyage de Lapérouse sur les Côtes de l'Alaska et de la Californie (1786). Baltimore:
        Johns Hopkins Press. 144 pp.
CLARKE, A. B.
    1852. Travels in Mexico and California. Boston: Wright and Hasty, Printers. 138 pp.
CLELAND, R. G.
    1929. Pathfinders. Los Angeles, San Francisco: Powell Publishing Co. 452 pp.
CLIFF, E. P.
    1939. Relationship between elk and mule deer in the Blue Mountains of Oregon. Trans. N. Am.
        Wildl. Conf. 4:560–569.
COMAR, C. L., L. SINGER, and G. K. DAVIS
    1949. Molybdenum metabolism and interrelationships with copper and phosphorous. J. Biol.
        Chem. 180(2):913–922.
CONAWAY, C.
    1952. The age at sexual maturity in male elk (*Cervus canadensis*). J. Wildl. Mgmt. 16(3):
        313–315.
COOK, S. F.
    1960. Colonial expeditions to the interior of California, Central Valley, 1800–1820. Univ.
        Calif. Anthro. Records 16(6):239–292.
COWAN, R. L., and T. A. LONG
    1962. Studies on antler growth and nutrition of white-tailed deer. Proc. Natl. White-tailed
        Deer Disease Symp. 1:54–60.
COY, O. C.
    1929. The Humboldt Bay region 1850–1875. Los Angeles: Calif. State Hist. Assoc. 346 pp.
DANA, R. H.
    1840. Two years before the mast. New York: Harper and Bros. 483 pp.
DARLING, F. F.
    1937. A herd of red deer. London: Oxford Univ. Press. 215 pp.

DE MASSEY, E.
  1931. To the diggings of the Trinity. Pp. 302–321 *in* The course of empire, ed. by V. Bari. New York: Coward-McCann. 368 pp.
DERBY, G. H.
  1932. The topographical reports of Lieutenant George H. Derby, with introduction and notes by F. P. Farquhar. Calif. Hist. Soc. Quart. 11(2):99–123.
DIETZ, D. R., R. H. UDALL, and L. E. YEAGER
  1962. Chemical composition and digestibility by mule deer of selected forage species, Cache La Poudre Range, Colorado. Colo. Dept. Game and Fish Tech. Publ. No. 14. 89 pp.
DONEY, A. E., P. KLINK, and W. RUSSELL
  1916. Early game conditions in Siskiyou County. Calif. Fish and Game 2(3):123–125.
DOUGHERTY, R. W., ed.
  1965. Physiology of digestion in the ruminant. Washington, D.C.: Butterworth. 480 pp.
DOW, G. W.
  1934. More tule elk planted in Owens Valley. Calif. Fish and Game 20(3):288–290.
DUFLOT DE MOFRÁS, E.
  1937. Travels on the Pacific Coast. Santa Ana, Calif.: Fine Arts Press. Vol. 1, 273 pp.; vol. 2, 352 pp.
DUHAUT-CILLY, A.
  1834. Voyage autour du monde. *In:* Calif. Hist. Soc. Quart. 8(2):130–166; (3):214–250; (4):306–336.
DYE, W. B., and J. L. O'HARRA
  1959. Molybdenosis. Univ. of Nev. Agr. Exp. Sta. Bull. No. 208. 32 pp.
EDGAR, W. F.
  1893. Historical notes of old land marks in California. Publ. Hist. Soc. of Southern Calif. 3(1):22–30.
EINARSEN, A. S.
  1946. Crude protein determination of deer food as an applied management technique. Trans. N. Am. Wildl. Conf. 11:309–312.
ELLERMAN, J. R., and T. C. S. MORRISON-SCOTT
  1951. Checklist of Palaearctic and Indian mammals, 1758 to 1946. London: British Museum. 810 pp.
ELLSWORTH, R. S.
  1930. Hunting elk for the market in the forties. Calif. Fish and Game 16(4):367.
  1931. Elk in Suisun marshes in late fifties. Calif. Fish and Game 17(2):224–225.
EVERMANN, B. W.
  1915. An attempt to save California elk. Calif. Fish and Game 1(3):85–96.
  1916. The California valley elk. Calif. Fish and Game 2(2):70–77.
FARQUHAR, F. P.
  1949. Up and down California in 1860–1864. The journal of William H. Brewer. Berkeley and Los Angeles: Univ. Calif. Press. 583 pp.
FERGUSON, A. D.
  1914. Fresno Division. General conditions and some important problems. Biennial Rept. of the Calif. Fish and Game Comm. 23:23–46.
FINLEY, E. L.
  1937. History of Sonoma County, California. Santa Rosa, Calif.: Press Democrat Publ. Co. 384 pp. + index.
FISHER, EDNA M.
  1930. The eary fauna of the Santa Barbara region, California. J. Mammal. 11(2):223–224.
  1934. Early fauna of the Monterey region, Califorina. J. Mammal. 15(3):253.
FLEROV, K. K.
  1952. Musk deer and deer. Fauna of USSR, Mammals. Vol. 1, No. 2 (New Series 55). 257 pp. Moscow and Leningrad: Acad. Sci. USSR. Translation publ. for the Natl. Sci. Foundation, and the Smithsonian Inst., Washington, D.C. (1960).

GEIS, A. H.
    1954. The food consumption and relative digestibility of various winter diets fed to elk (*Cervus canadensis, nelsoni*) under controlled conditions. Unpubl. master's thesis. Montana State University, Bozeman, Montana. 68 pp.
GIBBS, G.
    1860. Journal of the expedition of Colonel Redick McKee, United States Indian agent, through northwestern California. Pp. 99–177 *in* Archives of aboriginal knowledge, ed. by H. R. Schoolcraft. Philadelphia: Lippincott. Vol. 3. 642 pp.
GIFFORD, E. W.
    1940. California bone artifacts. Univ. Calif. Anthro. Records 3(2):153–237.
GILL, J., and Z. JACZEWSKI
    1958. Kapazität der verschiedenen Teile des Verdauungsupporates des Rothirsches (*Cervus elaphus* L.). Zeitschrift für Jagdwissenschaft 4(4):168–171.
GOSS, R. J.
    1961. Experimental investigations of morphogenesis in the growing antler. J. Embryol. and Exp. Morphol. 9(2):342–354.
    1963. The deciduous nature of deer antlers. *In* Mechanisms of hard tissue destruction. Publ. Am. Assoc. Advancement Sci. 75:339–369.
    1967. New light on mystery of antlers. Outdoor Life 139(3):54–55, 135.
GOSS, R. J., C. W. SEVERINGHAUS, and S. FREE
    1964. Tissue relationships in the development of pedicles and antlers in the Virginia deer. J. Mammal. 45(1):61–68.
GRAF, W.
    1955. The Roosevelt elk. Port Angeles, Wash.: Port Angeles Evening News. 105 pp.
GRAYSON, A. J.
    1920. Game in the San Joaquin Valley in 1853. Calif. Fish and Game 6(3):104–107.
GREER, K. R., and R. E. HOWE
    1964. Winter weights of Northern Yellowstone elk, 1961–62. Trans. N. Am. Wildl. and Nat. Resources Conf. 29:237–247
GREGSON, J., and E. M. GREGSON
    1940. The Gregson memoirs. Calif. Hist. Soc. Quart. 19(2):113–143.
GRINNELL, J.
    1933. Review of the recent mammal fauna of California. Univ. Calif. Publ. in Zool. 40(2):71–234.
HAHN, H. C., JR.
    1949. A method of censusing deer and its application in the Edwards Plateau of Texas. Texas Game, Fish and Oyster Comm., Fed. Aid Proj. 25-R:1–24.
HALAZON, G. C., and H. K. BUECHNER
    1956. Postconception ovulation in elk. Trans. N. Am. Wildl. Conf. 21:545–554.
HALL, E. R.
    1946. Mammals of Nevada. Berkeley and Los Angeles: Univ. Calif. Press. 710 pp.
HALL, E. R., and K. R. KELSON
    1959. The mammals of North America. New York: Ronald Press Co. Vol. II: 547–1083.
HARPER, J. A., J. H. HARN, W. W. BENTLEY, and C. F. YOCOM
    1967. The status and ecology of the Roosevelt elk in California. Wildl. Monographs No. 16. 49 pp.
HARRIS, L. E., C. W. COOK, and J. E. BUTCHER
    1959. Symposium on forage evaluation: V. Intake and digestibility techniques and supplemental feeding in range forage evaluation. Agron. J. 51(4):226–234.
HENNIG, R.
    1962. Über das Revierverhalten der Rehböche. Zeitschrift für Jagdwissenschaft 8(2):61–81.
HITTELL, T. H.
    1911. The adventures of James Capen Adams. New York: Charles Scribner's Sons. 373 pp.
HORMAY, A. L.
    1943. Bitterbrush in California. U.S. Forest Service, Calif. Forest and Range Expt. Sta. Note 34. 13 pp.

HOUPT, T. R.
1959. Utilization of blood urea in ruminants. Am. J. Physiol. 197(1):115-120.

HUMBOLDT, A.
1811. Essai politique sur le royaume de la Nouvelle-Espagne. F. Schoell, Paris, France. Vol. II (Livre III). 520 pp.

HUNTER, J. S.
1913. Game conditions in California. Biennial Rept. of the Calif. Fish and Game Comm. 22:17-25.

JENSEN, E. H., W. B. DYE, and R. A. MADSEN
1958. Molybdenum content of forage plants. Agron. Research Nev. Agr. Expt. Sta. Circ. 21:22-23.

JENSEN, E. H., A. L. LESPERANCE, and E. J. GREGORY
1961. Molybdenum in forage plants and how it affects animals. Nev. Ranch and Home Rev. 2(3):10-12.

JOHNSON, D. E.
1951. Biology of the elk calf, *Cervus canadensis nelsoni*. J. Wildl. Mgmt. 15(4):396-410.

JONES, F. L.
1950. A survey of the Sierra Nevada bighorn. Sierra Club Bull. 35(6):29-76.
1954. The Inyo-Sierra deer herds. Calif. Dept. Fish and Game, Fed. Aid Proj. W-41-R. 84 pp. Mimeo.

KIDDIE, D. G.
1962. The sika deer (*Cervus nippon*) in New Zealand. New Zealand Forest Service, Wellington, New Zealand. Information series No. 44. 35 pp.

KITTAMS, W. H.
1953. Reproduction of Yellowstone elk. J. Wildl. Mgmt. 17(2):177-184.

KLEIN, D. R.
1962. Rumen contents analysis as an index to range quality. Trans. N. Am. Wildl. and Nat. Resources Conf. 27:150-162.

KROEBER, A. L.
1953. Handbook of the Indians of California. Berkeley: Calif. Book Co. Ltd. 995 pp.

KRÖNING, F., and F. VORREYER
1957. Untersuchungen über Vermehrungsraten und Korpergewichte beim weiblechen Rotwild. Zeitschrift für Jagdwissenschaft 3(4):145-153.

LANGSDORFF, G. H.
1927. Narrative of the Rezanov voyage to Nueva California in 1806. San Francisco: Private Press of T. C. Russell. 158 pp.

LEIGH, R. W.
1928. Dental pathology of aboriginal California. Univ. Calif. Publ. in Am. Arch. and Ethnol. 23(10):399-440.

LENT, P.
1965. Rutting behaviour in a barren-ground caribou population. Animal Behaviour 13(2-3):259-264.

LESPERANCE, A. L., and V. R. BOHMAN
1963. Effect of inorganic molybdenum and type of roughage on the bovine. J. Animal Sci. 22(3):686-694.

LINSDALE, J. M., and P. Q. TOMICH
1953. A herd of mule deer. Berkeley and Los Angeles: Univ. Calif. Press. 567 pp.

LYMAN, G. D.
1931. John Marsh, pioneer. Chautauqua, N.Y.: The Chautauqua Press. 394 pp.

MALONEY, ALICE B.
1945. Fur brigade to the Bonaventura; John Work's California expedition, 1832-1833, for the Hudson's Bay Company. San Francisco: Calif. Hist. Soc. 112 pp.

MANLY, W. L.
1894. Death Valley in '49. San Jose, Calif.: Pacific Tree and Vine Co. 498 pp.

188   *University of California Publications in Zoology*

MATURANA, H. R., J. Y. LETTVIN, W. S. McCULLOCH, and W. H. PITTS
  1960. Anatomy and physiology of vision in the frog (*Rana pipiens*). J. Gen. Physiol. 43(6, pt. 2): 129–175.
MAYFIELD, T. J.
  1929. San Joaquin primeval, Uncle Jeff's story. Tulare, Calif.: Tulare Times. 88 pp.
MAYNARD, L. A., and J. K. LOOSLI
  1962. Animal nutrition. 5th ed. New York: McGraw-Hill. 533 pp.
McALLISTER, M. H.
  1919. Elk in Shasta County. Calif. Fish and Game 5(2):98.
  1924. Census of California's big game. Calif. Fish and Game 10(2):76–77.
McCAIN, R.
  1948. A method of measuring deer range use. Trans. N. Am. Wildl. Conf. 13:431–441.
McCULLOUGH, D. R.
  1964. Relationship of weather to migratory movements of black-tailed deer. Ecol. 45(2):249–256.
  1965a. Elk deposit on the San Francisco Peninsula. J. Mammal. 46(2):347–348.
  1965b. Sex characteristics of black-tailed deer hooves. J. Wildl. Mgmt. 29(1):210–212.
McCULLOUGH, D. R., and E. R. SCHNEEGAS
  1966. Winter observations of the Sierra Nevada bighorn sheep. Calif. Fish and Game 52(2): 68–84.
McCULLOUGH, M. E.
  1959. Symposium on forage evaluation: III. The significance of and techniques used to measure forage intake and digestibility. Agron. J. 51(4):219–222.
MERRIAM, C. H.
  1899. Results of a biological survey of Mount Shasta, California. N. Am. Fauna No. 16. 179 pp.
  1905. A new elk from California, *Cervus nannodes*. Proc. of the Biol. Soc. of Washington 18:23–25.
  1921. A California elk drive. Sci. Monthly 13:465–475.
MEYER, J. H., and L. G. JONES
  1962. Controlling alfalfa quality. Calif. Agr. Expt. Sta. Bull. 784. 72 pp.
MICHAEL, C. R.
  1966. Receptive fields of directionally selective units in the optic nerve of the ground squirrel. Sci. 152(3725):1092–1095.
MOFFITT, J.
  1934. History of the Yosemite elk herd. Calif. Fish and Game 20(1):37–51.
MOIR, R. J., and M. SOMERS
  1957. Ruminal flora studies. VIII. The influence of rate and method of feeding a ration upon its digestibility, upon ruminal function, and upon the ruminal population. Australian J. Agr. Res. 8(3):253–265.
MORRISON, J. A.
  1960a. Characteristics of estrus in captive elk. Behaviour 16(1–2):84–92.
  1960b. Ovarian characteristics in elk of known breeding history. J. Wildl. Mgmt. 24(3):297–307.
MORRISON, J. A., C. E. TRAINER, and P. L. WRIGHT
  1959. Breeding season in elk as determined from known-age embryos. J. Wildl. Mgmt. 23(1):27–34.
MUNZ, P. A., and D. D. KECK
  1963. A California flora. Berkeley and Los Angeles: Univ. Calif. Press. 1681 pp.
MURIE, O. J.
  1932. Elk calls. J. Mammal. 13(4):331–336.
  1951. The elk of North America. Harrisburg, Pa: Stackpole Co. and Washington, D.C.: Wildl. Mgmt. Inst. 376 pp.
MURPHY, D. A.
  1963. A captive elk herd in Missouri. J. Wildl. Mgmt. 27(3):411–414.

NAGY, J. G., H. W. STEINHOFF, and G. M. WARD
  1964. Effects of essential oils of sagebrush on deer rumen microbial function. J. Wildl. Mgmt. 28(4):785–790.
NATIONAL RESEARCH COUNCIL
  1963. Nutrient requirements of beef cattle. Natl. Acad. of Sci.-Natl. Res. Council Publ. 1137. 30 pp.
  1964. Nutrient requirements of sheep. Natl. Acad. of Sci-Natl. Res. Council Publ. 1193. 40 pp.
NEFF, D. J., O. C. WALLMO, and D. C. MORRISON
  1965. A determination of defecation rate for elk. J. Wildl. Mgmt. 29(2):406–407.
NEVINS, ALLEN, ed.
  1956. Narratives of exploration and adventure, by J. C. Frémont. New York: Longmans, Green. 532 pp.
NEWBERRY, J. S.
  1857. Report upon the mammals. Reports of explorations and surveys, to ascertain the most practicable and economical route for a railroad from the Mississippi River to the Pacific Ocean. U.S. War Dept. Vol. 6, pt. 4, No. 2:35–72.
PICKFORD, G. D., and E. H. REID
  1943. Competition of elk and domestic livestock for summer range forage. J. Wildl. Mgmt. 7(3):328–332.
PRESCOTT, H. S.
  1925. Del Norte County elk. Calif. Fish and Game 11(3):142.
PRIESTLY, H. I.
  1937. A historical, political, and natural description of California, by Pedro Fages. Berkeley and Los Angeles: Univ. Calif. Press. 83 pp.
QUAIFE, M. M.
  1934. Narrative of the adventures of Zenas Leonard. Chicago: Lakeside Press. 278 pp.
QUIMBY, D. C., and D. E. JOHNSON
  1951. Weights and measurements of Rocky Mountain elk. J. Wildl. Mgmt. 15(1):57–62.
REDDINGTON, P. G.
  1922a. Introduced elk thrive on Sequoia National Forest. Calif. Fish and Game 8(3):191.
  1922b. Elk on the Shasta National Forest. Calif. Fish and Game 8(3):192.
RERÁBEK, J., and A. BUBENIK
  1956. Untersuchungen des Mineralstoffwechsels bei Geweihträgern mittels radioaktiver Isotopen. Zeitschrift für Jagdwissenschaft 2(3):119–123.
REVERE, J. W.
  1922. A pioneer elk hunt. Calif. Fish and Game 8(1):35–37.
ROBBINS, W. W.
  1940. Alien plants growing without cultivation in California. Univ. Calif. Agr. Expt. Sta. Bull. 637. 128 pp.
ROBINSON, R. M., J. W. THOMAS, and R. G. MARBURGER
  1965. The reproductive cycle of male white-tailed deer in central Texas. J. Wildl. Mgmt. 29(1):53–59.
RODGERS, D. B.
  1929. Prehistoric man of the Santa Barbara coast. Santa Barbara, Calif.: Santa Barbara Mus. Nat. Hist. Special Publ. No. 1. 452 pp.
RYDER, D. W.
  1948. Memories of the Mendocino coast. San Francisco: Privately printed. 81 pp.
SCHENCK, W. E.
  1926. The Emeryville shellmound final report. Univ. Calif. Publ. Am. Arch. and Ethnol. 23(3):147–282.
SCHWARTZ, J. E., II, and G. E. MITCHELL
  1945. The Roosevelt elk on the Olympic Peninsula, Washington. J. Wildl. Mgmt. 9(4):295–319.

SHAW, J. C.
  1959. Symposium on forage evaluation: VIII. Relation of digestion end-products to the energy economy of animals. Agron. J. 51(4):242–245.
SHELLY, RUTH N., H. SALIVIN, and W. HORWITZ
  1963. Quantitative determination of formic, acetic, propionic, and butyric acids by gas chromatography. J. Assoc. Official Agr. Chemists 46(3):486–493.
SHORT, H. L.
  1963. Rumen fermentations and energy relationships in white-tailed deer. J. Wildl. Mgmt. 27(2):184–195.
  1966. Methods for evaluating forages for wild ruminants. Trans. N. Am. Wildl. and Nat. Resources Conf. 31:122–128.
SIMONNET, H., H. LeBARS, and J. MOLLÉ
  1957. Le cycle de l'urée administrée par voie buccale chez les ruminants. Comptes Rendus Académie Des Sciences, Paris 244(7):943–945.
SMITH, A. D.
  1952. Digestibility of some native forages for mule deer. J. Wildl. Mgmt. 16(3):309–312.
  1964. Defecation rates of mule deer. J. Wildl. Mgmt. 28(3):435–444.
SMITH, A. D., R. B. TURNER, and G. A. HARRIS
  1956. The apparent digestibility of lignin by mule deer. J. Range Mgmt. 9(3):142–145.
SMITH, ESTHER R.
  1953. The history of Del Norte County, California. Oakland, Calif.: Holms Book Co. 224 pp.
SMITH, W. P. U.
  1932. The development of the San Joaquin Valley 1772–1882. Ph.D. thesis. Univ. Calif., Berkeley, Calif. 238 pp.
STEVENS, D. R.
  1966. Range relationships of elk and livestock, Crow Creek Drainage, Montana. J. Wildl. Mgmt. 30(2):349–363.
STONE, W.
  1904. On a collection of birds and mammals from Mount Sanhedrin, California. Proc. Acad. of Nat. Sci. of Philadelphia 56:576–591.
STRUHSAKER, T. T.
  1967. Behavior of elk (*Cervus canadensis*) during the rut. Zeitschrift für Tierpsychologie 24(1):80–114.
SULLIVAN, M. S.
  1934. The travels of Jedediah Smith. Santa Anna, Calif.: The Fine Arts Press. 195 pp.
TALBOT, M. W., H. H. BISWELL, and A. L. HORMAY
  1939. Fluctuations in the annual vegetation of California. Ecol. 20(3):394–402.
TAYLOR, W. P.
  1916. The conservation of the native fauna. Sci. Monthly 3:399–409.
TEGGART, F. J.
  1914. Dairy of Nelson Kingsley, a California argonaut of 1849. Publ. Acad. of Pacific Coast Hist. 3(3):237–413.
THOMPSON, R. A.
  1877. Historical and descriptive sketch of Sonoma County, California. Philadelphia: L. H. Everts and Co. 104 pp.
  1896. The Russian settlement in California known as Fort Ross. Santa Rosa, Calif.: Sonoma Democrat Publ. Co. 34 pp.
TILLOTSON, M. R.
  1916. Elk in Shasta County. Calif. Fish and Game 2(2):111.
TOWNSEND, C. H.
  1887. Field-notes on mammals, birds and reptiles of Northern California. Proc. U.S. Natl. Museum 10:159–241.
VAN DYKE, T. S.
  1902. The deer and the elk of the Pacific Coast. Pp. 167–256 *in* The deer family, by T. Roosevelt, T. S. Van Dyke, D. G. Elliot, and A. J. Stone. New York: MacMillan. 334 pp.

VIZCAINO, S.
  1891. Letter to King of Spain (1603). Publ. Hist. Soc. Southern Calif. 2(1):70–73.
WALDO, C. M., and G. B. WISLOCKI
  1951. Observations on the shedding of the antlers of Virginia deer (*Odocoileus virginianus borealis*). Am. J. Anat. 88(3):351–395.
WATSON, E. B., and R.E. STORIE
  1928. Soil survey Bishop area, California. Washington, D.C.: U.S. Dept. Agr., U.S. Govt. Printing Office. 95 pp.
WILKES, C.
  1845. Narrative of the United States exploring expedition. During the years 1838, 1839, 1840, 1841, 1842. Philadelphia: Lea and Blanchard. Vol. 5. 558 pp.
WINANS, W.
  1913. Deer breeding for fine heads with description of many varieties and cross-breeds. London: Rowland Ward. 105 pp.
WISLOCKI, G. B.
  1942. Studies on the growth of deer antlers. I. On the structure and histogenesis of the antlers of the Virginia deer (*Odocoileus virginianus borealis*). Am. J. Anat. 71(3):371–415.
  1943. Studies on growth of deer antlers. II. Seasonal changes in the male reproductive tract of the Virginia deer (*Odocoileus virginianus borealis*) with a discussion of the factors controlling the antler-gonad periodicity. Pp. 629-653. *in* Essays in biology in honor of Herbert M. Evans. Berkeley and Los Angeles: Univ. Calif. Press. 687 pp.
WISLOCKI, G. B., J. C. AUB, and C. M. WALDO
  1947. The effects of gonadectomy and the administration of testosterone propionate on the growth of antlers in male and female deer. Endocrinol. 40(3): 202–224.
WOOD, W. E., C. W. ZUMWALT, and W. P. DASMANN
  1960. Range analysis field guide. Div. of Range and Wildl. Mgmt., U.S. Forest Service, Calif. Region. 184 pp.
WRIGHT, B. S.
  1960. Predation on big game in East Africa. J. Wildl. Mgmt. 24(1):1–15.
YOUNG, S. P., and E. A. GOLDMAN
  1944. The wolves of North America. Washington, D.C.: Am. Wildl. Inst. 636 pp.

PLATES

PLATE 1

a. A newborn tule elk calf, Female No. 2, weighing 18 pounds. It was able to stand, but could hobble only a few yards before it would drop to the ground. Note the faint spotting on the coat.

b. Same calf as above. Note typical lack of cover and exposed position of calf.

PLATE 2

PLATE 2

Alarm behavior in tule elk.
a. Notch in mild alert.
b. Notch in full alert.
c. Notch with nose high, beginning retreat.

PLATE 3

a. and *b.* Notch retreating cautiously moving head to and fro. These pictures are taken from a series showing the head movements.

c. Tritops giving mouth open response at beginning of alarm.

PLATE 4

a. Sequence of events occurring on August 29, 1964, showing the general confusion with bull cohort in the milling herd. Tritops at rear facing away; Five-point and Small Five-point in foreground.

b. Tritops bugling. Note head high, stationary position of two spikes. The spike on the left, Bent-left, has a deformed antler pedicel.

c. Five-point dominates Extra-trez, a bull of about the same size.

PLATE 5

a. Sequence of events occurring on August 29, 1964 (continued from pl. 4).
Sport bugling.

b. Sport bugling. Note his mud-caked coat.

c. Sport and Tritops clash.

PLATE 6

a. Tritops' decline in condition. On August 15, 1964, early in rut, Tritops is still in good condition. Note distended abdomen indicating feeding.

b. August 22. Tritops still in fair condition. Note all tines are still present.

PLATE 7

a. August 29, 1964 (continued from pl. 6). Tritops in poor condition (see also pls. 4 and 5), belly retracted. Note broken tines. Extra-trez and Five-point in background.

b. September 12. Tritops, 12 days after his defeat. Note poor condition, scars, broken antlers, and distended abdomen with resumption of feeding (see also pl. 3c).

PLATE 8

a. and *b.* Vegetation cones in two locations on one of the best forage sites of the cow pasture. Pictures taken on October 27, 1964, following summer elk use. Utilization cannot be detected.